Wakefield Press

'A Great and Glorious Reformation'

Six Early South Australian Legal Innovations

Dr Greg Taylor is a senior lecturer in Law at Monash University. Born in South Australia, he was educated at the University of Adelaide, where he has also taught. He has published essays on South Australian legal history in a number of scholarly journals.

T0363975

'A Great and Glorious Reformation'

Six Early South Australian Legal Innovations

Greg Taylor

Wakefield
Press

Wakefield Press
1 The Parade West
Kent Town
South Australia 5067
www.wakefieldpress.com.au

First published 2005

Copyright © Greg Taylor, 2005 and/or the journals
of first publication listed in Acknowledgements.

All rights reserved. This book is copyright. Apart from any fair dealing for the
purposes of private study, research, criticism or review, as permitted under the
Copyright Act, no part may be reproduced without written permission. Enquiries
should be addressed to the publisher.

Cover designed by Liz Nicholson, designBITE
Text designed and typeset by Clinton Ellicott, Wakefield Press
Printed and bound by Hyde Park Press
Indexed by Bill Phippard, Seaview Press

Published with the assistance of the Monash University Publications Grants
Committee and the Law Foundation of South Australia Inc.

National Library of Australia
Cataloguing-in-publication entry

Taylor, Greg.
A great and glorious reformation: early South Australian legal innovations.

Includes index.

ISBN 1 86254 675 4.

1. Law – South Australia – History. 2. Aboriginal
Australians – Legal status, laws, etc. – South Australia.
I. Title.

349.9423

Piam in memoriam
Illa Nicholls (*née* Gervasi), LL.B. (Hons.)
a friend in need
Alles Vergängliche ist nur ein Gleichnis

Contents

Foreword

By the Honourable Michael Kirby, AC, CMG,
B.A., LL.M., B.Ec. (Sydney), D.Litt. (*h.c.*), LL.D. (*h.c.*),
D.Univ. (*h.c.*), Hon. F.A.S.S.A.,
A Justice of the High Court of Australia

History is a marvellous discipline. If I could have my life over, it would be history, not law, that would capture my heart.

The history of most countries is lost in the mists of time. When parts of it are discovered, they reveal gruesome stories of oppression, violence and brute power, as humanity clawed its way from the dark ages into the muted light that is the current era.

On a recent visit to Berlin, I explored the new facilities of the *Deutsches Historisches Museum* on Unter den Linden. What was boasted to be an exhibition on the history of Germany in the twentieth century turned out to be a disappointing assembly of unremarkable photographs. No newsreels. No interviews with the Kaiser in exile at Doorn. None of the terrifying harangues of Hitler at places close nearby. No mementos or personal stories to explain how the land of Luther, Bach and Schrödinger had fallen, successively, into such autocratic and evil hands. Perhaps the story was too recent to tell. Or too painful.

On my return to Australia, I read Dr Taylor's book. It lifted my heart to realise what advantages the settlers enjoyed in opening up our continental country. Nowhere else were the blessings of rational government and systematic self-improvement for the settlers more evident than in the pre-federation Province of South Australia.

Even for the Aboriginal people, who long preceded the European settlers, the government that expanded from Adelaide into the hinterland made fewer mistakes than its counterparts elsewhere. Not long after the establishment of South Australia, a settler was hanged for the murder of an Aboriginal. The hanging made a point. The Chief Justice intoned that this was to be a place of 'superior morality and freedom'. There is evidence throughout Dr Taylor's book of the measure of enlightenment that came with economic and political power and confidence in the British mastery of the waves and dominion over palm and pine. Ironically, as Dr Taylor emphasises, many of the innovations that marked the early years of South Australia were influenced, if not shaped, by contributions of the German settlers who came to the Province in large numbers. Many of them were escaping religious or political oppression at home. To South Australia, they brought their devotion to rationality and conscience and their memories of laws in Germany on subjects as diverse as land title registration and the incorporation of clubs and societies.

This happy combination of a free settlement, spared of convict origins and committed to sensible reforms of inappropriate Imperial laws, led to many changes which it is the purpose of this book to describe. Whereas in most societies, the records of the founders are lost in time (being no more than legend and tradition) in South Australia, in their methodical way, the early settlers recorded nearly everything. We are the beneficiaries of their records. They take us into their controversies, their bright ideas, their bold innovations and their occasional failures. Yet all of this would be as hidden from us as the history of the Medes and the Persians, were it not for the enthusiastic scholarship of the author.

South Australia has long been a centre of Australian legal history. Professor Alex Castles of the University of Adelaide, whose recent and untimely death we mourn, took the story of the State's history a long way. Now, Dr Taylor has elaborated Alex Castles' record. By further research, he has qualified some of the doyen's conclusions. Through the Internet and electronic publication, we will never now lose the record of the great and glorious reformation in the law in South Australia as it was established. Perhaps the boast of 'great' and 'glorious' overstates things a trifle. By comparison to Martin Luther's Reformation – or even to the struggles of the English Commons against the Stuart kings – the story of legal reforms in South Australia looks rather tame. But at a time of Imperial complacency, in which laws long settled were accepted unquestioningly although manifestly unjust and inefficient, it is a mark of the people who established the community around Adelaide that they embraced reform so enthusiastically. Indeed, as Dr Taylor shows, in many things it is not too much to say that they led the world.

Interestingly, the greatest of the innovations, the Torrens system of land title by registration, bears close similarity to the system of land title earlier observed in the Hanseatic towns of Northern Germany. Here, we discover a mystery. Was it Robert Torrens after all who invented the land title system that universally bears his name? Or was Dr Ulrich Hübbe, from Hamburg in Germany, who invented or adapted the system in Australia and was cheated of the credit? The reader will find the analysis of this puzzle intriguing.

Quite as innovative as Torrens was the demand of an early grand jury in Adelaide for instruction about the customary laws of Aboriginal people hauled before them for punishment according to English law. The jurors could see the injustice of imposing on the indigenous people the punishments applicable to the settlers. At least they could see the unfairness where the Aboriginals were charged for doing no more than upholding their own laws according to their ancient ways.

The introduction into South Australia of the first statute anywhere in the British Empire permitting a subject, as of right, to sue the government proved an innovation that quickly spread. It was urged on by its manifest fairness, modernity and procedural simplicity.

In addition to these important reforms, there were many others. The registration of unincorporated associations enhanced the right of association which is the key to the success of a modern civil society. The right of a defendant to give evidence in criminal trials was a mighty change in established English trial procedures. It demonstrates, once again, the need for lawyers constantly to stand back and apply the test of rationality to the system of the law that they help to administer.

Whilst Dr Taylor acknowledges failures, notably in the attempt to overcome the inefficiencies of the separate administration of common law and equity, his book captures the mood of the province of South Australia as it grew from its rustic origins in the nineteenth century. Here were free people, making a prosperous home in a new land. They created the building blocks of institutions essential for the rule of law. Fortunate are we in Australia that the thread of lawfulness and constitutionalism has been unbroken since that time. Like all peoples, we have dark corners in our history. The treatment of the indigenous races, of women, of aliens and other minorities are amongst them. But here are early chapters of a story in which we can take much pride.

This book will prepare the reader for the celebration in 2007 of the sesquicentenary of South Australia's first Parliament. This event opened a long and honourable period of representative government that continues. As the author points out, South Australia has had other instances of great legal innovation. Encouraged by this book, it may be hoped that today's citizens in the State will rekindle the scrutiny of unjust laws and find anew the sense of determination to put rational and fair provisions in their place.

Michael Kirby
Canberra, 27 July 2004

Author's note

The author's grateful thanks are extended to those who assisted in the research on which this book is based. For their assistance in the work required to make this book possible, or for helpful suggestions, the author wishes to thank Pat Dening; Lynn Drew of the History Trust of South Australia; John Gava; Master Peter Norman of the Supreme Court of South Australia; Dr Pam O'Connor; Brian Taylor; Dr John Williams; and the staff of the Law Library of Monash University, Melbourne. Special *ex post facto* thanks are also due to the staff of the Law Library of the University of Adelaide, whose help and advice have been so valuable to the author throughout the years.

The author also warmly thanks the Law Foundation of South Australia and the Monash University Publications Grants Committee, whose generous support has made this book possible, and all who have worked on the book at Wakefield Press for numerous excellent suggestions on a draft of the text.

A note on spellings: in early South Australia, it was usual to spell words such as 'honour', 'misdemeanour' *etc.* without the 'u'. (Hence the spelling of 'Victor Harbor'.) These spellings have of course been retained where they occur in original sources quoted in the text, but correct (non-American) modern spelling is used elsewhere.

Sometimes the reader will find a reference to the Province of South Australia. This was the formal name of what is now the State of South Australia before Federation in 1901.

It is a matter of some regret that this distinctive title for South Australia was given up, and all the Australian colonies became, without distinction, States of the Commonwealth of Australia.

It should also be pointed out that the Vice-Regal office now known as that of Governor of South Australia is referred to by that title in this book, regardless of the title adopted at the time in question. During some of the events dealt with in this book, the office was in fact called Lieutenant-Governor (and was not the equivalent of today's office with the same title, but was the principal Vice-Regal office in South Australia). The office underwent minor changes of title in the nineteenth century.[1] In this book, however, the office is always referred by what is now its current name.

Adelaide/Melbourne, 8 June 2005

Note

1   The change in question was connected with the appointment of Sir Charles Fitzroy as Governor-General of the Australian colonies in 1851, with the consequent adoption of the title of Lieutenant-Governor in some of the other colonies. The appointment of a Governor-General, although little more than titular, caused some offence in South Australia at the time, where it was considered to denigrate a free colony and impose oversight from afar on it: see, *e.g. Register*, 18 July 1851, p. 2 (noting the enthusiastic reception for a toast to 'Sir Henry Young [the Governor of South Australia], and no Viceroy over him' at a dinner for A.H. Davis, on whom see chapter 3); *South Australian*, 30 May 1851, p. 3; *South Australian Gazette and Mining Journal*, 29 May 1851, p. 22; *Adelaide Times*, 28 May 1851, p. 3; 29 May 1851, p. 3; Pike, *Paradise of Dissent* (2nd ed., Melbourne U.P., Carlton 1967), p. 439 (noting, however, that the gold rushes contributed to breaking down this sentiment); Ward, *Australia's First Governor-General: Sir Charles Fitzroy 1851–1855* (University of Sydney, Sydney 1953), pp. 11f. See also Castles/Harris, *Lawmakers and Wayward Whigs: Government and Law in South Australia 1836–1986* (Wakefield, Adelaide 1987), p. 37.

1. Early South Australia – an innovatory place

1. Recovering the memory of innovation

Sometimes it is hard to believe that Adelaide, and South Australia, are only just over two human lifetimes old. The city and State seem so well-established to those living in them today that one could be forgiven for thinking that they have been there forever.

But of course they have not been. They had to be built up from scratch, a task which it is now difficult for us to conceive. The magnitude of this task was however brought home vividly to me when I read the newspaper report of Mr Justice Jeffcott's address to the first grand jury of the Province of South Australia in May 1837. Among other things, his Honour called for the labouring classes to work hard, respect their betters and earn a share in the prosperity of the Province. But how prosperous the Province really was at this stage, and the conditions under which the early settlers lived, were made clear to me, working as I was then amidst the solid buildings of the city of Adelaide, when reading the Judge's directions on whether burglary could be committed by breaking into 'the huts and tents, in which the great body of our population now reside', and which were 'fastened . . . by strings tied together on the inside'.[1] (It was, incidentally, decided that burglary could indeed be committed in this way.)

The distance between us and the generation that founded South Australia in 1836 is enormous, despite the relatively short period of time that has elapsed since. We tend to take their achievements for

Sir John Jeffcott,
the Colony's first judge, c. 1836
Photograph courtesy of the State Library of South Australia, SLSA: B 464

granted. Many of their legal innovations fall into the same category: today no one thinks twice, for example, about a defendant giving sworn evidence in his trial. But, as readers of this book will discover, it was pioneering South Australian legislation which permitted this to occur for the first time anywhere in the British Empire. And this legislation was an important stimulus to reform in other Australian colonies and even in England, then the centre of a great and powerful Empire.

The same generation which established the city and State also did many other remarkable things. But this book is a selection of their achievements in the field of law reform only. With one exception – the legislation about defendants just mentioned – all of those things are reforms that were achieved in the 1850s, when the Province of South Australia was a teenager and young adult, in the period of time just before and after the opening of the first South Australian Parliament in April 1857.

The fruits of South Australia's youthful reforming vigour have enriched the rest of Australia, and, in some cases, the rest of the world. The most obvious example of this is the system of title to land by registration – the Torrens system – which has spread to an incredibly large number of jurisdictions throughout the world. But there are others. The clubs and societies legislation conceived in Adelaide in the same year as the Torrens system has spread more slowly, but just as surely, around Australia. That legislation makes it much easier to form and to run clubs and societies, and thus greatly enriches the social fabric of society. The South Australian legislation greatly enhancing the citizen's rights to sue the government spread more rapidly around Australia, and to one or two other jurisdictions as well.

In most cases – the Torrens system is the exception – virtually everyone, including leading writers on the topic, has forgotten that the legislation concerned even originated in South Australia. Indeed, Professor Alex Castles expressed the view that Australian legislatures in the nineteenth century tended to be over-reliant on British statutes and failed to develop an independent body of statutory law.[2] This may perhaps be true as a general proposition. This book shows, however, that it was not true of the early legislatures in South Australia.

This book is accordingly an attempt to recover the memory of South Australia's innovative legal past. Not that the more recent past should be entirely forgotten either: another burst of reform and innovation occurred in the 1970s, and there have been achievements both before and since. Consumer protection and residential tenancies legislation are only two of many possible examples from the 1970s.[3] But this book is about innovations in what, in South Australian terms, is the distant past, innovations that occurred before anyone alive today can remember them and which are, therefore, often not even credited as South Australian achievements.

What we consider today to be a natural part of the legal landscape, such as the Torrens system, or the clubs and societies legislation, had to be invented by someone somewhere. It was not inevitable that such things would be invented; their invention required (first of all) inventiveness, but also attention to detail and persistence in having proposals accepted in the community as desirable and passed by Parliament. All these qualities were available in early South Australia, as this book records. In the result, a colony which, in all cases but one, was not even or just barely out of its teens, barely on the radar screen of human civilisation, was able to make several important contributions to legal progress.

Two notable South Australian achievements from the nineteenth century have been omitted. The first is the secret ballot. There is competition with our friends in Victoria for the honour of originating this. The second is that South Australia – as many readers of this book will know – was the first State to give the vote to women (and also permitted Aborigines to vote; indeed, it provided special polling stations for them).[4] The vote was conferred on South Australian women in 1894,[5] well before Victoria finally got around to doing it in 1908. These two innovations have been omitted partly because they have been discussed extensively elsewhere,[6] and partly because they are reforms which, while made by means of the law, did not result in the introduction of any new principles or institutions of the law. They were political reforms rather than law reform.

2. A common theme

This book may appear at first glance to contain a somewhat random collection of South Australian legal innovations. Closer inspection, however, will reveal a common theme – over and above the obvious theme of legal innovation in early South Australia, the coincidence of their dates and the fact that almost all of them spread well beyond the State's borders. This common theme has escaped notice because of the lack of research devoted to the topic of early local legal innovation by legal historians such as Professor Castles.

All of the legal innovations dealt with here enlarged the rights of the citizen – to sue the government, to give evidence in Court – or provided the citizen with a legal facility – to register title to land, to have a club or society legally recognised – which had not existed before. Each of them, therefore, enhanced the contribution that the law makes to the freedom of the individual.

Rather than just telling people what to do and threatening them with prison if they refused to obey, law reforms in early South Australia made citizens freer; it made them more fully citizens; it assisted them in more fully taking part in the life of the community and in doing productive work. The words of Professor H.L.A. Hart, one of the twentieth century's most influential legal philosophers, could easily be applied to these South Australian innovations from the nineteenth century: they were 'laws which provide[d] facilities or powers and sa[id], "If you wish to do this, this is the way to do it"'.[7]

The very enterprise of going to a new country and starting afresh requires, of course, some willingness to break with established patterns of behaviour and thought, and encourages the development of these qualities. But legal innovation to enlarge the capacity of the citizen to function as a citizen was especially appropriate in South Australia. It was entirely consistent with South Australia's self-image as a place of 'superior morality and freedom'[8] – a legacy of its birth free of the convict stain, and as a community of equals. No doubt this characteristic of the reforms considered here also explains why all the innovations described here survive in the modern law, which mirrors the society it serves by placing such a high premium on self-determination by the citizen.

In his masterly study of the character of early South Australian society which concludes his history of the early days of the Province – a study which was first published in 1957, but is still the standard reference – Professor Douglas Pike makes particular note of the independence which the early South Australians manifested, even going so far as to describe it as 'the worst of their faults'.[9]

Pike was not referring to the law in early South Australia at all when he expressed that view. When it came to legal reform, this independent attitude was not a fault only. It expressed itself both in the willingness of the early South Australians to make reforms which were untried in England, not merely following the leader as the other colonies mostly did; and in the nature of the reforms they made, promoting as they did the autonomy of the individual under, and as a result of the assistance of, the law.

That is not to say that the founders of South Australia in general, or those who introduced legal innovations in particular, were always motivated by high principle only. It comes across very clearly in a number of instances here that very concrete interests of influential people were served by legal innovation. The most obvious example of this is the *Claimants Relief Act* of 1853, the legislation dealt with in chapter 4, which permitted people to sue the government: as we shall see, it was introduced by someone whose company wished to claim money by suing the government.

There is at least one other less obvious example of the same thing – the Torrens system itself. Professor Douglas Pike, in detailing the early history of the Torrens system, waspishly started his discussion by pointing out that 'in its beginnings South Australia was a land job'.[10] The interests of those who were involved in land speculation go some way to explaining why the Torrens system was introduced at all. Speculators wanted secure title and a cheap and simple means of facilitating land speculation by making a legally effective sale of land easier to achieve.

But that too would be only half the story. Land speculators may have brought the Torrens system on to the agenda, but it became law because it appealed to a much broader section of the population. Land ownership in early South Australia was quite widely spread, not just among the 'land jobbers' or speculators. The Torrens system served the needs of the large number of people who owned land, mostly for their own personal use rather than as speculators. Moreover, it was something of a leap in the dark at the time, as no other English-speaking community had a system quite like Torrens's proposal. It was a brave step that could be taken only by those who were confident in their ability to re-design the law and make it more rational and a better servant of the community.

One further theme which recurs repeatedly in looking at South Australian legal innovations is that the reforms sometimes turned out, when applied, to be imperfect. Often, South Australian legislation, when picked up inter-State or overseas, was improved. This in itself is not a surprising order of events. Experience generally makes everyone wiser, and the first place in which something is done has, by definition, no relevant experience. Anyone can improve on an idea that someone else has conceived. The real credit belongs to the person who had the ingenuity to think of the idea in the first place.

Notes

1   *Register*, 3 June 1837, p. 5.
2   Castles, *An Australian Legal History* (Law Book, Sydney 1982), pp. 453–455, although note his qualifications of this general proposition.
3   One thinks of statutes such as the *Residential Tenancies Act* 1978 and the *Consumer Transactions Act* 1972.
4   An interesting summary of the history here may be found on the web site of the Australian Electoral Commission at:
    http://www.aec.gov.au/_content/when/history/ab_vote.htm.
5   *Constitution Amendment* 1894.
6   See, for example, McKenna, 'Building a "Closet of Prayer" in the New World: The Story of the "Australian Ballot"' and Sawer, 'Pacemakers for the World?', pp. 18–20, both in Sawer (ed.), *Elections: Full, Free and Fair* (Federation, Sydney 2001).
7   Hart, *The Concept of Law* (Clarendon Press, Oxford 1991), p. 28.
8   As Mr Justice Cooper once put it (*South Australian*, 27 November 1846, p. 6) in the proceedings which led to the hanging of one of the settlers for the murder of an Aborigine.
9   Pike, *Paradise of Dissent* (2nd ed., Melbourne U.P., Carlton 1967), p. 501; see also at p. 499.
10 Pike, 'Introduction of the *Real Property Act* in South Australia' (1962) 1 Adel LR 169, 169.

2. Hamburger to go?
The Torrens system

1. The need for reform

Of all South Australian legal innovations, the Torrens system of land titles is by far the best known and most widely copied. Introduced in South Australia by the *Real Property Act*, which came into force on 1 July 1858, it had spread to all the other Australian colonies except Western Australia within four years[1] (and Western Australia adopted it in 1875).[2] New Zealand adopted it in 1870 after the failure of an earlier reform of 1860 based on an English model.[3] English proposals fared no better in England either: in a report published in 2004, the Scottish Law Commission contrasted the 'immediate success' of the South Australian Torrens system of 1858 with the 'failure'[4] of the almost contemporaneous, but different attempt at reform embodied in the English *Land Registry Act* 1862.

The reform's success spread far beyond South Australia. After its initial success in the rest of Australia, the Torrens system then spread to several provinces of Canada,[5] some States of the United States,[6] and, in one form or another, to many Commonwealth countries such as Papua New Guinea, Malaysia, Kenya and Uganda.[7] Reports of its existence even extend to countries as diverse as Tunisia, Ethiopia, Madagascar and Iran.[8] In 1996, it was reported that 'Russia has been assessing the utility of adopting a Torrens-based system to regulate the registration of private land holdings. Similar proposals have been tabled in [the] Ukraine.'[9] Although the legislation has never been adopted in England, it has inspired notable modern reforms of English law.[10]

The Torrens system of land titles is, therefore, a South Australian innovation which, in the century and a half since it was invented, has spread into virtually all corners of the world, and has been a success in most of them. 'Torrens' is almost certainly the only name associated with South Australia which has received the honour of an entry both in the Oxford English Dictionary[11] and the *Oxford Companion to Law*.[12] As we have seen, the Torrens system has become the basis of land titles law in a great many jurisdictions.

In the United States, it must be said, the system has not been as successful as in most other places. A recent survey reports that nine American States still have Torrens system statutes[13] (although that does not necessarily mean that the Torrens system is the dominant system of land titles in those States). The relative failure of the Torrens system in the United States is not due to any intrinsic flaws in the Torrens system.[14] Rather, it is due to a combination of vested interests which oppose its extension (and have been accused of 'systematic sabotage of the American Torrens system');[15] inadequate drafting of the legislation and poor maps; public ignorance of what the system means and how it works; constitutional problems unique to American law which require expensive, tedious judicial proceedings for essential steps in setting up the system; and, finally, a lack of political will to overcome these hurdles.[16] In the Australian States and in many other jurisdictions around the world, however, it is hard to conceive of any system for managing ownership of land other than one dominated by the Torrens system.

To appreciate why the Torrens system has been so widely copied, consider the one it replaced. Under the law which South Australia inherited from England, land was sold by deed entered into between the existing owner and the new owner. The existing owner's right to sell the land had to be proved to the new owner, and the existing owner could do this only by proving that the person who sold the land to *him* had the right to sell it. And so on back into the mists of time, or rather, in South Australia's case, back to the first sale of the land by the

Crown to the first owner of it.[17] This was accurately described by Torrens as a system of dependent titles,[18] that is, a system in which everyone's title to land depended on the validity of the title of all the people who had sold it before.

The documents which proved the earlier sales were the deeds of sale, which were agreements made between the buyer and the seller as parties to the sale. The deeds were, as a rule, in private hands, normally the hands of the current owner or the owner's bank.

Proving the existence of a right to sell was known as establishing the 'chain of title'. This could be quite expensive, as the seller and buyer each had to employ a lawyer to examine the deeds and to make sure that each earlier seller of the land had had a complete right to sell it.[19]

There were three other major difficulties with this system of dependent titles. If documents were lost, problems arose in proving an owner's title. And because the documents were in private hands, the potential for fraud and forgery was great. Further, some mortgages or leases, and similar claims on land, could be created without noting them on the deeds and affect a new owner's title even if he knew nothing of them.

These problems were felt particularly acutely in South Australia. The Wakefield system of colonisation on which South Australia had been founded proposed, as its basic idea, that advance sales of land would be used to begin a fund to pay the costs of setting up the colony.[20] People buying land in this way received 'land orders', which could be sold and re-sold on the private market. The intention of the founding theorists was that the purchasers of land would use it themselves. Soon, however, speculation in land was rife, with properties being carved up and constantly bought and re-sold. This, of course, meant that the system of dependent titles quickly became as difficult to administer as in England, as it was necessary to trace each transaction and prove that it was not affected by some defect which would invalidate all later transactions.

Additional difficulties in determining ownership of land were created by South Australia's unreliable survey maps and other slack practices. Douglas Pike describes some of them:

One amateur vendor [of subdivided land] sold his township from a map that showed north pointing due south ... The township of Walkerville, purchased by Governor Hindmarsh and his wife, was sold to a surveyor who subdivided it into acre allotments, one of which had three owners before passing to two illiterate labourers as part payment for the sinking of a well. Before leaving Adelaide they sold the acre for £20 to a clerk fresh from England, giving him a verbal account of the earlier trans-actions and a receipt adorned with crosses and the undecipherable signature of a witness. On the strength of this title the clerk contrived to raise a loan. ... One agreement was for land 'about seventy paces from the N.W. corner of the Sheoak Log Hotel' (since burnt down); another, 'adjoining the lot late in the possession of William Smith' (since departed for the Californian diggings).[21]

Such inexact practices would be unsatisfactory anywhere, but they could affect the principal asset of many people in a colony in which land ownership was within the reach of many members of society rather than being confined to the well-off who could take the occa-sional loss and afford the occasional law-suit.[22] It was therefore in the interests of many ordinary people as well as land speculators to have a better, more certain and more secure system introduced.

Various remedies designed to fix the problems were tried before 1858. A statute of 1842,[23] based on precedents from assorted parts of the United Kingdom as well as New South Wales legislation of 1825,[24] required all deeds and some other documents affecting title to land to be registered by a government official. If they were not, the statute made them ineffective against anyone who bought the land later on. However, as Douglas Pike pithily and accurately comments, 'The Act was five years too late. It was not retrospective and gave little satisfac-tion. Registration was no more than a record which did not supersede deeds, make titles legal or define doubtful boundaries and locations.'[25]

The system introduced in 1842 was different from the Torrens system in a crucial respect: registration of deeds did not confer any additional validity on the deed. If a deed was invalid because it was forged, for example, or signed by someone without a right to sell, registration did not make it valid.[26] Registration merely prevented deeds that were *already* valid before registration from being set aside by later valid transactions. So buyers who accepted invalid deeds still found that they did not have any, or a complete, title to the land which they thought they had bought. Registration of the deed was of no use to them.

As someone said about another system of land titles, the registration-of-deeds system 'was no "hospital": it could not be used to elevate "bad" titles to "good" ones; rather it was directed at saving good titles'.[27] So the whole chain-of-title process had to continue. What the colonists needed was a system that rendered the process of establishing a chain of title entirely obsolete.

2. The Torrens system

The fundamental change introduced by the Torrens system was that the legal ownership of land could no longer be changed by private agreements between buyers and sellers, but only by the act of registration on a public register. The title of a registered owner is independent of the previous owners' titles: registration itself confers title. Simply being registered as the owner cures any defects that would otherwise exist in the title. All that you have to do, therefore, as a buyer of Torrens system land is to check that the person selling you the land is the person named in the public register as the owner of it. There is no need to check whether that seller bought it from the true owner of the land, for as long as the seller is the person named in the register you can be quite sure that you will get a good title from that seller.

This basic principle was expressed in s 31 of the *Real Property Act* of 1858,[28] and may now be found in s 67 of the current South Australian statute embodying the Torrens system, the *Real Property Act* 1886. In case anyone failed to understand the fundamental change wrought by the system, s 37 of the 1858 Act repeated that 'upon such entry [of a transfer in the register book] being made by the Registrar-General, the land, or the estate or interest therein, as set forth and limited in such memorandum of sale as to be transferred, shall pass to and vest in the purchaser'. Section 33 of the original version of the Act supplemented this principle by specifying that what appeared on the register was to be conclusive evidence of all the interests that existed in the land concerned.

Here, then, is the important change expressed in statutory language: once a change of ownership has been registered in the public register book *the fact of being registered as the owner – not the previous agreements between the buyer and the seller – is itself the source of the new owner's good and independent title to the land.* So the Torrens register *is* a 'hospital'.

Any agreements and deeds entered into by the parties themselves remained private arrangements, enforceable only between the parties themselves, until the ownership was legally transferred by an entry in the register book. Thus, the responsibility for keeping a record of the ownership of land, and ensuring that the ownership of land was changed effectively, was transferred from private to public hands.

That meant, in turn, that it was not necessary to investigate whether any private agreement or document was valid, for everything was shown on a public register.

Naturally this principle cannot be applied without any reservation. There had to be exceptions for what s 33 of the Act of 1858 called 'the case of fraud and error', or, more accurately, fraud (including out-right forgery) *or* error. If it were open to anyone to forge a transfer of land and have it registered, and then to claim a good title based on the fact that that person's name appeared in the register book, anyone could easily amass a substantial property holding with little effort (although no doubt such a person might soon find himself looking after his property holdings from prison).

The person who really needs protection in such a situation is not the fraudster, of course, but anyone who may buy the land from the fraudster in good faith – believing that the fraudster, who after all is registered as the owner of the land, is a legitimate seller. Accordingly, s 94 of the Act allowed the title registered by the fraudster to be cancelled up until the time that he sold the land to someone acting in good faith, but also said that a buyer, if acting in good faith, obtained the ownership of the land.

The principle that the register book is, subject to the limited exception also outlined, the independent source of an owner's title to land has been memorably subdivided by a commentator into two sub-principles, the 'mirror principle' and the 'curtain principle'.[29] The mirror principle means that the register book kept under the Torrens system should be an accurate reflection of the state of title to the land. It should show not only who the owner is, but whether he has mortgaged the land, or leased it, or in any other way done something which restricts his rights as the owner.

This is the principle to which s 33 of the original Act, with its emphasis on the conclusive nature of the register book, attempts to give effect. But again it is not possible for this principle to be applied without any exceptions. For example, it is usual for Torrens statutes nowadays to contain an exception to the mirror principle stating that people who have short-term leases over land and are actually in occupation of it do not have to register their leases for them to be valid. This is because, first, registering a short-term lease would be tiresome, unnecessarily complicated and expensive; and, secondly, people intending to buy land should notice if someone other than the owner is actually occupying it, and make further enquiries. The current South Australian statute accordingly protects people with leases for a year or less who are in actual occupation of the land.[30]

Equally (although the legal effect of this situation may be somewhat different from that of the last), people who wish to buy land should notice if the owner's copy of the certificate of title cannot be produced by the owner, and that should lead them to enquire whether someone else has it, perhaps because that other person has an interest in the land such as a mortgage which has not been registered. But subject to these and similar exceptions, the register book should mirror the state of title to the land.

The curtain principle marks a further, even more important departure from the old system: it states that a person wanting to buy land should not be concerned about transactions preceding those on the register nor (subject to the sorts of exceptions just mentioned) need to enquire about whether there is anything not on the register. A person wanting to buy land (or otherwise deal with land, for example by taking a mortgage over it) is entitled to draw a 'curtain' in front of everything which is not on the register book and to regard the register as the sole source of information about the land in question. Under the old system, that would have been fatal if there lay hidden, in deeds ten or fifteen years old, some defect in the title of the seller which would, so to speak, infect any potential buyer.

A further innovation – the 'insurance principle' – was contained in the Act to protect those who lost their land through the registration of incorrect details on the register, whether by fraudsters or by accident. A tax of one farthing in the pound – about 0.104 per cent – of the value of land brought under the system established by the Act was to be levied and paid into an Assurance Fund. Under ss 35 and 96 of the Act, this money was to be used to compensate people who had lost their land through fraud or error.

Thus, the Act established not only a state-run register of titles, but also a state guarantee that landowners would not be deprived of their land because of the operation of the system. This was obviously a very important part of the operation of the system. From the point of view of the landowner joining the Torrens system, it provided some assurance that nothing could be lost by joining the system.

Joining the Torrens system was a voluntary process for all land first sold by the Crown before July 1858, that is for all land which the Crown had sold in the first 21 years of settlement in South Australia. (It was not until the *Real Property (Registration of Titles) Act* 1945 that any attempt was made to compel people to bring their land within the Torrens system, although the overwhelming majority had done so voluntarily by then.) Owners of land already sold under the old system had to take the initiative and apply to receive a Torrens title instead of an old system title. So some guarantee had to be held out to existing landowners to persuade them to join the new system. And from the point of view of the state, having to pay compensation in the case of fraud or error obviously created an incentive to run the system with care.

The possibility of claiming on the Assurance Fund still exists, but under s 201 (7) of the current statute[31] no further taxes to top it up have been levied since 1988. That is how infrequently this form of insurance has been needed.[32]

The second piece of legal history which has had lasting consequences in South Australia is the initial opposition of some – perhaps most, but by no means all – South Australian lawyers to the Torrens system. Lawyers' opposition to the Act was strong enough to bring about the creation of a new para-legal profession in the shape of the land broker,[33] who could conduct business under the Act instead of solicitors. The Torrens system was simple enough to allow non-lawyers to carry on the business of transferring land, even land of very significant value. And land brokers, of course, are cheaper to employ than solicitors.

3. Torrens – man and system[34]

The Torrens system has nothing to do with the River Torrens – or, to be more precise, the River Torrens was named after the father of the man who developed the Torrens system, after Colonel Robert Torrens F.R.S. rather than his son, Sir Robert Richard Torrens.

The family came from what is now Northern Ireland, although Robert Richard Torrens was born in Cork. Colonel Torrens, the father, was a political economist of some repute in his day, and not entirely forgotten even today. Eight volumes of the *Collected Works of Robert Torrens*[35] were published as recently as 2000, at the forbidding price of £750. Torrens *senior* comes into the story, and appears on the map, of South Australia because of his unremitting labours in promoting the settlement and growth of the colony in its early years. He was Chairman of the Colonisation Commissioners, but he never visited South Australia.

However, his son arrived in Adelaide in 1840 aged 26. Very quickly Robert Torrens started on his career in the public service, as Collector of Customs. Almost as quickly he acquired a reputation as a somewhat headstrong and difficult man, and was regularly complained about by his subordinates, reprimanded by his superiors, and ridiculed in the newspapers, some of which thought him lazy and grasping. Once, he was even sued successfully for assault.

Sir Robert Richard Torrens (left) and
Colonel Robert Torrens, c. 1860.
Photograph courtesy of the State Library of South Australia, SLSA: B 7557

One thing stands out in the life of this most successful of South Australian legal reformers: Torrens had no legal training whatsoever.

Torrens became interested in the reform of lands titles law when, as he stated, a friend of his had suffered 'a grievous injury and injustice'[36] when a flaw was discovered in his title to land which he had not only purchased, but also improved. He, Torrens, said that he resolved to do something about the state of lands titles law as a result.

The issue of lands titles reform had been broached very early on by a number of colonists.[37] The Commissioner of Public Lands, J.H. Fisher, had drafted a Bill for the registration of titles in 1836, even before the first settlers sailed, which had 'the blessing of his lawyer friends in London and the Colonisation Commissioners',[38] the Chairman of which, it will be recalled, was one Colonel Torrens. Another legal luminary, Charles Mann, called as early as 1838 in his newspaper for the introduction of a system for registration of dealings in land.[39] This earnt him a sharp rebuke from the *Register*,[40] South Australia's first, and Adelaide's leading, newspaper.

The issue of registration of lands titles became one of the major issues in the election campaign for the first Parliament of South Australia which opened in April 1857. This is not surprising in a society in which all but the very poor were, or could hope to be, landowners, and given that virtually all adult men in South Australia had the vote. Land ownership was in fact one of the things that the common man could aspire to in a colony like South Australia, as distinct from England; it was a source of pride, and a reason to come here in the first place. Lands titles reform was therefore not just a question of helping big land owners or land speculators; it was an issue that affected many people. By advocating reform and registration of lands titles, and by clever campaigning, Torrens was the first candidate elected for the seat of Adelaide.[41] This indicates the importance of the issue of lands titles reform in the election.

An outline of Torrens's Bill for land titles reform had been published well before the election in the *Register*, then the principal newspaper of the colony, on 17 October 1856.[42] The editor hailed it as the start of 'a great and glorious reformation'.[43] (Perhaps the author of those words, which might well have seemed something of an exaggeration at the time, would still be astonished if he could know how successful, and how widely copied, that reformation has been.) An extended summary of the provisions of a revised version of the Bill was published in April 1857.[44]

Although we have these early sources for the Bill which became the *Real Property Act*, we do not know very much about the behind-the-scenes process of drafting the Bill. No written records of any of the early drafting were kept, and most of the early development of the idea probably took place in Torrens's head anyway. Virtually all we know about the development of the system until the introduction of the Bill into Parliament is what can be gleaned from public sources such as Parliamentary debates and newspaper reports. Even that is not very much. We are told, for example, in the newspaper report of 17 October 1856[45] that Torrens 'has, it seems, been devoting the Parliamentary recess to a consideration of the subject [of lands titles reform], and the result is now brought to light in the shape of a draft Bill, embodying a large number of salutary reforms'. But there is no record of how precisely that process was conducted, or who exactly, other than Torrens, was involved in it.

Three things can however be said about the process of developing the system. The first is that Torrens had help from many other people. This fact was clearly known to everyone at the time, but we know it even today partly because Torrens himself pointed it out.[46] John Baker, his predecessor as Premier, even accused him of being the head of a 'clique'.[47]

The newspaper report of 17 October 1856 records a recent meeting at Torrens's house of 'a party of influential gentlemen' to consider Torrens's proposals, of which, it is stated, they approved. Perhaps this was the same as, or perhaps it was a different gathering from, the dinner of nineteen people which John Baker also mentioned and at which those present are said to have pledged themselves to the Torrens system.[48] From the first, the Torrens system appears to have involved the effort of a number of people under the leadership of Torrens.

Some authors accordingly see the *Real Property Act*, in its final form,

as the result of the work of an informal committee.[49] We have no
record of a committee actually being formed, let alone holding regular
meetings, but clearly the Torrens system involved the co-operative
efforts of, and discussion among, a number of leading lights in early
Adelaide. The smallness of Adelaide at the time and the readiness of its
leading citizens to consider useful law reform, coupled with the well-
known need for it in lands titles law, facilitated this cross-fertilisation
process. That is one thing that makes the Torrens system a peculiarly
South Australian achievement.

Whatever other defects Torrens's character might have possessed,
unwillingness to seek advice from others does not seem to have been
one of them. Seeking advice and assistance from others was, however,
the only rational course given that his system could not be introduced
or hope to be a success without broad support in the community and
the legislature.

Secondly, there were also other systems of registration which
Torrens used to assist in the development of his system.[50]

Part II of the British *Merchant Shipping Act* 1854 is the most often
mentioned. That Act was mentioned by the *Register* as early as July
1856 as a possible model for a reform of land titles law,[51] and Torrens
certainly knew of it from his time as Collector of Customs.

However, there are considerable differences between ships and land,
and between the Torrens system and the system of shipping registration. In particular, the *Merchant Shipping Act* 1854 did not establish a
system of title solely by registration,[52] but it did include a register book
which was evidence (although not conclusive evidence) of the owner's
title. Dr Stanley Robinson's analysis shows that all but a very few of the
clauses of the first draft of the *Real Property Act* owed their origin to the
Merchant Shipping Act 1854.[53]

We cannot know whether Torrens saw the Act and then conceived
his system as a derivative from it, or whether he hit on the idea first and
then turned to the statute as providing a precedent for his desired
outcome. The latter is perhaps more likely. One of the first ways in
which the aims of the Torrens system were explained to the public was
as a means of making a registered title just as valid as a title newly

granted by The Crown.[54] Torrens himself compared the effect of adopting his system to a notional system in which each new owner of land would receive a new, and thus indisputably valid, grant of title from The Crown.[55] This idea – perhaps Torrens's original brainwave – cannot be adapted from a system for the registration of ships. Torrens also said in Parliament in November 1857 that 'it was nearly ten years since the ideas thrown together in [his] Bill had been first entertained by him',[56] and that he had tested the ideas on various of his contemporaries over the years. If this is right, his ideas pre-dated the Act of 1854.

Thirdly, Torrens appears to have circulated his Bill quite widely for comment to a number of people: in Parliament on 4 June 1857,[57] he refers to criticism of one specific provision, the preamble, by certain unnamed lawyers. No doubt Torrens knew that he would need the support of others to have his new system passed into law. No doubt he also accepted suggestions from a number of people about the shape of the system as time went on and it was refined.

After the elections of 1857, matters stood still for a few months; Torrens became the third Premier of South Australia in September 1857, his government lasting almost the entire month, and most of his attention was doubtless absorbed in trying to keep his government together. (However, this was not by any means the record for brevity in office, not even at this early stage, as his predecessor as Premier, John Baker, had remained Premier for only eleven days.)

Torrens's Bill was, however, eventually introduced in November 1857, and was passed by Parliament on 27 January 1858. During its passage, it was severely criticised from some quarters as a half-baked madcap idea of Torrens, a non-lawyer dabbling in legal affairs with insufficient knowledge and experience, but a vested interest in making his own property holdings more secure.

The *Adelaide Times* – an early newspaper which ceased publication before the Torrens system even came into operation – dismissed the Bill as 'the production of a non-legal mind'[58] and '"a thing of shreds and patches", picked up wherever he [Torrens] could lay his hands upon them'.[59] It expanded on its opposition in another editorial:

Our objections ... to this measure, then, are:– 1st, the large addition it will make for years to come to the legal expenses incurred in the transfer of real estate; 2nd, the deprivation of the holders of real estate of one of their inalienable rights, that of being the sole depositaries of their own secret as to the extent of their possessions, and the title on which they hold them, by a compulsory registration; and 3rdly, the setting up, at an enormous expense, of a great Government Establishment, as the workshop at which all conveyances of real estate are to be manufactured, and all transfers and encumbrances compulsorily registered.[60]

The leader writer's objections were two-sided: first, the system would not achieve what it was supposed to achieve, and secondly it would take away the advantages of the old system such as privacy. The newspaper was also suspicious of the motives of the Bill's promoters, and accused its rival in the newspaper business, Anthony Forster M.L.C. of the *Register*, of promoting the Bill in Parliament in the hope that he would receive income from the newspaper advertisements that would be required as part of the procedure envisaged by the Bill.[61]

Some lawyers, too, opposed the Bill. The unkind view was that some of them feared a loss of fees if the new system took hold – they were the only people who could operate the old chain-of-title system. But there were less unworthy motivations for their opposition as well, such as an emotional attachment to the intricacies of the old system,[62] or genuine (if mistaken) scepticism about whether a system designed by a non-lawyer could really work.

Historians are divided on the extent to which lawyers opposed the Torrens system, and there are few records of what they said or did. Fox[63] suggests that virtually the whole legal profession was opposed, whereas Pike[64] records that, once it had been enacted, 'most of the legal profession accepted the new law graciously and many constructive suggestions were offered'. In truth lawyers were divided in their opinions. Even the small colonial South Australian profession was not a monolith speaking with one voice. The *Register*[65] reported in January 1858 that the Torrens system was 'opposed by most of the lawyers in this Province' – most, but not all.

Having passed through Parliament, the Act came into force, under s 123, at the start of July 1858, and Torrens resigned his seat in Parliament to be the first Registrar-General under the Act. Once the *Real Property Act* had reached the statute book, it could be a success only if accepted by the community as an improvement on the old system and a secure means of holding land. It achieved this very quickly. The South Australian Company, a major – if not the major – landowner in early South Australia, astutely recognised that its holdings would be more easily marketable if it obtained Torrens titles than if they remained under the old chain-of-title system. By mid-1859 the Company was already making plans to acquire Torrens titles, bringing vast tracts within the system.[66] As Registrar-General, Torrens helped the new system to find its feet, and thus may claim some credit for the successful operation of the system in its first years.

Opposition to the Torrens system continued, however. Courts and lawyers discovered holes in the original Act, and the Supreme Court of South Australia began to pronounce crucial bits of it invalid. These defects, some real and some more or less invented by the Judges, meant that several amending Acts had to be passed from 1858 to 1861.[67] Torrens assisted in drafting these and in the defence of the system against those who argued that the need for amendments indicated that the whole principle was bad.

Torrens also went on 'missionary' expeditions in the late 1850s and early 1860s to the other Australian colonies and New Zealand,[68] persuading them to introduce a system similar to the South Australian one. This mission was completely successful by 1875, almost ten years before Torrens's death, so that, unlike many law reformers, he had the satisfaction of living to see his own success.

In the course of time, questions about the validity of the Act became subsumed in the larger issue of the extent to which the South Australian Parliament was permitted by the law of the British Empire to introduce innovations that were at variance with the law of England.[69] This controversy was eventually resolved by two events: the passing of the *Colonial Laws Validity Act* 1865 by the Imperial Parliament, and the death of Mr Justice Boothby in 1868 before his appeal against his removal from judicial office could be heard. Benjamin Boothby had been the major proponent of the view that the South Australian legislature's powers to deviate from the law of England were very limited indeed, and we shall meet him again in this book. His passing from the scene, and the *Colonial Laws Validity Act* 1865, confirmed the wide powers of the South Australian legislature to introduce virtually any legislation it liked, including the Torrens system, as embodied in the *Real Property Act* of 1858 and later amending legislation.

Torrens resigned as Registrar-General in 1865 after moving back to England. He entered the Imperial Parliament in 1868 as M.P. for Cambridge, but found that land titles reform did not excite as many people in England as it had in South Australia.[70] The class of property owners in England was proportionately smaller than it was in South Australia, and he found it impossible to stir up much popular interest in the subject. Torrens was knighted in 1872, but not re-elected to Parliament at the election of 1874. By then 60, he decided to retire from public affairs, and died in August 1884, aged 70, in Falmouth, Cornwall.

4. The Hamburg system?

In recent years, debate among legal historians has concentrated on the question of who really thought up the Torrens system. One legal historian, Dr Tony Esposito,[71] has claimed that the Torrens system was in all its essentials just a copy of the Hamburg system of lands titles registration. Another writer even goes so far as to suggest that 'Torrens must be vilified for his deceit'.[72] While there is no doubt that the role of people other than Torrens to the introduction of the Torrens system has been minimised in the past,[73] now it seems that the pendulum is swinging too far the other way, with some people keen to strip Torrens of any credit for originating the system at all.

There have long been competing claims to the invention of the Torrens system. This fact is not at all surprising given that 'success has a thousand fathers'. It is quite understandable that some of those who played a role in the creation of the Torrens system came with time, and the growing success of the system, to view their part in its creation as greater than an unbiased observer might have done. For example, the editor of the *Register*, Anthony Forster, claimed in 1892, once the success of the system was an established fact and Torrens himself was dead, that the system 'originated in a series of leading articles that I wrote'.[74] No doubt his agitation had helped keep the issue alive in the 1850s,[75] but would he have made such a claim had the predictions of the Torrens system's detractors been fulfilled and it had turned out to be a disaster and a flop?

In deciding who gets the credit for the Torrens system, something might also depend on the point of view of the observer: a lawyer will naturally concentrate on the details of the system as enacted and attribute the greatest credit to the person responsible for the detail, or the crucial principle, while a political scientist might be more concerned with the question of who persuaded the public and the legislature to undertake any reform at all and be less interested in the precise details of the reform.

As Hernando de Soto writes, 'Many [reforming lawyers] understand that the primary determinants of change rest outside the law'.[76] But commentators on the history of the Torrens system sometimes forget that. In debates about who wrote the words of the *Real Property Act*, it should not be forgotten that it would never have become law at all without the agreement of the Parliament of South Australia. Whatever our view is about who wrote the actual words of the *Real Property Act*, we should never forget that the main ingredient in its success and wide adoption throughout the world was Torrens's untiring promotion of it.

The claim that Torrens should be 'vilified' is perhaps suited to the iconoclastic age in which we have the good fortune to live. Even so, it does not seem to be in accordance with Torrens's considerable contribution to the development and passing of the new system of land titles law. Other recent contributions to this debate, not merely the one just quoted, appear to proceed from the assumption that it is simply unbelievable that a small community on the edge of Empire could have invented a system as successful as the Torrens system without outside help, or to wish to make a point, which in one recent contribution is rather laboured, about the multicultural nature of early South Australia, the defects of the English heritage and colonialism, and the great but sadly overlooked contribution of those who did not share that heritage.

Such wider issues cannot be resolved here, although obviously one of the aims of this book is to ensure that South Australia's considerable contribution to legal ideas in Australia and the wider world is not simply forgotten. A collection of a number of examples of South Australian legal innovations, such as this one, may also lead the reader to the conclusion that the idea that important original legal innovations can be thought up in South Australia is not necessarily a preposterous one. The contrary is the case. Early Adelaide was, for reasons given earlier, the ideal place for law reform to occur: the community both needed law reform and was bold enough to try it.

Nevertheless, a serious candidate as the 'outside' source of the Torrens system has been proposed. It is the land law of Hamburg, knowledge of which was brought to South Australia by Dr Ulrich Hübbe. Dr Hübbe, born in 1805 in Hamburg, immigrated to South Australia in 1842. He had a doctorate of law from the University of Kiel. In 1857 he published what was described as a pamphlet, but was in fact a book with the baroque title of *The Voice of Reason and History Brought to Bear against the Present Absurd and Expensive Method of Transferring and Encumbering Immovable Property, With some Comments on the Reformatory Measures Proposed in the Opening Speech of the Governor-in-Chief, and the Bill Recently Introduced by the Hon. R.R. Torrens, Esq., into the House of Assembly.*[77]

The similarity between the Torrens and Hamburg systems has been convincingly shown by Tony Esposito[78] and Murray Raff.[79] They have demonstrated how the Hamburg system evolved over time, and well before the invention of the Torrens system, into a system in which title was required to be registered and the register was conclusive evidence of what it contained.[80]

It is also clear that Torrens and Hübbe were in contact with each other. So is the Torrens system really just a copy of the Hamburg system, as explained by Dr Hübbe to Torrens? Has Hübbe been robbed of the credit for being the brains behind the system? I suggest not.

There are, firstly, differences between the Hamburg and the Torrens systems. There was, for example, no such thing in the Hamburg system as an Assurance Fund. One of the pillars of the Torrens system, the guarantee of title by the state not just in words, but by means of a fund of money produced by a very small tax on transactions under the system, is missing from the Hamburg model. Professor Whalan suggests that the Assurance Fund was a late addition to the scheme, and that the idea for it originated in England.[81]

Undaunted, Dr Esposito insists on the similarities, and says that the similarities show that the Torrens system was originally based on the system of title to land by registration then current in Hamburg. But similarity does not of itself establish copying. It could also just be coincidence. This is also not an unlikely explanation. For example, a system of title by registration like the Torrens system is obviously going to have some means of recording who is registered, and the limited technology available in the mid-nineteenth century makes it likely that that would be some sort of book. So the mere existence of a register book in each system does not prove very much at all beyond the fact that the systems happen to be similar, which we knew already. It does not prove that one is a based on another, which is what those pointing out such similarities wish to prove.

It is of course quite possible for two people to invent similar systems independently of each other – as, for instance, happened with the invention of calculus, which has been the subject of much dispute for centuries between the supporters of Sir Isaac Newton and Gottfried Wilhelm Leibniz (another competition between English- and German-speaking inventors). Indeed, in the same year as the introduction into Parliament of the *Real Property Act*, a report to the British House of Commons was published advocating a system of registration of lands titles.[82] This report did not reach Adelaide until November 1857[83] and thus cannot have been the source of the ideas behind the Bill (although it may have been used to effect one or two last-minute improvements, in particular the Assurance Fund).[84] But it demonstrates that it was quite possible for two sets of people to develop a similar idea independently of each other.

Common sense suggests that the hypothesis that a similar idea occurred to two different sets of people independently of each other is more plausible if the idea concerned is simple. And there is in fact nothing particularly complicated about the idea behind the Torrens system – registration as an independent source of title. In the view of one English commentator, the idea behind the Torrens system, especially in newly founded colonies such as South Australia, was 'so simple, and so obvious, that it is astonishing that it was not adopted long before'.[85] The same writer says, 'Basically the Torrens idea was that records of the sort normally kept by any competent land office in respect of Crown leaseholds should also be kept in respect of freehold grants. It was a very simple idea to comprehend.'[86]

At the time when the Torrens system was actually being conceived, considered by the public and Parliament and implemented, there is in fact no evidence at all that anyone thought that Dr Hübbe was the real brains behind the system, or that it was just a copy of the Hamburg system. Indeed, the reverse is the case: everyone at the time said that it was Torrens's system, including Hübbe himself.

In a letter to the *Register* in February 1857, Hübbe[87] refers to Torrens and 'the principle of his Bill, [which] he has plainly enough indicated ... both from the platform and in the papers'.[88] This hardly reads like the statement of someone who had done all the work himself and is finding that his idea has been taken over by an impostor. Rather, it confirms that Hübbe knew that he was not the author of Torrens's proposals.

The same conclusion must be drawn from references in Hübbe's book of 1857[89] to 'Mr Torrens's plan',[90] 'Mr Torrens's Bill'[91] and 'Mr Torrens's proposals'.[92] If the statements by Hübbe are to be reconciled with the thesis that Hübbe was the real brains behind the system, one must accept that, at this point in the development of the Torrens system (although not after its success was clearly established), he possessed a degree of diffidence comparable to that shown by only one other person in human history.[93]

Numerous speakers and writers referred to the Bill as Torrens's own creation in 1857 and 1858, as the Bill was going through Parliament.[94] No one objected to this appellation, neither the opponents nor the proponents of the Bill; no one even suggested that it was only a partial truth. No one ever proposed that it should really be called the Hübbe system or the Hamburg system. Criticism of the Bill concentrated rather on Torrens's alleged inability to draft a workable statute, given that he was not a lawyer – a point which Torrens might easily have answered had he been working from the start with a lawyer experienced in the system he wished to introduce.`

Nowhere does anyone attack the Torrens system as a mere translation of a foreign system. It would have been easy to attack the Hamburg system's suitability for South Australia. Not only are the languages and legal backgrounds very different; South Australia is also, without putting too fine a point on it, a bit larger than the city of Hamburg. There is, in other words, more land to register. Furthermore, the German settlers were sometimes looked at askance by the British settlers,[95] and some people might have tried, if they could, to discredit a legal idea by linking it with 'foreigners'. The enemies of the system never attacked it as a foreign import.

Why not? It could of course be that Torrens succeeded very well in hushing up the fact that his system was really based on Hamburg's. But far from trying to hush up any similarity between his system and the Hamburg one, Torrens openly admitted it. Responding to criticisms that his system was totally untried, he said in Parliament on 4 June 1857 that his system 'was not an untried measure, for although he was not at first aware of it, it had been in operation for 600 years in the Hanse Towns'[96] such as Hamburg.

This hardly suggests that he was reluctant to admit that a similar system was in operation in Germany in order to claim all the credit for himself. But Torrens also claims here that he was not at first aware of the parallel. The obvious conclusion is that Hübbe came into the picture only after Torrens had independently devised the basic principles of his system, and that it was an original proposal which just happened to be similar to an existing system found elsewhere. This conclusion is strongly supported by the fact that Torrens and Hübbe only met as a result of Hübbe's letters in the *Register* in February and March 1857 – as Hübbe himself confirms.[97] This meeting occurred just before Torrens's statement that he had only just become aware that his system was similar to the Hamburg one, but well after he had started to develop his system in mid-1856 at the latest.

Torrens's statement that he did not at first realise that the similarity existed is not at all implausible. When he proposed his system, Torrens was constantly faced with criticisms that it was untried and the product of a non-lawyer's bumbling attempts to reform the law.[98] If he had been able at an early stage in the debate to say, 'My proposal is based on a system in operation elsewhere and has been developed with the help of a lawyer experienced in that system', he would gladly have done so. That would have made the proposed system seem less of a leap in the dark and silenced the criticism that he was proposing a completely untried system. As soon as Torrens found out that his proposal was similar to the Hamburg one, he trumpeted that fact from the rooftops. Nor is there any record of enmity between Torrens and Hübbe which might have caused the former to wish to conceal the latter's contribution. Rather, Hübbe's account is that he and Torrens got on famously.[99]

If Torrens had presented what was essentially a copy of a foreign system, translated by a foreign lawyer (who, however, was fluent in English), is it really likely that that fact would not have speedily become known as the proposal to reform land titles law radically was subjected to a vast amount of debate in Parliament and the broader community, and as the system began to operate and problems with it had to be ironed out? We all know how efficient the rumour mill is in today's Adelaide. It was even more efficient when Adelaide was much smaller.

The drafting of the Torrens system also involved a wide circle of people. That means that many people would have known otherwise if Torrens's claim that he did not at first know about the similarity of his system to the Hamburg one had been false and he had at any stage abandoned his original idea and/or just copied another system explained to him by Dr Hübbe. It would have been, if false, a dangerous claim to make, easily liable to refutation by a fairly large number of people.

In short, we see Torrens in 1857 acting like a typical law reformer, seeking to claim support for his proposal from as many sides as possible and being only too glad to point out that he, a bumbling non-lawyer, had unwittingly created a system similar to an existing one. Only later, once his system was an established success, would Torrens have had any motive to downplay others' contributions. The reverse is also true: once the system had succeeded, everyone wanted to elbow Torrens aside and claim the credit for it. Anthony Forster tried to do that in the letters from 1892, quoted above. To find any statements that Hübbe was the real brains behind the system, or that it was based on the Hamburg system, we have to fast forward by over two decades after the Torrens system had come into operation on 1 July 1858 to the time when it was an established success.

Even then, the only statement that goes as far as stating that Hübbe was the real author of the system is a remark made in the South Australian Parliament in 1880 by a Rudolph Henning M.P., also an immigrant from Germany. He said that 'it was perfectly well known ... that Dr Hübbe provided the ideas, the brains and the work of [the *Real Property Act*], and that Sir R.R. Torrens merely fought the battle of the Bill in the House'.[100] His statement does suggest that Torrens merely promoted someone else's idea. But it was made twenty-two years after the events in question by someone who had no particularly central role in them: Henning was around twenty-four years old in 1858, and did not become a Member of Parliament until twenty years later, in 1878.[101]

The lack of any interjections during or contradiction of Henning's statements in this debate, to which Dr Esposito[102] points as proof of the persuasiveness of what Henning said among his contemporaries, is therefore much more likely to be due to the other parliamentarians' sense of politeness and their unwillingness to point out that Mr Henning was ignorant of what had occurred over twenty years ago when he was barely an adult. Or perhaps no one was listening to him at the time. We cannot draw any conclusion that Henning's listeners, if any, agreed with him from their silence.

Ulriche Hübbe, c. 1880
Photograph courtesy of the State Library of South Australia, SLSA: B 9042

Furthermore, other statements were made in the same debate which are not consistent with the thesis that Hübbe was the real author of the *Real Property Act*. Torrens was frequently mentioned by various speakers in the same debate as the originator of the Act. But apart from Mr Henning, no one mentioned Hübbe as providing anything other than assistance to Torrens; no one stood up and proclaimed him the real originator of the idea, as distinct from a helper.

The same thing can be said of a Parliamentary debate in 1884 about whether a pension should be provided to Dr Hübbe in recognition of his services in the drafting of the *Real Property Act*. The pension was granted, but again no one stood up and proclaimed Hübbe the real author of the principle behind the Act. A debate on recognising Dr Hübbe's contribution would have been the ideal opportunity to do so, but no one did. Rather, the case for Dr Hübbe was made exclusively on the basis of his assistance to Torrens. Even Rudolph Henning now said merely that Dr Hübbe 'had materially assisted in the passing of the *Real Property Act*'[103] – a much more realistic assessment of events, and this in a debate in which some exaggeration of Dr Hübbe's contribution might be pardoned. Another Member of Parliament came just as close to my own opinion in saying that 'Dr Hübbe did assist the late Sir R.R. Torrens to work out the *details* of the measure'.[104] (The reference here is to the 'late Sir R.R. Torrens' because he had died in the month before this debate on Dr Hübbe's petition seeking payment for his role in the creation of the Torrens system; for one reason or another, Hübbe waited until very shortly after Torrens's death to claim compensation for his role in the creation of the Torrens system.)[105]

H.E. Downer, who had been admitted to the Bar of South Australia in 1858, noted that Dr Hübbe 'had probably rendered assistance to Sir R.R. Torrens's, but even then 'he thought a great deal too much had been made of the matter'.[106] Mr Coglin M.P. – who had been in Parliament since 1860 and thus caught the end of the debates about the refinement of the Act of 1858, a process which was completed in 1861 – said that, without Hübbe, Torrens 'would not have been able to frame this Act as perfectly as he did'.[107] 'From his own knowledge as an old colonist', John Colton, the Premier, said, 'there was no doubt

Dr Hübbe had been of considerable service to the late Sir R.R. Torrens in framing and passing the *Real Property Act*'.[108] And the *Register*,[109] in commenting on this debate, reflected the same general theme of Dr Hübbe as Torrens's valued assistant: its view was that 'Dr Hübbe's intimate acquaintance with the details of the [Hamburg] system gave to the agitation in favour of the Torrens Act [note the phrase!] a much more definite and practical shape than it could have acquired without these aids'.

So what was Dr Hübbe's role in the development of the Torrens system? Why did he get his pension in 1884?

It is clear that Dr Hübbe did not just point out to Torrens, in about March 1857, that he had coincidentally come up with a system very much like that of his native country. Hübbe, with his detailed legal knowledge, helped to fine-tune the Torrens system. The question is when and to what extent this occurred. It is certain that any involvement by Hübbe began after the first drafts of mid-1856 and after he and Torrens met in the first quarter of 1857. It is not certain, but it is likely that it began before the first Bill was enacted in January 1858, and that he became more closely involved after the first Bill had been enacted and defects in it were revealed that required fixing by a technical expert.

We cannot be sure of Hübbe's involvement before the enactment of the first Bill, but it is likely that he was involved. Anthony Forster M.L.C., who had charge of the Bill in the Upper House, said in 1892 that 'the provisions of the Bill were settled by Mr Torrens and a few friends and put into proper form by Dr Hübbe'.[110] Another source from 1883 suggests that the drafting was divided between Hübbe and R.B. Andrews, a practising South Australian lawyer.[111]

Memories might have faded in the interval between 1858 and the making of those statements; Forster might have confused one of the later amending Bills with the first one; and we must not forget that Hübbe had published a book – at the urging of Torrens, in fact[112] – so that some of his influence may have been exercised in the public forum rather than as a collaborator behind the scenes.[113] But, assuming it is accurate, Forster's statement indicates that, even if involved as early as mid-1857, Hübbe was at most no more than a legislative drafter, who in the course of translating other people's ideas into legislative form helps them to refine their ideas and suggests improvements consistent with the scheme. Here, however, we know that a Bill existed in 1856, well before Hübbe came on to the scene, so he did not start drafting from scratch (as a drafter might today), but rather improved an existing Bill.

Caution needs to be exercised in relation to some other statements that are sometimes quoted as supporting a greater role for Dr Hübbe in the original Bill. For example, his daughter is recorded in 1931 as saying that 'the late Sir Edwin Smith used to tell how Dr Hübbe sat outside the bar of the House during the passage of the Bill in 1858 and was frequently consulted there by Sir Robert R. Torrens'.[114] Even if the date in this statement is correct – for there were several amending Bills shortly after 1858[115] – it may refer either to the original Bill debated in late 1857 and January 1858 or to the later amending Bill passed in 1858. If the latter, the statement says nothing about Hübbe's involvement in the original scheme. If the reference is to the first set of debates, then there is still reason for caution. Edwin Smith was only twenty-seven then. He did not become a member of Parliament until 1871. Unless he took time off from his business affairs, went along to the debates and saw Hübbe being consulted with his own eyes, Hübbe's daughter's statement is double hearsay – a most unreliable form of evidence, especially when first recorded three-quarters of a century after the events it purports to describe. Equally, Dr Hübbe's claim to have re-drafted the whole Bill from scratch after the abandonment of attempts to adapt the *Merchant Shipping Act* 1854[116] is not plausible given that the Act passed in January 1858 is recognisably the descendant of the Bill that existed well before his involvement began.

After the enactment of the first Bill, however, Hübbe was certainly involved as an adviser rather than a mere drafter. (Possibly he was consulted at the bar of the House by Torrens, if at all, at this later stage.) Hübbe's greater involvement is reflected in the incorporation of further suggestions from Hübbe into the system, which of course would have been there from the very start had he been its sole author.

The existence in South Australia of the land broker, for example, is probably the result of Hübbe's description of a similar vocation in Hamburg. This improvement in the system was made in 1860.[117] Torrens was asking Hübbe for advice on the public record in 1861.[118]

Even if the entire process of drafting the Torrens system had been recorded on film, and it was roughly as is suggested here, people could no doubt still argue about who should take the credit. But the process was not recorded on film, and probably most participants did not even realise the great historical importance of what they were doing at the time (as distinct from later, when the system had succeeded beyond the wildest dreams of its promoters and everyone rushed to claim credit for it). On the evidence, the better view is that the South Australian system was not originally based on the Hamburg one, and Hübbe's influence on the concept, as distinct from the detail, was minimal.

The Torrens system is not, from start to finish, a mere translation into English of a ready-made German system. Dr Hübbe merely fine-tuned someone else's brainwave, and the original form of that brainwave may well have been to give each buyer a title as good in effect as that of the first buyer from the Crown – an idea which cannot be taken from Hamburg, but which, rather, is very obviously suggested by the circumstances of a new colony in which Crown grants of land were a regular occurrence and always gave a good title. Hübbe's contribution, like that of others who helped Torrens, was no doubt immensely valuable, but it was not the origin even of the principles behind the system – let alone the cause of its adoption in South Australia, which for a number of reasons mentioned above was ideally placed to be the home of this great and truly South Australian work of law reform. Its rapid spread to other jurisdictions was also the result of Torrens's work.

The Torrens system is thus correctly named after its inventor and principal advocate.

This does not mean, of course, that the Torrens system was an entirely original invention. It was a 'mongrel' which owed its origins partly to Torrens's own contribution – his understanding of the defects of the old system and invention of the basic principle that should replace it; partly to the efforts of his assistants; and partly to copying from various existing systems. The *Adelaide Times*, one of its leading critics, was right to call it ' "a thing of shreds and patches" '.[119]

Just as there is no call to exaggerate Torrens's copying from sources such as the *Merchant Shipping Act* 1854, there is also no reason to play it down. Some degree of copying is hard to avoid. Anyone with any experience in legal history knows that there is so much law about the place that there probably never has been, nor can there ever be, an entirely original new legal idea, one uninfluenced by any other existing legal institutions. All law reformers, to adapt the words of Sir Isaac Newton, advance the law, and achieve what they do achieve, only 'by standing on the shoulders of giants' of the law who have preceded them. In this case, there were a number of other systems of registration in existence at the time, and it would have simply been foolish not to recycle whatever useful ideas and wording could be found in them. This not only saves work; it also enables the law reformer to argue (as indeed Torrens did) that his ideas are not as untried as they might otherwise appear to be.

Nevertheless, the Torrens system was much more than just a cut-and-paste job from any one source. It was a creative synthesis from several sources, one of which was Torrens's own original ideas; and the synthesis was developed in South Australia and contained improvements on the previous achievements of legal science. The Torrens system was something new under the sun, and the sun that first shone upon it was not the weak cold sun of Hamburg, but the harsh hot summer sun of Adelaide in January 1858. That sun which first rose in Adelaide now shines over countless acres of land in dozens of States, provinces, countries and territories all around the world.

Notes

1   The circumstances surrounding the adoption of the Torrens system in Tasmania are recounted in particular detail in Petrow, 'Knocking Down the House? The Introduction of the Torrens System to Tasmania' (1992) 11 U Tas LJ 167; see also Petrow, 'Responses to the Torrens System in Tasmania, 1862–1900' (1997) 5 Aust Prop LJ 194.

2   Whalan, *The Torrens System in Australia* (Law Book, Sydney 1982), pp. 8–11.

3   Whalan, 'The Origins of the Torrens System and its Introduction into New Zealand' in Hinde (ed.), *The New Zealand Torrens System: Centennial Essays* (Butterworths, Wellington 1971), pp. 12–32; Whalan, 'Immediate Success of Registration of Title to Land in Australasia and Early Failures in England' (1967) 2 NZULR 416, 424f.

4   Scottish Law Commission, *Discussion Paper on Land Registration: Void and Voidable Titles* (Discussion Paper no. 125; Stationery Office, Edinburgh 2004), p. 4.

5   Ziff, *Principles of Property Law* (3rd ed., Carswell, Scarborough 2000), pp. 422. A survey of the position in Canada not long after the adoption of the system there is Hogg, 'Uniformity in Registration of Title Law' (1917) 37 Can LT 374.

6   See below, fnn 13–16.

7   Cooper, 'Equity and Unregistered Land Rights in Commonwealth Registration Systems' (2003) 3 Ox U Clth Law Jo 201, 209–211; O'Connor, *Security of Property Rights and Land Title Registration Systems* (Ph.D. thesis, Monash University, July 2003), pp. 165–167; Raff, *Private Property and Environmental Responsibility: A Comparative Study of German Real Property Law* (Kluwer, the Hague 2003), p. 9; Ruoff, *An Englishman Looks at the Torrens System, being Some Provocative Essays on the Operation of the System after One Hundred Years* (Law Book, Sydney 1957), p. 7. In relation to Ghana, see Agbosu, 'Land Registration in Ghana: Past, Present and the Future' [1990] Jo Af Law 104, 104f, 123.

8   Garro, *The Louisiana Public Records Doctrine and the Civil-Law Tradition* (Paul Hebert Law Centre Publications Institute, Baton Rouge 1989), p. 75 fn 5; Raff, *Private Property*, p. 9; Simpson, *Land Law and Registration* (Cambridge U.P., 1976), p. 77–85, Ch. 21. I have no means of checking these claims, and it is possible that the word 'Torrens' is being used for systems which bear only the vaguest resemblance to the original version.

9   Ziff, *Principles of Property Law* (2nd ed., 1996), p. 412. The third edition (above, fn 5) is vaguer about this: at p. 423.

10   Gray, *Elements of Land Law* (3rd ed., Butterworths, London 2001), p. 192.

11   2nd ed., Clarendon, Oxford 1989, Vol. XVIII p. 273. The statement that Torrens was the first Premier of South Australia is, however, incorrect.
        The name of Torrens has also found its way into the French language judging by the title of a recent article: Brochu, 'Le système Torrens et la publicité foncière québécoise' (2002) 47 McGill LR 625. However, the content of this article, being in French, is not accessible to me.

12   Clarendon, Oxford 1980, p. 1224.

13   O'Connor, *Security of Property Rights*, p. 162

14   In addition to the references cited below, see Upham, 'An Introduction to the Principles of Private Land Ownership, Transfer and Control in the United States' in Jordán/Gambaro (eds.), *Land Law in Comparative Perspective* (Kluwer, the Hague 2002), pp. 48f.

15   Goldner, 'The Torrens System of Title Registration: A New Proposal for Effective Implementation' (1982) 29 UCLALR 661, 670. The reference is not to the legal profession, but to the title insurance industry, which

provides insurance to owners of land against defective titles to land and thus has a lot to lose from a system which largely eliminates such defects.

16 See, for surveys of these difficulties, Browder *et al.*, *Basic Property Law* (5th ed., West, St Paul 1989), pp. 912f; Casner *et al*, *American Real Property: A Treatise on the Law of Property in the United States* (Little, Brown & Co., Boston 1952), Vol. IV p. 640; Garro, *Louisiana Public Records*, pp. 90f; Goldner, (1982) 29 UCLALR 661; Grimes/Thompson, *Commentaries on the Modern Law of Real Property* (Bobbs-Merrill, Indianapolis 1963), Vol. 8A pp. 86–95 (on the constitutional objections in particular).

17 The position is somewhat better now that there is a real chance of a limitation period limiting the extent to which the backwards search has to be conducted (see *Limitation of Actions Act* 1936 s 4), but this was scarcely a possibility at the stage in South Australia's history dealt with here.

18 Harrison, 'The Transformation of Torrens's System into the Torrens System' (1962) 4 U Qld LJ 125, 125 (quoting Torrens's work).

19 Stein/Stone, *Torrens Title* (Butterworths, Sydney 1991), pp. 6–8; Whalan, *Torrens System*, pp. 14–16.

20 The legal framework for this was to be found in the Imperial statute 4 & 5 Wm IV c. 95 (1834) s 6. See also Castles, *An Australian Legal History*, p. 311; Pike, *Paradise of Dissent*, pp. 120f; Pike, (1960) 1 Adel LR 169, 171.

21 Pike, (1962) 1 Adel LR 169, 173f. See also Fox, 'The Story Behind the Torrens System' (1950) 23 ALJ 489, 491; Robinson, *Transfer of Land in Victoria* (Law Book, Sydney 1979), p. 2.

22 Pike, (1962) 1 Adel LR 169, 169; Whalan, (1967) 2 NZULR 416, 423. The view has also been expressed that the Torrens system was designed to deprive Aboriginal people of land: Ainger, 'Aboriginal Trailblazer Uncovers "Extraordinary Conspiracy["]' [1991] Syd Uni Gazette 18. Despite the respect I have for the person mentioned in that article as putting forward the theory (Mr Noel Pearson), it seems to me to draw a very long bow indeed, and the promised elaboration of the theory does not appear to have appeared.

23 No. 8 of 1841–42; see now the *Registration of Deeds Act* 1935.

24 6 Geo. IV No. 22 (1825). For further information, see Sykes/Walker, *The Law of Securities: An Account of the Law pertaining to Securities over Real and Personal Property under the Laws of Australian Jurisdictions* (6th ed., Law Book, Sydney 1993), p. 409.

25 Pike, (1962) 1 Adel LR 169, 176.

26 Stein/Stone, *Torrens Title*, p. 4; Whalan, *Torrens System*, p. 13.

27 Stein/Stone, *Torrens Title*, p. 13.

28 Section 31 began: 'No instrument [such as a deed] shall be effectual to pass any estate or interest in any land under the operation of this Act, or to render such land liable as security for the payment of money, but so soon as the Registrar-General shall have entered the particulars thereof in the book of registry, and made endorsement on such instrument as hereinafter directed to be made in each such case respectively, the estate or interest shall pass or, as the case may be, the land shall become liable to security in manner and subject to the conditions and contingencies set forth and specified in such instrument . . .'.

29 This terminology was first coined by Ruoff, *An Englishman*, p. 8, and the explanation here takes account of later contributions by commentators.

30 *Real Property Act* 1886 ss 69 VIII, 119.

31 *Real Property Act* 1886.

32 See also, for a fuller history and more details, South Australian Parliamentary Debates, Legislative Council, 23 March 1983, p. 563; 19 April 1983, p. 831; Ruoff, *An Englishman*, p. 33, and, in relation to the American Torrens systems, Goldner, (1982) 29 UCLALR 661, 706 fn 216.

33 *Real Property Act* 1860 s 133. See further Whalan, (1967) 2 NZULR 416, 419f.

34 The biographical sources used for this part include the *Australian Dictionary of Biography*, Vol. 2 pp. 534–536; Vol. 6 pp. 292f; *Dictionary of National Biography*, Vol. XIX, pp. 993–995; Pike, *Paradise, passim*.

35 Giancarlo de Vivo (ed.), *Collected Works of Robert Torrens* (Thoemmes Continuum, Poole 2000).

36 See Fox, (1950) 23 ALJ 489, 489f.

37 See, for later proposals and/or discussion, South Australian Parliamentary Debates, House of Assembly, 17 November 1857, col. 658; 18 November 1857, col. 660; 27 November 1857, col. 678; *Register*, 23 July 1856, p. 2; 31 July 1856, pp. 2, 3; 23 September 1856, p. 2; 24 October 1856, pp. 2f; 25 November 1856, p. 3.

38 Pike, (1962) 1 Adel LR 169, 175.

39 *Southern Australian*, 15 September 1838, p. 3.

40 *Register*, 22 September 1838, p. 3, which is the basis for the statement about Mann's views in Pike, (1962) 1 Adel LR 169, 176. Mann's views should however also be read in the original (see the previous footnote for reference).

41 Pike, (1962) 1 Adel LR 169, 179. The use of multi-member electorates in South Australia at this time explains the fact that Torrens was the *first* candidate elected.

42 *Register*, 17 October 1856, p. 2.

43 *Register*, 17 October 1856, p. 2.

44 *Register*, 14 April 1857, p. 2; 15 April 1857, p. 2.

45 *Register*, p. 2.

46 For example, in his speech recorded in the *Register*, 13 November 1857, p. 3, where he renders 'thanks to those gentlemen who first supported the measure, and to a member of the legal profession from whom he had received great assistance, but whose name he was not at liberty to mention'. One might wish that he had been more specific here.

47 South Australian Parliamentary Debates, Legislative Council, 22 January 1858, col. 779.

48 *Register*, 20 January 1858, p. 3; Mr Baker adds that this was now 'some time ago'.

49 Robinson, *Transfer of Land*, pp. 9f, 15; Whalan, *Torrens System*, p. 6; Whalan, 'Origins', pp. 5–8, 12.

50 In addition to the other models mentioned in the text, the idea of making every transfer a re-grant may also have been suggested by the archaic English tenure system of copyhold, on which see Simpson, *An Introduction*

to the History of Land Law (Oxford U.P., 1961), pp. 160f. An explanation of
the complexities of this system is outside the scope of this book.

51   *Register*, 31 July 1856, p. 2.

52   As ss 57 and 107 of that Act show.

53   Robinson, *Transfer of Land*, p. 8. A more detailed, clause-by-clause
comparison may be found at pp. 480–484, and in Dr Robinson's doctoral
thesis: *Equity and Systems of Title to Land by Registration* (Monash University,
1973), pp. 117–123.

54   Harrison, (1962) 4 U Qld LJ 125, 125f, 130.

55   See further Cooper, (2003) 3 Ox U Clth Law Jo 201, 205; *Register*,
17 October 1856, p. 2 – Torrens title should 'hold good in reference to all
legal processes equally with the original title itself'.

56   *Register*, 13 November 1857, p. 3.

57   South Australian Parliamentary Debates, House of Assembly, 4 June 1857,
col. 202.

58   *Adelaide Times*, 23 November 1857, p. 2.

59   *Adelaide Times*, 30 November 1857, p. 2. See also *Adelaide Times*, 15 January
1858, p. 2 (a confession that some of the provisions of the Bill adopted from
those of R.D. Hanson).

60   *Adelaide Times*, 23 November 1857, p. 2.

61   *Adelaide Times*, 15 January 1858, p. 2.

62   *Cf.* Offer, 'Lawyers and Land Law Revisited' (1994) 14 OJLS 269, 270; and
see Torrens in the South Australian Parliamentary Debates, House of
Assembly, 4 June 1857, col. 201.

63   (1950) 23 ALJ 489, 490–492.

64   (1962) 1 Adel LR 169, 182.

65   14 January 1858, p. 2.

66   Pike, (1962) 1 Adel LR 169, 184.

67   They were the *Real Property Law Amendment Act* [1858], the *Real Property
Act* 1860 and the *Real Property Act* 1861.

68   On the expedition to New Zealand, see Whalan, 'Origins', p. 13.

69   A good summary of the travails of the Torrens system in this context may
be found in Pike, (1962) 1 Adel LR 169, 183–189.

70   See, for example, Anderson, 'The 1925 Property Legislation: Setting
Contexts' in Bright/Dewar (eds.), *Land Law: Themes and Perspectives* (Oxford
U.P., 1998), pp. 117f; Dowling, 'Of Ships and Sealing Wax: the Introduction
of Land Registration In Ireland' (1993) 44 NILQ 360; Whalan, (1967)
2 NZULR 416.

71   Esposito, *The History of the Torrens System of Land Registration with Special
Reference to its German Origins* (LL.M. thesis, University of Adelaide,
January 2000); Esposito, (2003) 7 Aust Jo Leg Hist 193. A sequel to this
piece is forthcoming in the *Adelaide Law Review*, and Dr Esposito's doctoral
thesis will be published in German in due course.

72   Geyer, *Robert Richard Torrens and the* Real Property Act: *The Creation of a
Myth* (B.A. (Hons.) thesis, University of Adelaide, 1991), p. 73. This
Honours thesis might simply be ignored as insufficiently well argued and
researched were it not for the fact that a later writer does it too much
honour (Esposito, *The History*, p. 70).

73 Fox, (1950) 23 ALJ 489, 492; Robinson, *Transfer of Land*, p. 11; Whalan, (1967) 2 NZULR 416, 416 fn 2.

74 Forster to Miss A. Ridley, 15 May 1892, South Australian Archives A792; quoted in Esposito, *The History*, p. 24.

75 Pike, (1962) 1 Adel LR 169, 178; Robinson, *Transfer of Land*, p. 3.

76 *The Mystery of Capital* (Bantam, London 2000), p. 183.

77 Gall, Adelaide 1857.

78 Esposito, (2003) 7 Aust Jo Leg Hist 193.

79 Raff, *Private Property*.

80 Esposito, (2003) 7 Aust Jo Leg Hist 193, 206; Raff, *Private Property*, p. 95.

81 'Origins', p. 9.

82 'Report of the Commissioners Appointed to Consider the Subject of the Registration of Title with Reference to the Sale and Transfer of Land', House of Commons Sessional Papers, 1857 vol. XXI, pp. 245ff. See further, for a most helpful analysis, Raff, *Private Property*, pp. 47–54; *Dobbie* v. *Davidson* (1991) 23 NSWLR 625, 650f.

83 South Australian Parliamentary Debates, House of Assembly, 25 November 1857, col. 672; *Register*, 26 November 1857, p. 2 (Torrens received report yesterday, *i.e.* on 24 November); Pike, (1962) 1 Adel LR 169, 180 fn 78; Stein/Stone, *Torrens Title* (Butterworths, Sydney 1991), pp. 24f.

84 Whalan, 'Origins', pp. 7–9.

85 Simpson, *Land Law*, p. 76.

86 Simpson, *Land Law*, p. 71.

87 See Robinson, *Transfer of Land*, p. 15 fn 13. This author has of course read the letters referred to in that footnote himself, except the letter which Dr Robinson states was published on 8 March 1857.

88 *Register*, 18 February 1857, p. 3.

89 Above, fn 77.

90 Hübbe, *Voice of Reason*, p. 90. (A similar phrase may be found at p. 97.)

91 Hübbe, *Voice of Reason*, p. 79 (similar: pp. 70, 78).

92 Hübbe, *Voice of Reason*, p. 3.

93 See Mark 8:30.

94 There are several examples (and many more could be given) on one page of one newspaper – in the editorial and Parliamentary debates appearing in the *Register*, 13 November 1857, p. 2.

95 Esposito, *The History*, pp. 75–80; Raff, *Private Property*, pp. 29, 33–35.

96 South Australian Parliamentary Debates, House of Assembly, 4 June 1857, col. 210.

97 Robinson, *Transfer of Land*, p. 15 fn 13. Hübbe himself is unsure of the date in (1931) 32 Proceedings of the Royal Geographical Soc of A/asia (S.A.) 109, 110, but he is sure that the Bill was already a work in progress.

98 This may be found in many contemporary sources, and was pointed out by Hübbe himself: (1931) 32 Proceedings of the Royal Geographical Soc of A/asia (S.A.) 109, 111.

99 (1931) 32 Proceedings of the Royal Geographical Soc of A/asia (S.A.) 109, 111.

100 South Australian Parliamentary Debates, House of Assembly, 20 July 1880, col. 427.
101 See Coxon/Playford/Reid, *Biographical Register of the South Australian Parliament 1857–1957* (Wakefield, Netley 1985?), pp. 105f; Loyau, *Notable South Australians* (Carey & Page, Adelaide 1885), p. 34.
102 Esposito, *The History*, pp. 75–80.
103 South Australian Parliamentary Debates, House of Assembly, 17 September 1884, col. 1025.
104 South Australian Parliamentary Debates, House of Assembly, 17 September 1884, col. 1024. Emphasis added.
105 See also Whalan, 'Origins', p. 6.
106 South Australian Parliamentary Debates, House of Assembly, 17 September 1884, col. 1026.
107 South Australian Parliamentary Debates, House of Assembly, 17 September 1884, col. 1025.
108 South Australian Parliamentary Debates, House of Assembly, 17 September 1884, col. 1024.
109 18 September 1884, p. 5.
110 Forster to Miss A. Ridley, 15 May 1892, South Australian Archives A792; quoted in Esposito, *The History*, p. 25.
111 Loyau, *Notable South Australians*, pp. 156f.
112 (1931) 32 Proceedings of the Royal Geographical Soc of A/asia (S.A.) 109, 111f.
113 Robinson, *Transfer of Land*, pp. 15–19.
114 (1931) 32 Proceedings of the Royal Geographical Soc of A/asia (S.A.) 109, 110.
115 See above, fn 67.
116 (1931) 32 Proceedings of the Royal Geographical Soc of A/asia (S.A.) 109, 112.
117 See above, fn 33.
118 Robinson, *Transfer of Land*, p. 20.
119 See above, fn 59.

3. Recognition of Aboriginal Customary Law

1. The grand jury system

Unlike the convict colonies, South Australia inherited the grand jury system from England from its beginnings.[1] The first grand jury sat in May 1837, and its foreman was Colonel Light.[2] The adoption of the grand jury system meant that until it was abolished in 1852[3] – England followed this step belatedly in 1933[4] – no one could be tried in South Australia for a serious offence unless at least twelve members of a grand jury of up to twenty-three people had, after listening to the evidence for the prosecution, decided that it was sufficient to justify holding a full-scale trial.

Just before grand juries were abolished – although these events are not connected – one South Australian grand jury distinguished itself by calling for, and achieving, the recognition of Aboriginal customary law. First, however, some further background on the grand jury system is needed.

Nowadays, people who are accused of serious criminal offences appear before a magistrate, who decides whether there is enough evidence to put them on trial.[5] In South Australia's early days, it was instead the function of the grand jury to make this decision. The jury of twelve that still exists today – which decides whether or not the defendant is guilty or innocent – decides issues of fact afterwards, once the trial goes ahead. It was distinguished from the grand jury by the title 'petty jury' – not, one hopes, in the ordinary meaning of that word, but in an archaic sense meaning, more or less, 'small'. A grand jury had up to twenty-three members, and so it was larger than the petty jury of twelve. Accordingly, under this system two juries were required to find someone guilty of an offence – a grand jury had to put them on trial, and a petty jury had to find them guilty.

South Australian grand juries, under a statute of 1843,[6] consisted of male South Australians who held the rank of Esquire or any higher rank (such as a knighthood); or were a Justice of the Peace, a merchant (other than the keeper of a general retail shop), a bank director or manager; or who possessed real estate of the value of £500 or personal property to the value of £1000. This excluded a large number of people, of course (many of whom would no doubt have had better things to do than sit on a grand jury and were not displeased at their omission). But it embraced many ordinary people, such as farmers and small businessmen. The statute was not designed to assemble only the richest people, but was rather directed to identifying the 'independent' members of the community, those in charge of their own destiny.

2. Presentments

Although not necessarily wealthy, grand jurors were used to exercising their own judgment about the affairs of life. They were, or at least could be, quite articulate people. Because of this, the law enabled them to make what was known as a 'presentment'. When they had finished deciding whether to put people on trial for serious offences, they were permitted to hand in a statement, called a presentment, commenting on the law or its administration, or, indeed, anything at all that took their fancy.

Grand juries made several presentments throughout their history in South Australia. The first was at the end of the first sittings. The foreman of the first grand jury, Colonel Light, came into Court and thanked Mr Justice Jeffcott in the name of the grand jury, which thanks were cordially reciprocated.[7]

The first recorded presentment of any significance occurred at the third sessions of the Court in March 1839. The grand jury expressed its approval of the idea of creating a Court of Quarter Sessions to try the less important cases which had just troubled them, and began a tradition of grand jury presentments on the topic of Aborigines by pointing out the need to ensure the tranquillity of the Aboriginal natives, the colony's security from possible endangerment by them and the desirability of good relationships with them.[8] This produced a reply from the Governor, in which he praised the colonists on their 'degree of judgement and of humanity scarcely ever equalled'[9] in maintaining good relationships with the Aborigines.

The grand jury of March 1840 continued this enlightened tone by making a presentment to the Judge on the state of the gaol and its religious facilities. This document received the unusual honour of being reprinted in the British Parliamentary Papers.[10] At the next criminal sessions, the Judge informed the grand jury of the remedial action that had been taken as a result of that presentment.[11]

The grand jury of August 1841, according to the caption of a drawing in *The Adelaide Independent*, 'presented to his Honor [the Judge] the house on North Terrace, acre no. 6, formerly occupied by Messrs Mann & Gwynne', two leading early legal luminaries. This sounds rather generous until we read the report and discover that the house was 'presented' by the grand jury because it was 'a public nuisance, extremely destructive to the morals of the community, and tending, in a very great degree[,] to depreciate the value of the neighbouring property'.[12] The original of the grand jury's presentment about this 'House of ill Fame and Repute'[13] has been preserved together with the papers that went to the grand jury. It is signed by the foreman, A.H. Davis, and many of the grand jurors. The result of this presentment, at all events, was that the Advocate-General said that he would look into it.

After some years without presentments of any sort, the grand jury of September 1849 returned to the theme of relations with the Aborigines. This presentment was prompted by a number of cases involving killings and violence between settlers and Aborigines or among the Aborigines themselves. The jury expressed the view that previous to these melancholy events of murder of and by the Aborigines, the districts in which they occurred were not sufficiently under police control, or the oversight of an officer, whose humane duty it is to protect the savage, and to guard the settlers from the incursions of the natives.[14]

The Acting Judge (Charles Mann, one of the early legal luminaries just mentioned) considered this presentment important enough to transmit it to the Governor.[15] The presentment also suggests that these colonists felt some confidence in the ability of the police to prevent outrages against the Aborigines if they were only present in a particular district in sufficient numbers, a statement that is in accord with the results of a recent study by Alan Pope.[16] Commenting in a more general fashion on the performance of the police was something in which other grand juries also indulged.[17]

3. A grand jury speaks out about Aboriginal customary law

By far the most important presentment made by a grand jury was also on the theme of relations with the Aborigines.

The grand jury of May 1851 had been directed by Mr Justice Cooper to treat two cases involving killings of Aborigines by Aborigines as subject to the colony's law – that is, to the recently imported British law. The evidence suggested that Tukkurru, Ngalta Wikkanni and Kanguworli had killed Maltalta on Yorke Peninsula – we are not told exactly where on the Peninsula – by spearing because he was a stranger and it was their custom to kill strangers who had intruded into their territory.[18] Four other Aborigines, whose tribal names are given as Ngai-e-me, Weepin, Tarroot and Penchungy, were accused of killing Mayponin near Robe.[19]

The newspaper reports give very little information about these Aborigines. There is hardly anything in the surviving sources to indicate what sort of people they were. They come across as passive objects of the white justice system; but that may be partly because, at this stage in legal history, no accused person (Aboriginal or not) was permitted to give evidence[20] – it took another South Australian innovation of 1882 to accomplish that. That fact, as well as perhaps language difficulties, meant that there was little opportunity for them to speak in open Court and leave traces on the public record. Nevertheless, the white justice to which they were subject was hardly a heartless uncaring Eurocentric system, as we shall now see – and no doubt the accused Aborigines did speak to the Protector of Aborigines, Matthew Moorhouse, who in turn gave evidence and appears to have put their case to the grand jury.

The attempt to subject these seven Aborigines to the white man's law for allegedly killing other Aborigines provided the grand jury with an opportunity to speak to the Protector. As the foreman of the grand jury later told the story, 'It was from the answers elicited from Mr Morehouse [*sic*] in the Grand Jury Room as Protector of the Aborigines that myself and the other Jurors were led to the conclusions at which we arrived'.[21] Those conclusions were expressed in a remarkable presentment which gives a fascinating insight into the attitudes of a representative group of early South Australian settlers towards the Aborigines as they came into contact with the British settlers.

It is worth noting that this grand jury had initially been discouraged by Mr Justice Cooper from doing more than deciding whom to put on trial, their basic function. A contemporary newspaper reports the following exchange on 15 May 1851:

> The foreman said it was their wish to make a presentment on the subject [of the gaol], as was the custom of Grand Juries in England.
>
> His Honor – It is not the province of the Grand Jury to make presentments on any subject not given to them in charge.
>
> The foreman said the Grand Jury had no wish to do anything irregularly; but they felt bound to mention that matter in what they considered the proper manner.[22]

They thereupon left the Court in the company of the head turnkey and returned after a couple of hours[23] with a presentment on the gaol (in which they found certain fairly minor defects), complimentary remarks on the work of the police force and their presentment on the liability of Aborigines to the sanctions of the criminal law. Given its

Cover of the indictment against the Aborigines accused of the Robe killing. It is signed by the foreman and other members of the grand jury as 'a true Bill', which authorised a trial before a jury of twelve. Source: *see* p. 63 fn 19.

length, it must have been written in advance. They presented these remarks in an open and 'crowded'[24] Court. It might be thought that it shows some cunning to ask simply to visit the gaol, a task which the grand jury had undertaken occasionally in South Australia, and then to spring a written presentment on Aborigines on a reluctant Court.

The presentment was very long, thirteen paragraphs in fact. It was reproduced, despite its length, in at least six contemporary Adelaide newspapers,[25] and it amply justified the description of it in one newspaper as 'the very distinct opinion of an intelligent Grand Jury'.[26]

In the presentment, the grand jury recorded that they had, in accordance with his Honour's instructions, found a case to answer in the two separate cases of violence among Aborigines. But in doing so, many of the grand jurors had done 'violence to their own natural feelings of equity and justice'. They thought that it was 'morally incumbent' on the colonists

to confine their interference to the mutual protection of both races in their intercourse with each other, and not to meddle with laws or usages having the force of laws among savages, in their conduct towards their own race.

The Grand Jurors believe, from the evidence adduced, especially of the Protector of the Aborigines, that the slaying of the native at Yorke's Peninsula was in accordance with a law common in all the native tribes – a law analogous to that which regards spies in civilised countries – that the native who was killed knew the law – that he ran the risk of violating it, and suffered in consequence: and that in the other case, the native seems to have been the victim of a prevalent superstition among the Aborigines.

That the Grand Jurors apprehend that, prior to the occupation of this country by the colonists, all these native tribes, as distinct communities (however small)[,] would have been held by all jurists to be in a situation to make laws and adopt usages for their own protection and government – that it can scarcely be even assumed that the limited intercourse which has yet subsisted between the colonists and the Aborigines, especially on the confines of the province, should have sufficed to impart such information to these uncivilised men as would justify us in breaking up their own internal system for the punishment of offences to which all their previous traditions and habits give force and sanction.

That if the character of British subjects is to be enforced upon them, and they are at once to be made amenable to the severe penalties of British law for moral offences between themselves, then it becomes a serious question whether we ourselves are not committing a similar offence (presuming the extreme penalty of the law were inflicted) by punishing that as a crime which, in the minds of the persons punished, was simply the enforcement of their own mode of justice.

That, admitting the Aborigines are to the fullest extent entitled to the protection of British law, it is but reasonable that before the awful severities of its infraction are enforced, the blessing and advantages in relation to personal protection and security which it affords, should be made appreciable to those whom by our own voluntary act, and without provocation, we have forced to submit to our sway, and now seek to coerce to our habits.[27]

The grand jurors accordingly called for mercy to be shown to the Aborigines concerned if they were sent to trial and for further consideration to be given to the extent to which the colonial Courts should deal with cases of violence among Aborigines.

Today, of course, it is easy to recognise the grand jury's opinion for what it is: a call for the recognition of Aboriginal customary law by the Anglo-Australian legal system.

The presentment attracted the signatures of eighteen grand jurors; two others were absent. Two further grand jurors dissented from the presentment on the gaol, but, significantly, not from that on Aboriginal customary law.

To this presentment, Mr Justice Cooper responded with his standard argument that Aborigines were British subjects now too and were therefore liable to criminal punishment as the settlers were. This was the principle under which Aborigines were punished for crimes against white people and *vice versa*. His Honour added that he had always been vigilant to ensure that Aborigines received justice at the hands of the colonial Courts and had counsel assigned to defend them. He also said, confusingly, that he was of the view that Aborigines were subject to the sanctions of the criminal law only if they were aware of them.[28]

(Some years before, Mr Justice Cooper had expressed the opinion that the Aborigines alleged to have maltreated some Europeans who had been shipwrecked were not liable to criminal punishment by the official Court system. That prompted the sending out of a punitive expedition outside the law by the South Australian government, which earned it the severe censure of the Colonial Office. So laying down a general proposition that all Aborigines were not capable of being punished by the criminal law for criminal offences was not a mistake that his Honour was going to make again in a hurry.)[29]

4. The grand jury gets results

While his Honour thus defended the law in public, he wrote a letter to the Governor essentially agreeing with the grand jury's view on the advisability, as distinct from the legality, of subjecting to British law Aborigines such as those he had just tried.[30] This view is not surprising given his Honour's general reservations about placing Aborigines on trial in similar circumstances.[31]

The Judge gave a strong hint in summing up to the petty jury in the case involving the Yorke Peninsula killings that he would recommend clemency if the accused were found guilty, and referred to the distinction between legality and wise policy in putting Aborigines on their trial.[32] The other set of defendants, those accused of the killing at Robe, were acquitted by the petty jury after Mr Justice Cooper directed the petty jury strongly in their favour.[33] They accordingly play no further role in this story. But the Aborigines in the Yorke Peninsula case were found guilty by the petty jury.

The mandatory sentence (for all – not just Aborigines) was death. But it was soon announced that the death penalty would not be carried out. The *Register*[34] noted that this would meet with 'the unanimous approval of the community' and avoid 'manifest injustice and inhumanity'. The Executive Council (the Governor and his officials) then met on 11 June 1851 and resolved in favour of a full pardon, as recommended by Mr Justice Cooper, for the Aborigines under sentence of death.[35] Executive Council noted that the Aborigines had acted in accordance with their custom. The pardon was duly issued, the Governor asking the responsible official 'to see to the safe return'[36] of the Aborigines.

It is clear that the grand jury's presentment had some considerable effect on this result.

This result was achieved, and the opinions about Aboriginal law and custom earlier quoted were held, by some quite ordinary people. None of the grand jurors who made the presentment had a particularly high rank in colonial society or, with the notable exception of F.H. Faulding, left any other significant trace on South Australia. The occupations of most of the grand jurors are listed in the newspaper[37]: they were drapers, merchants, stationers and so on – a typical South Australian grand jury consisting largely of small businessmen, Justices of the Peace, and, in this case, three grand jurors who gave their occupation simply as 'gentleman'.[38]

Reference to the *Biographical Index of South Australians 1836–1855*[39] shows that the grand jury also included a number of people who had lived in places such as Port Lincoln, Mount Gambier, McLaren Vale and Kingscote – places that are well away from the City of Adelaide and in which the average settler might well have had considerable contact with Aborigines who were still in their pre-settlement state.

The foreman, A.H. Davis Esq., is listed in the *Biographical Index* as a teacher, publisher, gardener and merchant.[40] Earlier, he had been an unsuccessful applicant for the position of Protector of Aborigines,[41] and in 1839 he gave a speech opposing retaliation against the Aborigines at a well-attended public meeting to consider the killings of settlers by Aborigines.[42] He was, however, no follower of every latest fad; after the secret ballot had been introduced in South Australia, for example, he called (unsuccessfully) for the Province to revert to the earlier system of open voting.[43] Shortly after his death, he was described in Parliament as a man of 'intelligence and … thorough conservativeness'.[44] That makes the opinions expressed in the presentment all the more remarkable.

Davis later claimed the presentment as his own composition, saying, 'I took some pains at the time to draw up this document'.[45] This statement was made in February 1858 during another campaign for mercy in another black-on-black violence case that had led to convictions and a sentence of death. In support of this campaign, the presentment of May 1851 was wheeled out almost seven years after it was made.[46] The campaign against the death penalty for the convicted Aborigine based in part on the grand jury's presentment of May 1851 was again successful. Acting Chief Justice Boothby[47] attended before the Executive Council when it considered the 'numerously and respectably signed'[48] petitions for clemency.

5. The wider context

It is interesting to observe that, in early July 1851, A.H. Davis stood for election to the Legislative Council for the district of West Torrens. He lost by two votes to C.S. Hare, one of the other grand jurymen of May 1851 and fellow-signatory of the presentment.[49]

The election of July 1851 has, at first sight, little to do with the grand jury's presentment (although it may be that it was fear of election-related grandstanding that explains Mr Justice Cooper's initial half-hearted attempt to prevent the making of the presentment). But it is certainly unlikely that either Hare or Davis would have been keen to associate himself with an unpopular cause just before the election; we may conclude that the opinions which the grand jury espoused in May had considerable support in the community, and were not an eccentric view held only by the grand jurors who signed the presentment.

How broadly the support reached for the views expressed in the presentment may only be guessed at. It is however noticeable that the Chairman of A.H. Davis's election committee was none other than R.D. Hanson,[50] who in July 1851 was appointed Acting Advocate-General and later became South Australia's second Chief Justice. It would be interesting to know whether he had any influence on the opinions expressed by the grand jury, especially as he was a man of very modern views in some respects.[51]

Although petitions for mercy towards particular Aborigines were 'not uncommon'[52] in early South Australia, this presentment is unique: it was not confined to an individual case but made broad and sweeping claims about the nature of Aboriginal society and law; it attracted support from a broad cross-section of the community in the grand jury and three newspapers. The opinions expressed are surprisingly ahead of their time. It would take only a change of dates, and certainly some polishing of language to remove references to superior peoples, savagery and so on, to convert what was said in May 1851 into a debate about the recognition of Aboriginal customary law in the early twenty-first century. (We should not imagine, however, the grand jury lacked respect for Aborigines on the grounds that they used an occasional word which would be unacceptable today, but in their time excited no indignation or surprise. There is an interesting contrast between the generally respectful tone of the grand jury and, for example, that of a petition for mercy in a Victorian case almost fifty years later, which called for a reprieve 'having regard to the well-known intense animal passions of the Aborigines, their degraded ancestry and evil tribal influences'.)[53]

As there are today, there were good arguments back then both in favour of and against the recognition of Aboriginal customary law as proposed by the grand jury. All these arguments were canvassed in the public discussion that followed the grand jury's presentment. Recognising Aboriginal customary law in cases involving violence among Aborigines might be represented either as the law's declaring that Aboriginal life was of lesser value[54] and/or as a breach in the 'one law for all' policy on which South Australia claimed to operate.[55] Or it might be seen as a merciful indulgence towards the Aborigines, or, even more significantly, as a recognition of the existence and status of their law alongside or outside the British law (which was essentially the position taken by the grand jury).

The newspapers were divided in their views. The *Register*[56] and the *South Australian*,[57] the Province's two oldest newspapers, disagreed with the grand jury. The *South Australian* put forward the view that the criminal liability of Aborigines even for offences committed among themselves should continue in order to protect Aboriginal women, 'who', it said, 'are regarded by the brutal males as property over whom they have the power of life and death'. The *Register* was of the view that cases of murder, at least, were in a special category which no custom could excuse. On the other hand, the *South Australian Gazette and Mining Journal*,[58] the *Adelaide Times*[59] and the *Austral Examiner*[60] all essentially agreed with the grand jury,[61] and the great detail and thought which the grand jury had shown made it difficult for those newspapers to add much more by way of comment or argument.

However, the *Adelaide Times*, in its editorial, took the opportunity to suggest other topics, such as the bridge over the River Torrens, the law of debtor and creditor and so on, on which future grand juries could make a presentment, and hoped 'to see all future grand juries in the Province alive to their position as the conservators, not only of our judicial, but of our constitutional and moral rights'. This was supported by a letter to the editor in which the author suggested that 'the few persons'[62] who wished to see grand juries abolished were wrong, and that the existence of grand juries helped to keep prison managers on their toes and added to public confidence in the prisons. (In fact grand juries were abolished the next year, but that had nothing to do with the story told here, but was rather connected with the discovery of gold in Victoria later in 1851.)[63]

Despite the extensive debate and the pardoning of the Aborigines, it is uncertain whether there was any long-term result of the grand jury's presentment. If the grand jurors had wanted lasting change in the law they might more appropriately have directed their pleas to the legislature (of which, after all, C.S. Hare was shortly to become a member). The law as laid down by the Judges was tolerably clear; although there were arguments against as well as in favour of the law as it stood, they were unlikely to sway those who had laid it down in the first place. It may be, however, that prosecutors took the sentiments of the jury into account in considering future prosecutions of Aborigines; after all, even after the abolition of grand juries in the following year, petty juries continued to exist. And, at least in the early days of South Australia, there was perhaps a lot to be said for dealing with such cases as they arose rather than try to lay down in advance a rule to deal with all of them. That enabled the law to remain flexible as events unfolded and knowledge about the Aborigines and their customs accumulated. It therefore made sense not to have a statute laying down the law in advance, but rather to rely on a decision by the Executive in each case about whether the Aborigines in question should be pardoned.

In the case just referred to, however, the Executive's decision was that such a pardon should be issued, and in that it agreed with the forthright opinion of the body of ordinary citizens who constituted the grand jury. And its decision was supported by everyone who expressed an opinion on the question which has survived.

Notes

1   For an analysis of the South Australian grand jury system as it operated from 1837 to 1852, see the author's 'Grand Jury of South Australia' (2001) 45 Am Jo Leg Hist 468.

2   The report may be found in the *Register*, 3 June 1837, p. 4; 8 July 1837, p. 4.

3   Act No. 10 of 1852 s 1.

4   *Administration of Justice (Miscellaneous Provisions) Act* 1933 s 1, supplemented by the *Criminal Justice Act* 1948 s 31 (3).

5   *Summary Procedure Act* 1921 ss 101–107.

6   Ordinance No. 12 of 1843, s 34.

7   *Register*, 8 July 1837, p. 4.

8   *Register*, 23 March 1839, p. 2.

9   *Register*, 23 March 1839, pp. 3f; *Southern Australian*, 3 April 1839, p. 3.

10 No. 394 of 1841, Appendix, p. 315.

11 *Register*, 11 July 1840, p. 6; *Southern Australian*, 10 July 1840, p. 3.

12 *Adelaide Independent and Cabinet of Amusement*, 5 August 1841, p. 2.

13 State Archives of South Australia, GRG 36/1/2. (All sources prefixed 'GRG' may be found in the State Archives of South Australia.) The wording of the original presentment differed slightly from that in the newspaper report quoted.

14 *Register*, 19 September 1849, p. 3; *South Australian*, 18 September 1849, p. 3; *South Australian Gazette and Mining Journal*, 20 September 1849, p. 3.

15 *Register*, 19 September 1849, p. 3; *South Australian*, 18 September 1849, p. 3; *Adelaide Railway Times, Mining Record and Weekly Political Register*, 19 September 1849, p. 2.

16 Pope, *Aborigines and the Criminal Law in South Australia: the First Twenty-Five Years* (Ph.D. thesis, Deakin University, 1998), pp. 244f, 252, 257–260.

17 *Register*, 13 February 1851, p. 3; *South Australian Gazette and Mining Journal*, 13 February 1851, p. 3.

18 *Register*, 20 May 1851, p. 3.

19 *Register*, 21 May 1851, p. 2. The names are given as found in the indictments preserved in the State Archives of South Australia, GRG 36/1.

20 Grand juries did not take evidence of any sort on behalf of the accused, as their task was only to assess the prosecution's case; the accused however could not give evidence at the trial before the petty jury either until 1882.

21 GRG 24/6/1858/247.

22 *Register*, 16 May 1851, p. 3. Similar: *Adelaide Times*, 16 May 1851, p. 2.

23 *Adelaide Times*, 16 May 1851, p. 2.

24 *South Australian Gazette and Mining Journal*, 17 May 1851, p. 3; *Adelaide Times*, 16 May 1851, p. 3.

25 See below, fn 27.

26 *South Australian Gazette and Mining Journal*, 17 May 1851, p. 2.

27 *Register*, 16 May 1851, p. 3; *Observer*, 17 May 1851, p. 8; *South Australian*, 16 May 1851, p. 3; *South Australian Gazette and Mining Journal*, 17 May 1851, p. 3; *Adelaide Times*, 16 May 1851, p. 2; *Austral Examiner*, 23 May 1851, p. 11.

28 See further Bennett, *Sir Charles Cooper: First Chief Justice of South Australia 1856–1861* (Federation, Sydney 2002), p. 71. The statement about counsel being assigned to defend Aborigines is corroborated in the *Adelaide Times*, 15 August 1850, p. 3, where Mr Justice Crawford was told that the provision of counsel paid for by the government was 'customary in cases where the Aborigines were implicated' and that it was paid for 'liberally'. See further Pope, *Aborigines and the Criminal Law*, pp. 262f.

29 On this, see, for example, Bennett, *Cooper C.J.*, pp. 59–62; Castles/Harris, *Lawmakers and Wayward Whigs: Government and Law in South Australia 1836–1986*, pp. 13–16; Foster, *Fatal Collisions: the South Australian Frontier and the Violence of Memory* (Wakefield, Adelaide 2001), pp. 13–28; Pope, *Aborigines and the Criminal Law*, pp. 55ff and the references cited there.

30 GRG 24/6/1851/1564, 1721.

31 Pope, *Aborigines and the Criminal Law*, Ch. 4.

32 *Register*, 20 May 1851, p. 3; and see the letter to the editor of the *Austral Examiner*, 6 June 1851, p. 10.

33 *Register*, 21 May 1851, p. 2; see further Pope, *Aborigines and the Criminal Law*, p. 137.

34 7 June 1851, p. 2.

35 GRG 40/1/3/334f; Pope, *Aborigines and the Criminal Law*, p. 140.

36 GRG 24/6/1851/1721, 1752.

37 *Register*, 13 May 1851, p. 2.

38 This ignores J.O. Lines, who is listed in the *Register* but not in the Court's records. Possibly he was excused, or did not turn up.

39 Statton (ed.); S.A. Genealogy and Heraldry Society, Adelaide 1986.

40 See also Pike, *Paradise of Dissent*, pp. 141, 328.

41 Pike, *Paradise of Dissent*, p. 439.

42 *Register*, 11 May 1839, pp. 3, 5.

43 South Australian Parliamentary Debates, House of Assembly, 29 April 1859, col. 4; Legislative Council, 2 May 1859, col. 5; House of Assembly, 4 May 1859, col. 9. This request 'was received with bursts of laughter by the House': *Register*, 30 April 1859, p. 2.

44 South Australian Parliamentary Debates, House of Assembly, 28 June 1866, col. 125.

45 *Observer*, 27 February 1858, p. 5.
46 A summary may be found in the *Observer*, 27 February 1858, pp. 5f.
47 As his Honour became during the absence of Chief Justice Cooper: *South Australian Government Gazette*, 12 February 1857, p. 142.
48 GRG 40/1/4/412.
49 Pike, *Paradise of Dissent*, pp. 430f, 433.
50 *Register*, 15 July 1851, p. 3; 18 July 1851, p. 2.
51 As well as being a lawyer and first Chancellor of the University of Adelaide, he participated energetically on the side of the modernists in the controversies connected with the critical analysis of the Bible that began in the nineteenth century. His efforts in this field earnt him the praise of, among others, Bishop Colenso of Natal, conveyed to him by the noted suffragette Catherine Helen Spence: Spence, 'Sir Richard Hanson' (1876) 1 Melbourne Review 427, 431. Spence's article contains a detailed summary of Sir Richard's religious writings.
52 Pope, *Aborigines and the Criminal Law*, p. 80; see also pp. 80–83, 161; Cranston, 'Aborigines and the Law: An Overview' (1973) 8 U Qld LJ 60, 62f. Occasionally, too, Judges in other colonies might say things almost (although not quite) as bold as the grand jury's statements here, but a consensus to the contrary emerged. On the position in other colonies, see *R* v. *Murrell* (1836) 1 Legge 72, 73, the case reports from contemporary newspapers reproduced in (1998) 3 Aust Indig Law Rep 410ff and Castles, *An Australian Legal History*, pp. 526–532.
53 Douglas/Laster, 'A Matter of Life and Death: the Victorian Executive and the Decision to Execute 1842–1967' (1991) 24 A & NZ Jo Criminology 144, 153.
54 *Cf.* Pope, *Aborigines and the Criminal Law*, pp. 148–152.
55 Pope, *Aborigines and the Criminal Law*, p. 47 *et passim*.
56 17 May 1851, p. 2; but see *Register*, 28 May 1853, p. 2.
57 16 May 1851, p. 2.
58 15 May 1851, p. 2.
59 21 May 1851, p. 3.
60 23 May 1851, p. 6; see also the letter to the editor published on 6 June 1851, p. 10.
61 See also the *Deutsche Post für die australischen Colonien*, 6 December 1849, p. 107 (opposing the infliction of the death penalty on Aborigines).
62 *Adelaide Times*, 21 May 1851, p. 3.
63 See the author's article referred to above, fn 1.

4. Rights to sue the Government

1. The need for reform

Dr Peter Howell has rightly said that 'one of the most valuable parts of the United Kingdom's legacy to Australia has been the principle that all officials are under the law and must perform their duties according to law'.[1] Nevertheless, the law as Australia received it from the United Kingdom was not perfect in this respect. One of the most glaring imperfections in the inherited rule of law was the immunity of the Crown (in other words, the government) from the legal liability that applies to individuals. This meant that the Crown was often not required to pay damages to people who had suffered as a result of its actions in the same way as an ordinary person or company would be.

Under the old law, the Crown was not, it is true, entirely exempt: people claiming to have contractual rights against the Crown could sue under an antiquated procedure called the 'petition of right'. This involved a very time-consuming, cumbersome and expensive process including the issuing of a commission to determine the facts of the case. In addition, the Crown had various rights in the process superior to those of its opponent. Professor Holdsworth summarises some of the difficulties facing a person wishing to sue the Crown using the petition of right:

> In the first place, there was a lengthy preliminary procedure before the legal question at issue could be brought before the Court. The petition

must be endorsed. A commission must issue to take an inquest to find the facts. If the facts were not found satisfactorily, a second commission might issue to find them again. If they were found satisfactorily, it was sometimes necessary to put in a second petition to stir up the Crown to take the next step of answering the petitioner's plea, and coming to an issue, which could be sent to the King's Bench for trial; and in all cases begun by petition the Crown could delay the petitioner by instituting a search for records which would support his title. In the second place, [the King's prerogatives] placed a very heavy burden on the petitioner. ... When this fence had been successfully surmounted, the petitioner was further handicapped by the fact that the King had many advantages in pleading which he had not. ... At any time he could stop the proceedings by the issue of a writ *rege inconsulto*; and the Judges could not then proceed without an order from the King.[2]

That describes the process in England. There were additional doubts in early South Australia about whether the procedure was available outside England – in the South Australian Courts, for example – at all.

There was a further problem: the grace-and-favour procedure of the petition of right was available in contractual disputes, but there was no redress, even in England, against the Crown for those claiming that the Crown had committed a tort (a civil wrong not arising from a contract, but from negligence or trespass, for example). People with such claims could admittedly sue the public servant who actually committed the tort, such as the person who actually trespassed on their land, for example. The government then, as the phrase went, 'stood behind' the public servant – in other words, conducted the case and paid any damages awarded. Sometimes, however, it was hard to find an individual responsible who could be sued in that way – the person who did the act concerned (say, failed to build a structure properly at some unknown time in the past when it was built) might not be very easy to identify, or the person might be the victim of a complex system not under the control of any one person such as the railways.

Accordingly, it was necessary to reform the law quite radically in order to bring about equality of rights between the government and the citizen.

The first statute in Australia – and the British Empire as a whole, it seems[3] – ending these anomalies and making the government liable as if it were a normal person is Act No. 6 of 1853 of South Australia. That Act is the ultimate ancestor of present-day Australian statutes on the liability of the government. Professor (now Justice) Paul Finn has traced the manner in which the South Australian statute spread throughout all the Australian colonies[4]: it was copied more or less faithfully in New South Wales in 1857, in Tasmania in 1859,[5] and in Queensland in 1866. An altered version of it was enacted in Victoria in 1858[6] – altered so as to include only contractual claims within the ambit of the legislation. The Victorian legislation was copied with variations on this point to include some additional claims in Western Australia in 1898,[7] New Zealand in 1871[8] and Natal in 1894.[9]

Some credit for the reform of the law of the United Kingdom by the *Crown Proceedings Act* 1947 – which finally abolished the petition of right there in favour of a more modern and rational procedure – may also be claimed for the Australian line of statutes commencing with the South Australian one. This is because the principle adopted in Australia became fairly well known in the United Kingdom[10] after the decision of the Privy Council in *Farnell* v. *Bowman*[11] in 1887, which dealt with the variant on the South Australian innovation adopted in New South Wales. Indeed, in introducing the Bill for the *Crown Proceedings Act* 1947, the Lord Chancellor said that the 'experiment we are now making has already long been the law in some of His Majesty's Dominions and Colonies – particularly in Australia and South Africa. They have Acts on the lines of this Bill, and they have worked well.'[12]

The influence of the pioneering South Australian Act of 1853 on the law of the rest of Australia can be traced back to the period very shortly after it was enacted. John Baker, who was its chief promoter in Parliament, and later became the second Premier of South Australia, referred in a later debate to the means by which the South Australian innovation began to spread to the other Australian colonies:

The Act of 1853 provided the means of affording relief to persons having particular claims upon the government; but the Attorney-General of the day objected to that part of it which, as he [Baker] introduced it, made provision for granting relief to persons having other than pecuniary claims on account of an outstanding land-order then held in the name of Mr Matthew Smith. At that time a friend of his residing in Hobart Town wrote to him upon the subject, and in his reply he explained the reason for that exception. Subsequently, and as the result of the correspondence, a Bill was passed in Tasmania and another in New South Wales, which was a *verbatim* copy of our own Act, with the exception to which he had referred.[13]

John Baker was an influential businessman, farmer and politician in early South Australia, and, as mentioned, its second Premier. He was a man of 'firmness and energy'.[14] It has been said of him that he combined 'intense[] loyalty to the Crown and established English traditions' with suspicion of 'the arbitrary powers of governors'.[15] It is therefore not surprising that he should have felt keenly the injustice produced by the inability of the citizen to sue the government and resolved to do something about it.

But the motives behind the reform he introduced also included a considerable degree of self-interest by those responsible for its enactment. John Baker was interested in this topic because he was a creditor of the South Australian government. In this respect, the Act did not differ from the Torrens system. It too served a wide variety of vested interests from those of existing land-holders to those of Torrens himself, the first Registrar-General (and also a landowner). Perhaps, therefore, we should not be too judgmental: cases in which an entirely disinterested party has sufficient energy and enthusiasm to carry through a reform are probably relatively infrequent.

The origins of claims-against-the-government legislation in South Australia extend slightly beyond 1853, for the 1853 Act was largely based on South Australian 'Act' No. 14 of 1851, which, although described and numbered as an Act and bound in the statute book, never became law because it was never assented to by the Queen owing to objections by the British authorities to certain parts of it. The story of the enactment of the first claims-against-the-government legislation in Australia therefore also includes this episode and an explanation of why the British authorities objected to the first but not the second version of the legislation.

The Act passed in 1853 had no official name, but was 'popularly known',[16] at least in South Australia, as the *Claimants Relief Act*. As transformed into ss 74–77 of the *Supreme Court Act* 1935 (S.A.), it remained without major changes on the South Australian statute book[17] until the enactment of the *Crown Proceedings Act* 1972 which gave the law its modern shape.

The preamble to the Act recited that disputes had arisen, and may later arise, between 'Her Majesty's Local Government in the Province of South Australia' and citizens, and that the 'ordinary remedy', the petition of right, 'is of limited operation, is insufficient to meet all such cases, can only be obtained in England, and is attended with great expense, inconvenience, and delay'. Section 1 therefore gave a right to present a petition setting out the claim, supported by a barrister's certificate, to the Governor of the Province of South Australia. The Governor was then to refer the petition to the Supreme Court 'for trial by a jury or otherwise as such Court shall ... direct'. The exception to this – a crucial provision in the history of the Act – was for cases in which the Governor, advised by the Executive Council, certified that the petition 'affects the Royal prerogative', in which case it was to be sent to the Secretary of State for the Colonies in London for decision. In the case of a refusal to accept such a petition, the reasons were to be published. (In the original version, 'Act' No. 14 of 1851 had provided for claims that affected the Royal prerogative to be identified by means of a Judge's certificate to that effect rather than a decision by the Governor.)

Section 2 provided that, for the purposes of the trial, the Governor was to name a 'Nominal Defendant or Defendants', who was/were not to be personally liable but merely represented the government for the purpose of the Court case. Further provisions stated that those with claims existing at the passing of the Act were to have two years in which to present them before the usual limitation rules applied and that the parties to cases against the government 'shall have the same rights, either by way of appeal, rehearing, motion for reversal of verdicts, or otherwise, as in ordinary cases of law and equity'. Finally, s 7 stated that the Act was to commence 'immediately after the passing thereof', which was 23 November 1853. That, therefore, was the day on which claimants could take advantage of a new procedure for claims against the government of South Australia, a procedure which was significantly simpler than that existing in England at the time.

2. The claimants

Certain names occur with monotonous regularity in the period leading up to the enactment of the *Claimants Relief Act*. It was to the lobbying of those with real or imagined grievances against the Provincial government of South Australia that the Act owed its genesis.

a. Borrow & Goodiar

William Blake wrote that 'Prisons are built with stones of law'.[18] The *Claimants Relief Act* might be said to have been built with the stones of prisons, for the main lobbyists for such a law, the building firm of Borrow & Goodiar and their creditors, based their claim principally on their construction of the Adelaide Gaol in the early 1840s. The gaol was the first permanent gaol in the Province. Although no longer in use (except as a tourist attraction), it still stands just off Port Road to the east of Bonython Park.

Sir Henry Ayers, who arrived in South Australia in 1841, commented waspishly on the gaol project:

> The [gaol] I found on my arrival was certainly not adapted to the end in view – the safe-keeping of prisoners. It consisted of a tent, with an airing ground in front, enclosed with a rope, around which one or two turnkeys patrolled, armed with a Brown Bess musket. But while it will be acknowledged that [the earlier] accommodation was altogether inadequate for the purpose, there was no need why the other extreme should have been adopted. High walls and strong doors were doubtless

necessary, but no angle towers, surmounted with cut-stone embattlements, the stone alone costing 42s per cube foot to work, while for other services artisans were paid from £3 18s to £4 4s per week, and the cost generally was [so] greatly enhanced from the high price of labor and unforeseen contingencies, that it brought ruin upon a most respectable firm of contractors, and involved the colony in debt for years to come.[19]

This edifice was the most striking example of the over-expenditure by George Gawler, second Governor of South Australia, on public buildings. As Douglas Pike records[20] and the Colonial Office[21] and other records bear out, the claim for the construction of the gaol reached dizzy heights. By mid-1842, the claimants were claiming £32,022/2/9. An initial offer by the government, based on a suggestion from the creditors of the firm in December 1841[22] and approved at a meeting of the Executive Council on 1 March 1842,[23] to submit the remaining claims to trial using a nominal defendant to represent the Crown[24] – a precursor of the procedure adopted under the *Claimants Relief Act* – was withdrawn when rumours were bandied about that Borrow & Goodiar were fraudsters and grossly overcharging.[25] These rumours never seem to have been backed up with facts. Possibly the more compelling reason for the withdrawal of the offer was that given by Gawler's successor, George Grey, in a despatch to the Colonial Office:

the number of persons interested directly or indirectly in the settlement of this claim is so large, and the means which have been resorted to for the purpose of influencing the public mind through the Press and otherwise have been so improper and constant that I fear it would be hopeless to expect an impartial consideration of the subject from any Jury in this Colony.[26]

Lobbying for payment by Borrow & Goodiar came to a temporary halt when in April 1842, clearly pressed by their creditors for money, they signed a full discharge of their claim relating to the gaol in return for £6432/12/10 in government debentures, making a total payment of

£19,800 plus interest.[27] Competition for the remaining money allegedly owed to Borrow & Goodiar soon emerged: as well as having numerous general creditors, the firm had also executed an assignment of all sums due or to become due to it to cover its debts of about £7750 to the South Australian Banking Company.[28] For this reason, the debentures of April 1842 were made payable not to Borrow & Goodiar, but to the Bank, which received the money in full at the end of 1845.[29] Borrow and Goodiar themselves therefore became insolvent despite the payment.[30]

By a surprising coincidence, one of the principal general creditors of Borrow & Goodiar was the Adelaide Auction Company, the Chairman of Directors of which was a prominent local man of affairs, one John Baker. This was the very same man who, a few years later, introduced the *Claimants Relief Act* and pressed for its passage – despite, as we shall see, hurdles which might have daunted a lesser man. Also a creditor of the firm was John Neales M.L.C., claiming from his time as the auctioneer of the Adelaide Auction Company, while Anthony Forster M.L.C. had claims to urge as part-owner of the *Register*.[31] Other members of the local legislature in the early 1850s had somewhat different reasons for favouring the claim: the Borrow side of the firm had a daughter who had married Mr Gywnne M.L.C., a prominent local lawyer and later to be the first locally appointed Judge, in July 1854.[32]

The moral claim for the remaining sums allegedly due to Borrow & Goodiar, despite their giving of a full legal discharge, was kept in view by various methods until the start of the 1850s.[33] Those promoting the claims hoped that the discharge could be set aside or otherwise declared invalid by the Courts, or that the government would give them a grace-and-favour payment. It was the opening of the first part-elected legislature in 1851 that, as we shall see, finally permitted legislation to be proposed to allow the claim to be submitted to a jury. This became the *Claimants Relief Act*.

b. The land order cases

As we have seen,[34] one of the crucial stages in the commencement of settlement in South Australia involved advance sales of land to begin a fund to pay for the passage of emigrant labourers. By proclamations in February and April 1843,[35] the rights of priority in selecting land associated with the advance sales were to expire if not exercised by May of that year. Speaking rather generally, it might be said that the problems that had become apparent with the whole of Wakefield's theory of colonisation had occasioned this change; at the level of detail, one wonders why provision was not made in the original scheme for lapse of the rights of priority in selection under the pre-sold 'land orders' after the expiry of a reasonable time for selection.[36]

The legal effect of the proclamation first emerges as an issue, as far as can be determined, at the end of 1845, when the South Australian Company, as the holder of some preliminary land orders, sued the Governor for an injunction preventing the sale of certain land that the Company wished to select. The Advocate-General, William Smillie, accepted service of the proceedings under protest that the Governor could not be compelled to submit to the jurisdiction of the local Courts.[37] Mr Justice Cooper refused the injunction mostly because of delay by the company.[38]

In London, the Colonial Office was annoyed that the local government had agreed even to enter into such legal proceedings. The Secretary of State for the Colonies – W.E. Gladstone, later to be one of Queen Victoria's best-known Prime Ministers – told the Governor off:

> I cannot sanction the course which you followed in this case. By appearing, or permitting any officer of the Crown to appear in defence of such a suit, you virtually acknowledged that the head of the Local Government was amenable to the jurisdiction of the Courts of the Colony which he governs.
>
> ... I object to that acknowledgment, not on any ground of mere dignity, or usage, or precedent; but, because thus to break down the barriers which separate the judicial and the administrative authorities must result in great practical evils. The immunities of the Sovereign in

this country, and the corresponding immunities of a Governor in the Colony he rules, exist for the good of the people at large. If it were admitted that you, as Governor of South Australia, were amenable to the Courts of the Colony, you would of course be liable to fine, to distress, and to imprisonment at their bidding. Many of the grounds of public policy, on which you might well justify your acts to the Queen or to Parliament, would be altogether inadmissible as a defence at the trial of an action against you in those Courts. Nor can I omit to notice that a colonial Jury might, however unconsciously, be under a strong bias against a Governor in the character of a defendant; especially when they understood, or supposed, that the British Treasury would be really responsible.[39]

It is worth noting here in passing that William Smillie, the Advocate-General, was a Scots lawyer.[40] Scots law was by no means as restrictive as English law on the question of the citizen's rights to an injunction[41] against the Crown[42] – but the rule in the British Empire was that English and not Scots law applied in the colonies.

After its defeat in Court in December 1845, the Company tried again in early 1846, seizing a piece of land and suing for trespass when the Crown expelled it.[43] The Company lost again, although the case shows that Gladstone's fears about colonial juries were not necessarily justified, as this claim was rejected by one.

We find claims under the old land orders being urged to their conclusion not by the South Australian Company but by Matthew Smith, a lawyer. According to a later newspaper report,[44] he had bought his land order from the original grantee, a Mr Richmond, in May 1845 – about two years after its expiry under the notice of February 1843. (As a lawyer, Smith had coincidentally witnessed Borrow & Goodiar's declaration of insolvency[45] and acted for their assignees,[46] so he was well aware of the difficulties involved in enforcing legal claims against the government.) Smith's claims were summarily rejected in London when he urged them through his connexions there.[47] The Colonial Office referred Smith to the Courts and added for good measure that, if he had a claim, 'it must enure to the serious prejudice of the South

Australian Public at large'.[48] An attempt to have the matter resolved by petitioning the Imperial Parliament was also unsuccessful.[49]

The stage then shifted to South Australia, and in the Legislative Council on 23 August 1849 a motion was carried by the four votes of the non-government members to the three of the nominated officials that, as it was 'the birthright of every British subject who feels himself aggrieved' to sue, Smith should be permitted to sue a nominal defendant appointed to represent the interests of the government. But although the motion in favour of Smith's claim was passed,[50] this had no effect, for the Legislative Council at this time could only express its opinion. It could not compel the Governor to approve Smith's claim, and given the Colonial Office's attitude to such claims there was little likelihood of that.

As late as September 1852, Smith was still petitioning the Legislative Council for the appointment of a nominal defendant so that his case could be heard before the Courts.[51] And although his claim, at least to select land, was in the end excluded from the ambit of the Act of 1853 by the insertion of the provision that it was to apply only to 'pecuniary' claims (s 1), Smith received his remedy. The Advocate-General, R.D. Hanson, reported on 31 October 1853, a few weeks before assent was given to the *Claimants Relief Act*, that the proclamation of 16 February 1843 referred to above was 'absolutely nugatory, since it was in violation of the *Waste Lands Act*', 'an attempt by one of the parties to a contract to change its terms, without the consent of the other party, ... an attempt to substitute prerogative for legislation' and, if that were not enough, 'unjust in principle' given that no compensation was offered.[52]

Hanson's devastating assessment of the government's behaviour towards Smith doubtless sprang from conviction rather than professional friendship, for we find him repeating similar sentiments in an unrelated case almost twenty years later as Chief Justice.[53] At all events, the opinion of 1853 led to the granting of Smith's request to select land on 14 November 1853,[54] although the final resolution of the matter was delayed when Smith responded by selecting land on the Echunga Gold Field.[55] Smith, however, did not live long to enjoy the fruits of his struggle, for he died in November 1858 just after completing his term of service as Acting Commissioner of Insolvency.[56] Just as the testimonial presented to him on completion of that term was signed by many of the colony's lawyers,[57] his funeral[58] was attended by a veritable 'who's who' of the early South Australian legal profession, including Chief Justice Cooper,[59] Mr Justice Boothby and Mr Hanson.[60] Again we see that it was the well-connected who lobbied for the provision of a remedy for the subject against the Crown.

c. The dishonoured bill cases

The practice in very early South Australia was to draw on the account of the Colonisation Commission in England in order to pay government debts owed to South Australians. This was done by way of bills – essentially 'I.O.U.'s – which were sent to England for the Commission's acceptance. If the Commission failed to accept a bill, it was returned 'protested' and, after sixty days, became dishonoured and was 'sent back to the drawer who became liable for the face value of the draft and a penalty of twenty per cent'.[61] (It is interesting to note the scale of bank fees in the nineteenth century.) Bills were dishonoured on a massive scale in the wake of the financial collapse of the colony in 1840–41; the solution ultimately adopted was to issue debentures payable at the discretion of the colonial government in place of the repudiated bills.[62]

But this did not settle all the claims, for some holders of the debentures, although paid reasonably promptly, claimed the expenses they had incurred in consequence of the dishonour of the original bills, starting with the 20 per cent charge just mentioned.[63] The Colonial Office refused to authorise the reimbursement of these expenses, because, in the words of Earl Grey, the Secretary of State for the Colonies:

> The Colony having become wholly insolvent, Parliament had munificently granted an aid of no less than £200,000 to extricate it from its difficulties. But that grant had not been made without its limitation. In submitting the vote to Parliament, Her Majesty's Government had deemed it enough to propose that the principal of the various

demands, including the dishonored bills drawn upon the Colonization Commissioners, should be discharged, but not the interest, and only upon condition that the parties should give a receipt in full. In liquidating from the British Treasury debts, of which the payment must otherwise have been hopeless, the Government of that day were entitled to impose such terms as appeared to them reasonable; and they required, as is so common in similar cases, and from motives of mutual convenience, which are sufficiently obvious, that the settlement should be final. They paid off the principal, but not the incidental expenses, because they considered it not unfair that all parties concerned should bear some portion of the consequences of what was deemed a general improvidence.[64]

The holders of the dishonoured bills were not to be dismissed so easily. They also joined the claims-against-the-government bandwagon. One of the most persistent of such claimants was William Jacob,[65] who had done survey work for the Province in its very early days as a member of the staff of Colonel Light and resigned from the government service together with Light.[66] Afterwards, he had the good sense to join the surveying firm of B.T. Finniss, later first Premier of South Australia, and to marry a daughter of C.H. Bagot M.L.C.[67] Bagot was also referred to by another claimant against the government, R.F. Macgeorge, in a letter pushing his claim as a 'friend'.[68] Indeed, it was 'after an angry debate'[69] on Macgeorge's claim that John Baker obtained leave in 1851 to introduce what became the first version of the claims-against-the-government legislation.

Another holder of a dishonoured bill was Captain John Hart, later an M.L.C., although his claim was resolved in April 1845 and a receipt issued by his attorneys, one of whom was John Baker.[70] John Baker himself held dishonoured bills, and when his cheeky attempt to pay government charges by returning the bills for credit was refused, he added this to his list of complaints that he made against the Governor to London in 1844–45. (The complaints were rejected.)[71] Presumably he had a claim for expenses to urge on his own behalf. Certainly, at all events, he would have had great sympathy for those who did.

However, Jacob's claim at least could be resolved before the Act of 1853 finally came into effect: Jacob received his money in July 1852[72] after the Colonial Office decided that

> when a claim of this nature is again urged on Her Majesty's Government by the Legislative Council, representing, as it now does, the Community of South Australia, it should not be disregarded unless on stronger grounds than any of which I am aware in the present instance.[73]

The Colonial Office had not changed its mind about the merits of the claim, but rather gave effect to its well-established policy that local government was better than good government (by it). The *Register*[74] called the result 'a gratifying triumph of right against might'.

The fate of the other claims for expenses incurred is less certain.[75] In 1852 and 1853, some time after Jacobs' claim had been paid, Macgeorge and/or H.W. Phillips can still be found petitioning the Legislative Council for their claims to be dealt with.[76] Phillips was apparently advised against bringing a legal claim,[77] and this may well have deterred others. Furthermore, a Select Committee of the Legislative Council rejected Phillips' petition in 1854 as not worthy of the Council's attention; Phillips, they thought, should be confined to any remedy he might have in the Courts.[78] It is possible that he gave up, thinking that the cost of proceedings was not worth the risk of failure. Certainly, given the number of dishonoured bills, the number of claims lodged after the passage of the *Claimants Relief Act* appears surprisingly low. Another petition by H.W. Peryman and James Macgeorge, presumably the son of R.F. Macgeorge of that name,[79] which was based on a different claim, sank without trace in 1856.[80] Clearly, however, they played their role in the lobbying campaign that led to the enactment of the *Claimants Relief Act*.

3. The passage of the Act

Until the advent of representative government in South Australia in 1851, there was little that putative claimants against the government could do but present petitions to the nominated Legislative Council

John Baker, c. 1857
Photograph courtesy of the State Library of South Australia, SLSA: B 6692/2

and hope that something would be done about them. This was because the Governor had the sole right of proposing legislation under the pre-1851 arrangements.[81] Once, however, the part-elective Legislative Council had been set up in mid-1851, John Baker lost little time in proposing legislation to remedy the grievances with which he and some of his fellow members were so familiar.

Despite the united claims of self-interest and principle, continued Crown control of the Province's finances[82] made it difficult even after 1851 for the Legislative Council to provide money of its own motion to settle the claims. The Legislative Council could do things such as pass a motion 'praying that His Excellency [the Governor] will make early provision for the payment of the claim'[83] of Jacob and adopt a Select Committee report to the effect that the claim of Borrow & Goodiar should be submitted to a jury. (The Select Committee had reported also that, not being able to examine witnesses on oath, it had been unable to determine the truth.)[84] But, as John Baker pointed out when introducing the Claimants' Relief Bill on 7 October of that year, if the colonists were no longer to be prevented by Downing Street from restoring the Province's honour and actually paying their debts to firms such as Borrow & Goodiar rather than just calling on the authorities to do so, 'some Court was necessary. In England the petition of right was a means of redress, but here the distance debarred claimants from its use. In the United States a Court had been appointed for the purpose.'[85] He added however that he would be satisfied with the provision of a nominal defendant who could be sued in the existing Courts.[86]

These debates took place in the single-chamber legislature, known as the Legislative Council, that existed in South Australia from 1851 until the opening of the first Parliament of South Australia in April 1857. Tracing the progress of the Bill for the 'Act' of 1851 through the Legislative Council is a difficult process given the need to rely, in the absence of official reports of the debates beyond the outline given in the 'Votes and Proceedings', on newspaper reports of the debates. Many of these are truncated, and they occasionally contradict each other. No copy of the Bill as it was originally introduced has survived.

It is clear, however, that it was given a cautious welcome by Acting Advocate-General Hanson and the government members generally. On its second reading, Mr Baker even said rather airily that he did not expect opposition to it, but Hanson feared that it might be rejected in London if it did not distinguish between claims against the Provincial and the Imperial governments. Baker had however already anticipated this possible objection, and pointed out that 'laws had been passed and acted upon in New South Wales, which were disallowed as contrary to British law, and yet they had been re-enacted, the colonists being determined to have the benefit of them'.[87]

The Bill of 1851, like the Act of 1853, provided for legal proceedings to be conducted against a nominal defendant. The creation of a nominal defendant had been suggested in previous correspondence on the case of Borrow & Goodiar. In proposing this solution, Baker was doubtless also thinking of the practice, followed in South Australia in the South Australian Company's action in trespass a few years before, of suing a public servant behind whom the Crown stood. Even more importantly, it was a neat solution to Gladstone's earlier objection to actions or suits against the Crown's representative personally. The local government would not have accepted any Bill which made the Governor personally a defendant. Indeed, the Registrar-General (B.T. Finniss) said that 'the Governor was above the law, and should not stoop to be made a defendant'.[88] (This rather tactless observation brought forth a furious editorial in the *South Australian Gazette and Mining Journal*[89] and a somewhat more restrained although still condemnatory one in the *Adelaide Times*,[90] which remind us that there was a principle at stake here, not just the claims of certain well-connected personages. The former editorial, headed 'Above the Law', accused the Provincial government of 'foul' conduct and of perpetrating 'undeviating injustice' and claimed that 'the colonists of South Australia are sick and weary of Downing-street government, and of continual references of their own exclusive business to men who can know nothing about it'.)

As the debate on Bill wore on, the government warned that it would advise the Governor not to assent to the Bill but to refer it to the

Colonial Office, which might well reject it.[91] Matthew Smith's claim,[92] for example, was considered to be one affecting Imperial rather than just local interests given that the Province did not at this stage control the disposal of Crown lands.[93]

The Bill of 1851 as finally passed provided that it applied only to claims against 'the Colonial Government of the Province of South Australia' (s 1). However, appearances were deceptive. Section 1 provided that claims against the local government 'the subject matter of which may lie or be within' South Australia could be made. This would still have given people such as Matthew Smith the right to sue for an order compelling the local government to permit him to select land,[94] at least if the Judges were prepared to conclude that land sales did not fall under the proviso protecting the Royal prerogative – 'whatever that might mean'.[95]

The proviso stated that, if a Judge certified that claims affected the Royal prerogative, they should be referred to the Imperial authorities. The Bill's drafters thought that this was security against objections to the Bill by the Imperial authorities on the grounds that the legislation invaded their territory. If that was the case, then, under the proviso, London would have the opportunity to decide on the claims. Nevertheless, 'affect[ing] the Royal prerogative' was a strange way of describing Imperial interests. Little thought seems to have been given to what the Royal prerogative actually was and how it might be affected by the legislation or to whether this provision would have had any effect on Matthew Smith's claim, for example.

Another crucial issue in the debates was whether to restrict the Bill to pecuniary claims, thus furnishing an impregnable defence against specific claims to the waste lands of the Crown and resulting Imperial complications. Such a restriction was first inserted into the Bill[96] and then taken out again[97] so that the 1851 Bill, unlike the Act of 1853, was not restricted to pecuniary claims. This too was obviously relevant chiefly to Matthew Smith's claim, as a Bill confined to pecuniary claims would have satisfied Borrow & Goodiar. The fact that Baker and Gwynne opposed the restriction to pecuniary claims indicates, incidentally, that they were not solely concerned with the claim of

Borrow & Goodiar, which was entirely a pecuniary one. For the sake of a principle – government liability in the civil law – they were prepared to make the Bill more comprehensive even if that decreased the likelihood that it would receive the Royal assent either locally or in London.

Baker's and other members' advocacy of the Bill was not driven solely by self-interest. When Baker was asked by a fellow member, 'Is it the old land grants at which the hon. Member for Mount Barker [Baker] is hammering away?', he responded that he was 'hammering away ... at every wrong that has been committed or that may occur within the Province of South Australia'.[98] Now Baker's interest in the Adelaide Auction Company's claim against Borrow & Goodiar was well known by this stage. It had been mentioned in an earlier debate when Baker stated that he was 'not personally interested in the claim of Messrs Borrow and Goodiar, but ... as the agent of others',[99] and the Adelaide Auction Company's name was thereupon introduced into the debate. So his 'hammering away' statement cannot have been an attempt to cover up this notorious fact. Indeed, the course of debate to that point, in which the government members pointed out that excluding Imperial claims would still give Baker what he wanted, strongly suggests that the questioner was puzzled about why Baker was so insistent on proposing a Bill which covered more than his 'own' case. But Baker was clearly interested in a broader principle as well.

Efforts made to produce a Bill that was acceptable to all sides were obviously in vain. On 28 November, as the debate approached its conclusion and the clauses of the Bill were being read in the Legislative Council, 'the officials, nominees, and a stray representative of the people ... sung [sic] out distinctly "No"'.[100] However, the Bill passed, and the hope was expressed that it would receive more favourable official consideration in England than it clearly had in Adelaide.[101] Baker's view was that the 'passing of the Bill would at least show Her Majesty what was wanted, and even should her assent be refused, it would occasion little more than a twelvemonth's delay'.[102]

The Colonial Office considered the Bill accordingly. The files present an interesting picture of paternal indulgence, one official commenting that if the South Australians 'choose to yield to pressure from people with old land-grievances' they should be permitted to do so – the revenues were now theirs rather than the Imperial Treasury's – 'although it seems a very unwise piece of legislation'.[103] But the Bill's fate was sealed when the Colonial Office referred it to the Law Officers of the Crown.[104] The Attorney-General and Solicitor-General reported that it

> does not provide a sufficient security against interference with the rights and Prerogatives of the Crown nor do we think that that it would be constitutionally right to entrust the Judges of the Supreme Court with the decision of such a question, as whether the subject matter of a Petition does or does not affect the Royal Prerogative.[105]

Assent should therefore be refused, they advised; and it was.[106]

At this stage in South Australia's history, judicial appointments were still made by the Colonial Office; the last, and disastrous, such appointment was that of Mr Justice Boothby in 1853. Therefore, the refusal to permit local Judges to determine whether 'the subject matter of' a claim for relief 'affects the Royal prerogative' implied no lack of confidence in the colonists, as it seems unlikely that the Colonial Office was looking forward to a time when judicial appointments were vested in the South Australian government. It seems much more likely that the objection was simply to the possibility that controversial or even political questions might be determined by Judges (no matter who appointed them) rather than politicians under a test which was as vague (even meaningless) as 'affect[ing] the Royal prerogative'. Seen in this light, the objection is by no means one that can easily be dismissed. It is exactly the sort of question that might be raised under modern jurisprudence about the sorts of quasi-judicial or non-judicial functions that can lawfully be vested in the Judiciary. The objection was therefore based upon a sound principle – even if it, too, involved a happy coincidence between principle and self-interest given that the Governor was amenable to Colonial Office instructions but the Judges were not.

On receipt of the Colonial Office's despatch notifying the refusal to assent to the Bill, the question for South Australians such as Baker was whether to try again. There could be little doubt about the answer to this question. A second attempt was indeed suggested by the statement in the despatch that

> I have [] to request you to bring the subject again before [the Legislative] Council, and whenever an Enactment containing the defined [unstated!] amendments shall reach this Department I shall be prepared to submit it for the Royal Assent.[107]

John Baker and Co. knew of this statement, as it was published in the South Australian Parliamentary Papers.[108]

The government back in Adelaide may well have been surprised that no more extensive objection was taken to making the local government liable in this way. However, that was perhaps not very surprising given that the Imperial Parliament itself was shortly to begin the process of making the law for claimants against the Crown more similar to that applicable between ordinary citizens. This process reached a temporary climax in the *Petitions of Right Act* 1860.[109] The Colonial Office therefore confined itself to objections relating to the procedural details of the Bill; on the question of principle – whether to have a statute about Crown liability at all – it was content to leave the South Australians to make their own mistakes (if mistakes they were). This deprived the South Australian officials of any real argument against the principle of the Bill.

Reading the Colonial Office's despatch, the South Australian advocates of the principle would have been able to conclude without great difficulty that, if the power to decide whether a claim affected the Royal prerogative were vested in the executive rather than the Judges, a different result would ensue. That is exactly what was done, the Bill for what became the *Claimants Relief Act* of 1853 vesting in the Governor rather than the Judges the power to refer a claim to the Colonial Office on the grounds that it affected the Royal prerogative. Although this discretion in the executive to refer claims against itself to the British authorities survived in the law of South Australia until

1972,[110] I have found no report of any injustice caused by its existence or even of its being exercised in a manner unfavourable to a claimant.

In light of the prior debate in 1851 and the despatch informing the colonists of the reasons for the disallowance of the Bill passed in that year, the Bill of 1853 enjoyed a smooth passage through the Legislative Council.[111] In addition to shifting responsibility for identifying prerogative claims, the Bill and Act of 1853 excluded all claims but those 'touching any pecuniary' claim and omitted the words in the 'Act' of 1851 permitting claims 'the subject matter of which may lie or be within' South Australia. This of course excluded Matthew Smith's claim, prompting him to petition the Legislative Council asking to be included again;[112] but, as we have seen, his claim was resolved shortly afterwards without the need for legal action.

After these exclusions, the Bill provided sufficient security for (Imperial) Crown interests in waste lands. Much later, in 1866 and 1867, by which time the waste lands were firmly in the colonists' control[113] and a case had emerged in which a suitor required relief going beyond the merely pecuniary relief permitted by the Act of 1853,[114] John Baker promoted a Bill to delete the restriction to 'pecuniary claims' and assimilate the South Australian law to that in New South Wales and Tasmania – which, as he pointed out in the extract quoted at the start of this chapter, was itself inspired by the South Australian innovation and (with that exception) was largely a copy of it.[115] This, too, shows that he was not entirely unconcerned with establishing the principle of Crown liability 'all round' as well as getting his money back from the estate of Borrow & Goodiar.

This proposal to supplement a South Australian innovation by an elaboration of it from elsewhere is also a very familiar process. When South Australian legal innovations were exported to other colonies or countries, they often underwent fairly minor but important improvements in their new homes, which were then re-imported back to South Australia. (The same thing happened to various aspects of the Torrens system, for instance.) But in this case, John Baker's campaign in the mid-1860s to adopt the improvements from New South Wales in the *Claimants Relief Act* was unsuccessful.

Once the Bill of 1853 had passed through the Legislative Council on 27 October,[116] the question arose whether it should receive Royal assent, and if so whether the local Governor could do it or the Bill should be sent to the Colonial Office with a recommendation. Advocate-General Hanson thought that the Bill could receive the Royal assent locally, as

> the present Bill does not really relate to the same objects [as that of 1851], since all questions with the Imperial Government which as arising in the Colony would have been within the scope of the former Bill are excluded from the present.[117]

That, it might be thought, was stretching the matter, but it was all in a good cause.

Accordingly, the Royal assent was given locally on 23 November 1853 to the first claims-against-the-government legislation passed on Australian soil. The Governor announced on proroguing the Legislative Council on 9 December that the Act would 'remove one great source of dissatisfaction which has existed in all British Colonies – the want of a local tribunal in which claims against the Government could be enforced'.[118]

4. The resolution of Borrow & Goodiar's claim

The passing of the Act enabled Borrow & Goodiar – in reality, their creditors – finally to bring a claim for the work done in the early 1840s. In so doing, they had obviously to surmount the obstacle that Borrow & Goodiar had previously signed a discharge. The claim that the discharge was somehow invalid or ineffective obviously took some time to prepare, and before the case came to Court at least one other matter had been resolved under the *Claimants Relief Act*. This involved William Humberstone, who sued R.R. Torrens, then Colonial Treasurer, as the nominal defendant under the Act. The claim was settled by arbitration, and the government's good faith was demonstrated by its prompt payment of the award.[119]

Borrow & Goodiar's case eventually came to trial in July 1856.

When it did, it was titled not Borrow & Goodiar v. Torrens (again the nominal defendant), but *Baker* v. *Torrens*. The plaintiff's leading counsel at the trial was Edward Gwynne M.L.C., who was Borrow's son-in-law. The trial took place before Chief Justice Cooper and a specially qualified jury from which Mr Justice Boothby had excluded all government officers and persons who had signed petitions in favour of the plaintiffs.[120] In opening for the plaintiffs, Gwynne stated that he 'had every confidence in the sympathy of all old colonists',[121] while the Advocate-General, Richard Hanson, appearing for the government, reminded the jury that damages would have to be paid by the taxpayer. He also stated that he:

> hardly knew whether he should most congratulate the Jury or himself upon the circumstance that that was the first occasion, he might say, in the history of the civilised world in which a Jury had been called upon, as a matter of right, to adjudicate a question between a Government and individuals. He believed this was the only country in the world where such a law existed.[122]

At least to a modern reader, this comes across as so smug that one wonders whether it endeared Hanson to the jurors at all. If the newspaper quoted Hanson accurately, his claim to be the first in the world, as distinct from the English-speaking world, is also startlingly broad. However, this statement does at least show how conscious, and proud, Hanson in particular and South Australians in general were of their role as legal pioneers. It also shows that the new statute was considered to have created a 'right' despite the existence of the residual discretion in the executive government to refuse to permit claims which might affect the Royal prerogative.

Chief Justice Cooper, in summing up to the jury, virtually directed them to find a verdict for the defendant, stating that he had consulted with Mr Justice Boothby and come to the conclusion that the discharge given by the firm in April 1842 was effective to extinguish all claims. The jury, acting it would seem as old colonists rather than taxpayers, came back with a verdict for Borrow & Goodiar on the grounds that the discharge had been given 'under force of circumstances'[123] and was therefore ineffective. Chief Justice Cooper thereupon argued with the jury. It emerged that the jury's verdict for the plaintiffs was based on an alleged promise by the government to forward a petition by Borrow & Goodiar to the Imperial authorities made at about the time of the discharge of April 1842:

> [Foreman –] We should be happy to follow your Honor's opinion so far as we can do so consistently with our sense of duty. We consider there is a balance of account still due; that the sum was received [pursuant to the discharge of April 1842] on the condition that the Governor should forward their memorial to the Home Government.
>
> His Honor – Gentlemen, there was no such promise.
>
> [Foreman –] There certainly was such a promise referred to in Mr Stephens's evidence.
>
> ...
>
> Mr Gwynne – Will your Honor allow me to observe that it is the privilege of an English jury to return a general verdict.
>
> His Honor – Certainly; and it is my duty to take their verdict, and I am endeavouring to do so.
>
> Mr Gwynne – Will your Honor excuse me for saying that you argue with the Jury, and do not take their verdict. .... This is a great constitutional question – the right of a Jury to return a general verdict.

Chief Justice Cooper was moved to remark shortly afterwards that he could forgive Gwynne's 'considerable energy and vehemence' in the exchange quoted above 'on account of the strong personal interest which he felt in the matter'.[124]

The jury was thereupon sent out again, but on its return stuck to its guns, the foreman repeating their earlier view that the 'receipt having been given under the force of circumstances, we wish to give a general verdict for the plaintiff'.[125] There was a verdict for the fantastic sum of £35,405/1/5, of which an award of interest made up more than half (£19,669/9/8).

That was not, however, the end of the matter. The government launched an appeal, and a new trial was ordered.[126] And although the award was that of a jury, it is clear that it caused some shock in the community. The amount awarded was about one-sixth of the Provincial government's entire yearly revenue in 1856 (excluding previous years' surpluses and other abnormals).[127] The *Register*[128] was moved to publish an editorial to quieten 'the fears of the community' that future huge sums could be awarded for long-finished works, and pointed out that the period of two years under which claims pre-dating the enactment of the Act could be brought – which was a wise addition to the Bill in 1853[129] – had by now expired. On the other hand, the *Adelaide Times*,[130] which once even called on the electorate to vote against candidates who opposed the claim of Borrow & Goodiar,[131] stated that a new jury would simply come to the same conclusion. Even it, however, printed a letter asking how much of the 'monstrous'[132] award would be received by Borrow & Goodiar and how much by the Adelaide Auction Company.

The matter was, however, foreshortened. A long debate in the Legislative Council on 4 December 1856,[133] during which the government was accused of attempting to wear out the claimants before the second trial could take place by seeking evidence from far-flung corners of the Empire,[134] was inconclusive as the Legislative Council could do no more than recommend payment. This it duly did in a debate in which John Baker moved the ultimately successful motion.[135] Once fully democratic government was inaugurated in April 1857, the creditors (although not including John Baker on this occasion) lost no time in petitioning the new Parliament for a settlement and pointed out that, as a litigator, the government possessed 'vast and crushing advantages ... in their having in the public funds an unfailing resource for the prosecution of litigation to an endless extent'.[136] On 11 June 1857, the House of Assembly (of which John Baker M.L.C. was not a member) agreed to a vote of £10,000 to the assignees of Borrow & Goodiar, on condition that £2000 be handed over to Borrow and Goodiar personally for their private use. This last proviso had been added at the instance of Attorney-General[137] Hanson, despite his opinion that 'the claim was emphatically a dishonest one'[138] and that the jury had made its award based 'not [on] the justice of the case, but the wealth of the other party'.[139] (Clearly, the government's unlimited resources could also be a burden in litigation.) Not all politicians, however, shared this view of the claim: during the debate, one member declared that the treatment meted out to Borrow & Goodiar was 'the blackest spot in the history of South Australia'.[140] Commenting on the Parliamentary vote, the *Adelaide Times*[141] declared sarcastically that Borrow & Goodiar would be 'utterly overwhelmed' by the generosity of the House.

Once the money was paid, that was still not the end of the matter. A further petition[142] from a certain John Baker and Thomas Waterhouse[143] pointed out that the South Australian Banking Company claimed almost the entire sum of £8000 voted for the creditors by adding interest to its original more modest claim.[144] The petition asked the House of Assembly to express its intentions about the use of the money it had made available. This the House quite properly refused to do, despite a motion in favour of the request by J.B. Neales. The House decided to leave the parties to fight the matter out in the Courts.[145]

The sum of £8000, which was originally paid to Baker and Waterhouse personally awaiting the outcome of the dispute with the Bank, had by this time been paid by them, by order of the Insolvency Court, to the Official Assignee, the official in charge of bankrupts' affairs.[146] The case before the Insolvency Court to determine the fate of this sum was heard at first before the Acting Commissioner, Matthew Smith,[147] and then before the Commissioner, Charles Mann, who had been legal adviser to Borrow & Goodiar and in that capacity had signed minutes of record with John Baker.[148] Mann refused to grant the Bank's claim for the sum of £8000,[149] and an appeal to the Supreme Court by the Bank was unsuccessful.[150] By the time the case re-appeared in the Insolvency Court before Mr Commissioner Mann, the Bank's claim was for only £2500.[151] Perhaps there had been a compromise. At all events, a distribution to the creditors of six shillings in the pound (30 per cent) was declared as early as February 1859.[152] One of the creditors which benefited from this dividend, almost twenty years after the gaol had been built, was the Adelaide Auction Company, which claimed for £1220/2/-.[153] A legal notice of April 1859[154] also refers to John Baker – together with the Hon. George Hall, presumably the same person as the M.L.C. from 1851 to mid-1853[155] – as a co-owner of the estate of the South Australian Marine and Fire and Life Assurance Company, which claimed for £1140/15/9.

Borrow and Goodiar themselves lived until 1862 and 1887 respectively. From their obituaries[156] we learn that neither was deterred by his experiences as a government contractor from entering the public service. Even before the claim against the government was resolved, Borrow became Secretary of Railways[157] and an official of the Births, Deaths and Marriages Office. Goodiar, after again becoming insolvent in the early 1860s,[158] became Superintendent of the Port Augusta Waterworks.[159] In his report for 1872, the Auditor-General wrote:

> In consequence of my frequent Reports as to the Superintendent's delay in remitting Waterworks Revenue from Port Augusta, and want of Collector's Accounts, correspondence ensued …
>
> On my becoming fully acquainted with the state of affairs, and reporting, the Superintendent was suspended from office, and subsequently removed. Meanwhile, I personally entered upon a tedious research, from the commencement of water supply in 1865; and, having corrected the local cash records (by such checking as was found possible, and by explanation readily afforded by Mr Goodiar), I submitted a balance-sheet. From time to time, as anything came to light, Mr Goodiar paid in sums which it appeared he *should* have collected; and eventually he completely satisfied the Government's claim, so far as I could establish it from the data in command. I should think he must have suffered considerable pecuniary loss, as well as deprivation of office, as the result of his laxity and want of business method.[160]

Probably Chief Justice Hanson (as Goodiar's principal foe in the battles of the 1850s had become) came to know before his death in 1876 of this damning assessment of Goodiar's business skills.

5. Effect and interpretation of the *Claimants Relief Act*

The precise effect of the Act was long uncertain. In particular, the question arose whether the Act removed the Crown's immunity in tort – in cases in which the government committed a civil wrong which was not a breach of contract. It was clear enough that it was intended to give rights to sue the local government for breach of contract. This was so not just because of its history – Borrow & Goodiar had a claim squarely in contract – which was well known to everyone in the first decades of its operation, but also because the procedure created by the Act could be seen as a greatly simplified version of the English petition of right,[161] and the principal area of operation of the petition of right was in contract. However, the Act's effect on the Crown's immunity in tort would depend on whether it was a merely procedural statute for enforcing the Crown's existing liability or, alternatively, one that created substantive rights beyond those already in existence as well as a way of enforcing them. The Act's preamble, with the reference to the difficulty of using the petition-of-right procedure in South Australia, and the fact that it provided a procedure to replace the petition of right, pointed to the Act's being procedural only and merely providing a more convenient means of enforcing the pre-existing liability of the Crown in contract and other areas in which the petition of right applied, without extending the Crown's liability into additional areas.

On the other hand, the procedure under the Act was far simpler than, and rather different from, that applicable in England under the petition of right. Furthermore, the Act's preamble complained about the 'limited operation' of the petition of right, and section 1 commenced by giving a right to sue in 'all cases of dispute or difference, touching any pecuniary claim'. These words were wide enough to include at least a claim for damages in tort. The South Australian Act did not expressly restrict itself to contractual claims only, as did the somewhat altered version of it enacted in Victoria in 1858.[162] In addition, on the second reading of the Bill in 1851, the following exchange had occurred:

MR GWYNNE observed that no case could be tried under the present Bill, but such as could be tried by a petition of right to the Queen. ... No case of tort, or personal damage [,] could be tried by petition of right, as it was presumed that the Queen could do no wrong. He would therefore suggest to the hon. mover [Baker] that the remedy should be extended to all cases of claim against the local government.

But the Act's principal advocate disagreed with this view:

MR BAKER ... had taken his view of the petition of right from Lord Coke, and it would be remembered that the petition of right arose on the illegal Acts [*sic*] of King Charles, and gave the subject the means of remedy in all cases of claims upon the Crown.[163]

And then there was Baker's line in the debate of 1851, quoted earlier, that he was 'hammering away ... at every wrong that has been committed or that may occur within this province of South Australia', although that could be seen as little more than an unconsidered remark without specific relevance to the question of Crown liability in tort.

It is perhaps not surprising that the precise extent of the Act's operation was not settled as it went through the legislature, despite the exchange between Messrs Gywnne and Baker just quoted. It appears, in the first place, that 'the question whether a petition of right would lie for damages in respect of a tort was *first* argued'[164] in England in 1843. If this is right, the issue of the liability of the government in tort had only just emerged. And, secondly, the issue was not at the forefront of the minds of those who debated the Act, for none of the claimants whose lobbying led to the enactment of the Act had a claim in tort.

Nevertheless, a consensus on this question appears to have developed during the first decades of the Act's operation. There appear to be no nineteenth-century judicial expressions of opinion about whether the Act excluded claims in tort.[165] However, there is even better authority available, namely the authority of Parliament. Act No. 17 of 1874 was 'An Act to provide for the Recovery of Damages caused by

Negligence on the part of Persons employed by the Government of South Australia in certain cases'. The first section provided that:

> Every person injured in his person or property by the wrongful act, neglect, or default of the Commissioner of Railways, or of any person or persons employed by him or by his authority, express or implied, upon any of the Government lines of railway in the said Province [of South Australia], or upon or in connection with any other undertaking on the part of the said Government having for its object the carriage of passengers or goods for reward, shall have a similar right of action against the Commissioner of Railways for the recovery of damages sustained by reason of such wrongful act, neglect, or default, to that which such person would have against a private company or companies if such railways or other undertakings were carried on by a private company or companies, any law or usage to the contrary notwithstanding; and no defence to any such action against the said Commissioner shall be available that could not be maintained by such company or companies.

Reference to debates on this Act show that it was intended to create Crown liability in tort where there was none before (if only, of course, against the Commissioner of Railways). Thus, the Commissioner of Crown Lands, in moving the second reading for the Bill which became Act No. 17 of 1874, stated that 'at present if an action was brought against the Government for an accident sustained on the railway the maxim that the Queen could do no wrong' – the classic means of expressing the Crown's immunity in tort – 'was pleaded'.[166] As a result of this, petitions were presented to Parliament by persons injured on the railways pleading for an *ex gratia* payment;[167] it is clear that their claims had been defeated by the maxim that the Queen could do no wrong. In commenting on the proposal to abolish this maxim in railway cases, the *Register*[168] welcomed this 'much-needed reform', the removal of the 'burning reproach to the administration of justice' constituted by the 'indefensible' and 'monstrous maxim that the Queen can do no wrong', a maxim that was 'constantly' working injustice. This leaves little doubt that the contemporary understanding of the

limits of the *Claimants Relief Act* just over twenty years after its enactment was that it did not apply in tort.

As time went on, however, lawyers realised that its terms were
actually wide enough to embrace liability in tort. As with other, similar,
later Acts of other colonies, the South Australian innovation was
accordingly applied in a way which 'went far beyond [what was] initially
intended'.[169] A series of cases in the first third of the twentieth century
expanded the Act's area of application and turned it from a procedural
statute into one creating substantive rights as well.

In 1913, the Full Court of the Supreme Court held in *Thomas* v.
Raymond[170] that the Act was available for enforcing a statutory claim
arising out of an injury sustained by a police officer during employ-
ment. Although this claim was statutory, it is analogous to a claim for
personal injury in tort. In 1922, in the case of *Bloch* v. *Smith*,[171] the
same Court held, in the words of the Chief Justice, Sir George
Murray,[172] that the restriction 'touching any pecuniary claim' in the
South Australian Act 'is not sufficient to exclude torts, for a claim for
damages for a tort is plainly a "pecuniary claim"'.[173] (Two later Judges,
speaking in 1955, said that this was the first time that the point had
been directly raised.)[174] From 1922 on, therefore, it was possible to sue
the Crown in South Australia in tort under the *Claimants Relief Act*.

Some later commentators did not realise that this had ever been
doubted. In 1948, an English commentator on the new British *Crown
Proceedings Act* 1947 dated the Crown's liability in tort in South
Australia to 1853.[175] In the High Court of Australia, Mr Justice
Windeyer said the same thing in 1971.[176] This was just before the
words first introduced into the law of South Australia by the Act of
1853 were finally expunged, after 119 years, from the State's statute
book by the *Crown Proceedings Act* 1972, which continued the principle
of Crown liability in tort and contract but expressed it in more modern
language and concepts.

It is, finally, a shame that John Baker did not leave behind a record
of who wrote those words in 1853 – in other words, who the drafter of
the Bill was. As with the *Real Property Act*, the process of drafting this
South Australian innovation is also shrouded in mystery, even if we can

be fairly sure, given his (self-)interest in the topic, that the idea behind the Act was Baker's.

The Act might have been written by Baker himself, or perhaps he asked a friendly lawyer to do it. There is just no direct evidence available on this point. However, the debate on the second reading of the Bill of 1851, part of which was quoted earlier,[177] strongly suggests that Mr Gwynne M.L.C., the obvious friendly lawyer who might have been the drafter, was not responsible for the Bill, and that Baker had educated himself on the law relating to claims against the Crown.

Although in other respects the drafting of the Bill was up to the usual standard, the somewhat inartistic reference to claims 'affect[ing] the Royal prerogative' suggests that the Act was drafted by a non-lawyer. Accordingly, the Bill may well be Baker's own handiwork – in which case, it would be a remarkable achievement for a non-lawyer, a record of achievement by a non-lawyer in reforming the law which is second, perhaps, only to that of Robert Torrens himself.

Whatever the solution to that mystery might be, it is clear that it was Baker's energy, persistence and self-interest that resulted in the enactment of this innovatory statute, which for the first time in the British Empire gave the citizen a right to sue the government when the government committed a civil wrong or failed to pay a debt, and vastly simplified the procedure for suing the government when it broke a contract. It might justly be called, in a dual sense, 'John Baker's Act'; and so might its numerous successors throughout Australia.

Notes

1   Howell, *South Australia and Federation* (Wakefield, Kent Town 2002), p. 133.
2   Holdsworth, *A History of English Law* (Methuen & Co., London 1926), Vol. IX pp. 22f. See also *Xenophon* v. *South Australia* (2000) 78 SASR 251, 261.
3   This qualification is occasionally necessary because of the vastness of the Empire and the possibility that, somewhere, someone else might have got in first.
4   Finn, *Law and Government in Colonial Australia* (Oxford U.P., Melbourne 1987), pp. 142–145.
5   *Crown Redress Act* [1859].
6   21 Vic. c. 49 (1858).
7   *Crown Suits Act* 1898.

8   *Crown Redress Act* 1871.

9   *Crown Suits Act* 1894. For a historical sketch of the development of the law of South Africa on this point, which post-dated that in (South) Australia by some decades, see *Mhlongo* v. *Minister of Police* [1978] 2 S Af 551, 563; Hahlo/Kahn, *The Union of South Africa: The Development of its Laws and Constitution* (London, Stevens & Sons 1960), pp. 194f.

10 Holdsworth, *History*, Vol. IX, pp. 44f.

11 (1887) 12 App Cas 643.

12 Parliamentary Debates, House of Lords, 4 March 1947, vol. 146 col. 67. See also Parliamentary Debates, House of Commons, 5 December 1946, vol. 431, written answers coll. 122f.

13 South Australian Parliamentary Debates, Legislative Council, 25 September 1867, col. 789.

14 Pike, *Paradise of Dissent*, pp. 431f.

15 Baker's entry in the *Australian Dictionary of Biography*, Vol. 3 p. 76.

16 South Australian Parliamentary Debates, House of Assembly, 30 June 1875, col. 298.

17 It remained on the statute book of the Northern Territory until repealed in 1965 by the *Supreme Court Ordinance Repeal Ordinance* 1965 Ord. 2 (2) & Second Schedule.

18 William Blake, *Proverbs of Heaven and Hell*, 'The Proverbs of Hell'.

19 Quoted in Blacket, *The Early History of South Australia: A Romantic Experiment in Colonisation 1836–1847* (Vardon & Son, Adelaide 1907), p. 121; see also Burgess (ed.), *Cyclop[a]edia of South Australia* Vol. 1 (Cyclopaedia Company, Adelaide 1907), p. 309; Pike, *Paradise of Dissent*, p. 294; Scheiffers, *Inside: A Brief History of the Adelaide Gaol* (Strathalbyn, 2002), pp. 7–10.

20 Pike, *Paradise of Dissent*, pp. 237f; see also pp. 185, 230–236.

21 CO 13/39/376–379 (A.J.C.P. 599).

22 CO 13/39/436 (A.J.C.P. 599).

23 GRG 40/1/121f.

24 CO 13/39/4362 (A.J.C.P. 599); see also GRG 24/6/1842/225?.

25 CO 13/39/364–366, 369 (A.J.C.P. 599).

26 GRG 2/5/6/No. 123 of 23 September 1844.

27 GRG 36/32/10/9; CO 13/39/376f, 502f (A.J.C.P. 599).

28 GRG 36/32/10/5.

29 GRG 24/4/1845/92.

30 *South Australian Government Gazette*, 29 June 1843, p. 167; South Australian Parliamentary Papers, no. 21/1856, pp. 4f, item 88; see also the notice of the sale of the premises by J.B. Neales in the *Register*, 24 April 1844, p. 2; *South Australian*, 3 September 1844, p. 2.

31 *Register*, 5 December 1856, p. 3; *Adelaide Times*, 5 December 1856, pp. 2f.

32 *Australian Dictionary of Biography*, Vol. 4, p. 312.

33 See, for example, the report of the proceedings of the Legislative Council in the Votes & Proceedings, 12 March 1850, p. 6; *Register*, 13 March 1850, p. 2; *South Australian*, 15 March 1850, p. 3; *South Australian Gazette and Mining Journal*, 14 March 1850, p. 2; *Adelaide Times*, 13 March 1850, p. 3. GRG 1/23 (bundle '1846 – Supreme Court') contains a writ issued by

Borrow & Goodiar to Charles Sturt dated 6 November 1846 and claiming £590/-/2.

34 See above, p. 15.

35 *South Australian Government Gazette*, 16 February 1843, p. 54; 6 April 1843, p. 95.

36 See the opinion of John Buckle, reproduced in the *Register*, 3 June 1846, p. 2; *South Australian*, 17 August 1849, p. 2.

37 GRG 2/5/7/No. 42 of 23 December 1845.

38 *South Australian*, 23 December 1845, pp. 2f, 3; see also edition of 16 December 1845, p. 3; *Register* 20 December 1845, pp. 2f, 3; *South Australian Gazette and Colonial Register*, 20 December 1845, p. 2; 27 December 1845, pp. 3f. In GRG 2/5/7/No. 42 of 23 December 1845, the Governor states that the case was 'fairly reported in the South Australian newspaper of today'.

39 South Australian Parliamentary Papers, 22 October 1851, reproducing GRG 2/1/6/No. 42 of 13 June 1846.

40 Hague, *A History of the Law in South Australia 1836–1867* (unpublished, Adelaide 1936), p. 1282; Taylor, 'South Australia's *Judicature Act* Reforms of 1853: The First Attempt to Fuse Law and Equity in the British Empire' (2001) 22 Jo Leg Hist 55, 63f.

41 In Scots law, referred to as an interdict.

42 For references to the pre-1947 Scots law, see *McDonald* v. *Secretary of State for Scotland* 1994 SC 234, 238–241, 246; *Mewett* v. *Commonwealth* (1997) 191 CLR 471, 544; Smith, *Scotland: The Development of its Laws and Constitutions* (Stevens & Sons, London 1962), p. 65.

43 *Register*, 30 May 1846, pp. 2–4 (note that the special jury here included R.F. Macgeorge, one of the other claimants). See also *Register*, 22 April 1846, p. 3; 15 April 1846, p. 3; *South Australian*, 17 April 1846, p. 3; 14 August 1849, p. 2; GRG 2/5/8/No. 64 of 2 June 1846; Pike, *Paradise of Dissent*, p. 334.

44 *South Australian*, 14 August 1849, p. 2.

45 *South Australian Government Gazette*, 29 June 1843, p. 167.

46 GRG 24/6/1844/812.

47 Pike, *Paradise of Dissent*, p. 193.

48 GRG 2/1/9/No. 20 of 2 March 1849.

49 GRG 24/6/1848/222, 263; 24/4/1849/340.

50 Minutes of the Legislative Council, 23 August 1849, preserved in the Library of Parliament House, Adelaide. See also the Minutes of 25 September 1849; *Register*, 26 September 1849, p. 3; *South Australian*, 24 August 1849, p. 2; 28 September 1849, Supplement, p. 1; *South Australian Gazette and Mining Journal*, 27 September 1849, p. 5; *Adelaide Times*, 27 August 1849, p. 4; 1 October 1849, p. 3.

51 Votes & Proceedings of the Legislative Council, 14 September 1852, p. 17.

52 GRG 1/1/1853/108 = GRG 24/6/1853/2616.

53 *North Australian Company* v. *Blackmore* (1871) 5 SALR 149, 153.

54 GRG 24/4/26/852; *Adelaide Times*, 22 November 1853, p. 3.

55 See, *e.g.*, GRG 24/4/1854/395; 24/6/1854/197; 24/6/1855/404, 2406 (the last of which appears to suggest that another claimant under another land order had also surfaced).

56 Loyau, *Notable South Australians*, p. 229.

57 *Observer*, 12 June 1858, Supplement, p. 1.

58 *Observer*, 27 November 1858, p. 6.

59 The title of Chief Justice was conferred on Mr Justice Cooper by Act No. 31 of 1855–56, s 1.

60 See also *Biggs* v. *McEllister* (1880) 14 SALR 86, 95.

61 Pike, *Paradise of Dissent*, pp. 185, 211.

62 *South Australia Act* 1842 (Imp.) s 10; Pike, *Paradise of Dissent*, pp. 185–192.

63 See Jacob's itemised claim for £768/15/8 in South Australian Parliamentary Papers, 19 September 1851, preserved in the Library of Parliament House; Macgeorge's itemised claim for £381/16/5, South Australian Parliamentary Papers, no. 40/1853, and GRG 2/1/5/No. 24 of 24 July 1845; Phillips' petition, South Australian Parliamentary Papers, no. 41/1853.

64 Despatch to the Governor of South Australia, 27 August 1850, reproduced in South Australian Parliamentary Papers, 19 September 1851, preserved in the Library of Parliament House; spelling as in Parliamentary Papers. For debate on this statement, see the *Adelaide Times*, 3 October 1851, p. 3; 4 October 1851, p. 5; 6 October 1851, p. 3; *Austral Examiner*, 4 October 1851, pp. 9, 12. The despatch was itself a response to the debate in the Legislative Council recorded in the Minutes of the Legislative Council, 19 February 1850; *Register*, 20 February 1850, p. 3; *South Australian*, 22 February 1850, pp. 2 (editorial comment), 4; *South Australian Gazette and Mining Journal*, 21 February 1850, p. 3; 23 February 1850, p. 3 (editorial comment); *Adelaide Times*, 21 February 1850, p. 3.

65 In addition to the other sources cited, see Minutes of the Legislative Council, 12 December 1849; the South Australian Parliamentary Papers for 1851, papers ordered to be printed on 19 September and 3 October 1851; Votes & Proceedings of the Legislative Council, 3 October 1851, p. 82 (and the correction to be found in the Votes & Proceedings, 7 October 1851, p. 85, and in sources such as the *Adelaide Times*, 8 October 1851, p. 3; *Austral Examiner*, 11 October 1851, p. 7).

66 Pike, *Paradise of Dissent*, p. 175; *Observer*, 10 August 1901, p. 32; 19 July 1902, p. 25. See also State Library of South Australia, Mortlock Library, PRG 558.

67 Statton (ed.), *Biographical Index*, Vol. 1 p. 54.

68 GRG 2/5/13/No. 141 of 27 October 1851 (attachment dated 17 October 1851).

69 *Austral Examiner*, 10 October 1851, p. 7.

70 GRG 24/6/1845/414. See also Baker's involvement in the claim the subject of the despatch in GRG 2/5/8/No. 63 of 28 May 1846, and note the implication in the *Register*, 12 June 1857, p. 3, that one of the Members of the House of Assembly was acting for Borrow & Goodiar.

71 GRG 2/1/5/No. 6 of 25 August 1845; 2/5/6/No. 163 of 19 December 1844; 24/6/1844/1442, 1463; 24/4/1844/336; 24/4/1846/159.

72 GRG 24/6/1852/2006.

73 GRG 2/1/12/No. 1 of 5 March 1852.

74 22 September 1851, p. 2.

75 There is nothing in the index to GRG 24/6 or GRG 24/4 at the State Archives of South Australia relating to either gentleman – and this may also indicate that no legal proceedings were taken, because such proceedings sometimes appear in the index in their own right, and usually led to the writing of letters which find their way into that index. The last entries for Macgeorge are GRG 24/6/1852/3017, 3054; GRG 24/4/1852/936, which again constitute a refusal. Macgeorge died on 26 October 1859 (Statton (ed.), *Biographical Index*, Vol. 3 p. 993), and it is possible that he gave up owing to ill health before he died.

76 Votes & Proceedings of the Legislative Council, 16 November 1852, p. 145; 13 September 1853, p. 81; 14 September 1853, p. 83; *Register*, 14 September 1853, p. 2; *Adelaide Times*, 14 September 1853, p. 2; 15 September 1853, p. 2.

77 South Australian Parliamentary Papers, no. 46/1854.

78 South Australian Parliamentary Papers, no. 120/1854. See also *Register*, 28 October 1854, pp. 2f; *Adelaide Times*, 28 October 1854, pp. 2f.

79 Statton (ed.), *Biographical Index*, Vol. 3 p. 993.

80 Votes & Proceedings of the Legislative Council, 20 February 1856, p. 167; South Australian Parliamentary Papers, no. 113/1856.

81 Castles/Harris, *Lawmakers and Wayward Whigs*, pp. 39f.

82 *Australian Constitutions Act* 1850 (Imp.) s 14.

83 Votes & Proceedings of the Legislative Council, 2 October 1851, p. 78; *Register*, 3 October 1851, p. 3; *South Australian Gazette and Mining Journal*, 4 October 1851, p. 3 (and see the report of the debate on 3 October 1851, *ibid.* p. 3, in which Mr Gwynne apologised for his 'warmth of language' in that debate); *Austral Examiner*, 4 October 1851, p. 9; *cf. Register*, 4 October 1851, p. 2; *Adelaide Times*, 4 October 1851, p. 5.

84 Votes & Proceedings of the Legislative Council, 2 September 1851, p. 29 (referring to the tabling of papers); 22 October 1851, p. 108; *Register*, 23 October 1851, p. 3; *South Australian Gazette and Mining Journal*, 23 October 1851, p. 4; *Adelaide Times*, 6 October 1851, p. 3; *Austral Examiner*, 24 October 1851, p. 8.

85 *Register*, 16 October 1851, p. 3; *Adelaide Times*, 16 October 1851, p. 3. See also *Adelaide Times*, 27 November 1851, p. 3 ('They only sought to pay their own debts out of their own money').

86 *South Australian Gazette and Mining Journal*, 9 October 1851, p. 3; *Adelaide Times*, 8 October 1851, p. 3; *cf. Register*, 8 October 1851, p. 3.

87 *South Australian Gazette and Mining Journal*, 9 October 1851, p. 3; *Adelaide Times*, 8 October 1851, p. 3; *cf. Register*, 8 October 1851, p. 3.

88 *South Australian Gazette and Mining Journal*, 23 October 1851, p. 4; *Austral Examiner*, 23 October 1851, p. 8. He also claimed that 'it was contrary to the law of the mother-country for a nominal defendant to be selected on the part of the Crown'. This view, in so far as it related to a nominal defendant who had in truth nothing to do with the case and the position at common law, appears to have been confirmed by *Adams* v. *Naylor* [1946] AC 543. See also *Royster* v. *Cavey* [1947] 1 KB 204; *Barnett* v. *French* [1981] 1 WLR 848.

However, it was not contrary to the law of South Australia to provide for a nominal defendant to represent the Crown once the law had been so altered.

89 25 October 1851, p. 2.

90 26 November 1851, pp. 2f = 29 November 1851, p. 1.

91 *Register*, 1 December 1851, p. 3; *South Australian Gazette and Mining Journal*, 27 November 1851, p. 3.

92 *Register*, 30 October 1851, p. 3; *South Australian Gazette and Mining Journal*, 27 November 1851, p. 3; 30 October 1851, p. 3; *Adelaide Times*, 30 October 1851, p. 3; *Austral Examiner*, 31 October 1851, p. 9.

93 *Australian Constitutions Act* 1850 (Imp.) s 14; Pike, *Paradise of Dissent*, p. 304; Pike, (1960) 1 Adel LR 169, 170. Control was vested in the local legislature under the *Australian Waste Lands Act* 1855 (Imp.) ss 2, 5.

94 See Hanson's opinion on the Act, reproduced in South Australian Parliamentary Papers, no. 32/1853.

95 South Australian Parliamentary Debates, House of Assembly, 13 October 1875, col. 1376.

96 *South Australian Gazette and Mining Journal*, 27 November 1851, p. 3; *Austral Examiner*, 28 November 1851, pp. 8f.

97 *South Australian Gazette and Mining Journal*, 29 November 1851, p. 3; *Adelaide Times*, 29 November 1851, p. 5; *Austral Examiner*, 5 December 1851, p. 7. The *Register* (1 December 1851, p. 2) presumably has its wires crossed when it states that words were retained that had earlier been struck out. It gets it right in the edition of 29 November 1851, p. 2.

98 *South Australian Gazette and Mining Journal*, 27 November 1851, p. 3; similar *Register*, 27 November 1851, p. 3.

99 *South Australian Gazette and Mining Journal*, 20 September 1851, p. 3; similar *Register*, 20 September 1851, p. 3; *Adelaide Times*, 20 September 1851, p. 5.

100 *South Australian Gazette and Mining Journal*, 29 November 1851, p. 3; similar *Adelaide Times*, 29 November 1851, p. 5; *Austral Examiner*, 5 December 1851, p. 7. 'Nominees' is a reference to the members of the Legislative Council nominated by the Crown, and 'officials' to the members holding office *ex officio* as a result of their occupation of what would now be called ministerial positions.

101 *South Australian Gazette and Mining Journal*, 29 November 1851, p. 3; *Adelaide Times*, 29 November 1851, p. 5; *Austral Examiner*, 5 December 1851, p. 7.

102 *Adelaide Times*, 29 November 1851, p. 5.

103 CO 323/73/No. 6309 (A.J.C.P. 2956).

104 CO 396/9/13 August 1852 (A.J.C.P. 878).

105 CO 13/79/98f (A.J.C.P. 787) (letter of 25 August 1852 from Law Officers to Secretary of State).

106 Secretary of State (Sir J. Pakington) to Governor, GRG 2/1/12/No. 64 of 15 October 1852 = South Australian Parliamentary Papers, no. 22/1853.

107 As above, fn 106.

108 No. 22/1853.

109 Other relevant statutes are 16 & 17 Vic. c. 107 (1853) s 263; *Crown Suits Act* 1855.

110 Latterly as the proviso to s 74 (3) of the *Supreme Court Act* 1935, and referring to the Secretary of State for the Dominions.

111 The main changes in the Bill resulting from the debate may be gathered from the *Adelaide Times*, 7 October 1853, p. 2; *Register*, 22 October 1853, p. 3.

112 Votes & Proceedings of the Legislative Council, 23 September 1853, p. 97; 5 October 1853, p. 119; *Register*, 6 October 1853, p. 3; *Adelaide Times*, 24 September 1853, p. 2; 6 October 1853, p. 2.

113 See above, fn 93.

114 South Australian Parliamentary Papers, nos. 64 & 64A/1865–66; see also no. 120/1868–69.

115 South Australian Parliamentary Debates, Legislative Council, 27 February 1866, col. 1143; 8 March 1866, col. 1261; 13 March 1866, col. 1314; 25 September 1867, coll. 789ff; 1 October 1867, col. 850; House of Assembly, 11 October 1867, col. 997; 5 December 1867, col. 1266. See also South Australian Parliamentary Debates, House of Assembly, 27 November 1866, col. 1075.

116 Votes & Proceedings of the Legislative Council, 27 October 1853, p. 153; *Register*, 28 October 1853, p. 3; *Adelaide Times*, 28 October 1853, p. 2.

117 GRG 1/6/3/329 (17 November 1853).

118 Votes & Proceedings of the Legislative Council, 9 December 1853, p. 248.

119 GRG 24/6/1856/118 (copy of a petition under the Act), 238, 1807, 1808, 1877, 2226, 2656 (indicates that Mr Justice Boothby was administering the Act without objection); GRG 24/4/1856/323, 334; *Register*, 8 April 1856, p. 3; *Adelaide Times*, 8 April 1856, p. 3. (For a later petition under the Act, see South Australian Parliamentary Papers, no. 72/1867.)

120 *Adelaide Times*, 12 July 1856, p. 3; 15 July 1856, p. 2. See also GRG 1/1/1856/59 and a book kept in the Library of the Supreme Court of South Australia containing Master Jickling's Court records from 1853 to 1860, which records the names of the special jury under the date 10 June 1856; the names crossed out in this record may be those thus excluded.

121 *Register*, 8 July 1856, p. 3.

122 *Register*, 9 July 1856, p. 3; see also *Adelaide Times*, 9 July 1856, p. 3.

123 *Register*, 12 July 1856, p. 3; *Adelaide Times*, 12 July 1856, p. 3.

124 *Register*, 17 July 1856, p. 3.

125 *Register*, 12 July 1856, p. 3.

126 *Register*, 22 July 1856, p. 3; 2 August 1856, p. 2; *Adelaide Times*, 2 August 1856, p. 4.

127 See South Australian Parliamentary Papers, no. 5/1857–58, p. 2 (revenue of £205,009/18/5).

128 19 July 1856, p. 2.

129 *Register*, 22 October 1853, p. 3.

130 2 August 1856, p. 2.

131 *Adelaide Times*, 10 December 1856, p. 2.

132 *Adelaide Times*, 16 July 1856, p. 2.

133 *Register*, 5 December 1856, pp. 2f; *Adelaide Times*, 5 December 1856, pp. 2f.

134 See also South Australian Parliamentary Papers, no. 43/1856, p. 1;
     no. 59/1857–58, p. 2 – petitions of the *creditors*, for some reason not
     including Baker.
135 Votes & Proceedings of the Legislative Council, 4 December 1856, pp. 45f;
     5 December 1856, p. 49.
136 South Australian Parliamentary Papers, no. 59/1857–58, pp. 2f.
137 The title of this officer changed from 'Advocate-General' to 'Attorney-
     General' with the advent of full democracy.
138 South Australian Parliamentary Debates, House of Assembly, 11 June 1857,
     col. 272.
139 South Australian Parliamentary Debates, House of Assembly, 11 June 1857,
     col. 273.
140 South Australian Parliamentary Debates, House of Assembly, 11 June 1857,
     col. 272.
141 13 June 1857, p. 2.
142 South Australian Parliamentary Papers, no. 94/1858.
143 Who seems not to have been a close relative of the politician
     G.M. Waterhouse judging from Statton (ed.), *Biographical Index*, Vol. 4
     p. 1679.
144 The sum actually claimed by the Bank was £7383/10/7: *Register*, 28 May
     1858, p. 3.
145 South Australian Parliamentary Debates, House of Assembly, 26 October
     1858, coll. 442f. The report in the *Register* (27 October 1858, p. 3) suggests
     that Neales' motion was in fact carried. It is not surprising that the unusual
     and confusing form of Parliamentary procedure adopted here should have
     confused the reporter. The true position can be determined in the Votes &
     Proceedings of the House of Assembly, 26 October 1858, p. 117 and
     Erskine May, *A Treatise upon the Law, Privileges, Proceedings and Usage of
     Parliament* (1st ed., Irish U.P. [1844] 1971), pp. 173f; and see also
     Limon/McKay (eds.), *Erskine May's Treatise on the Law, Privileges,
     Proceedings and Usage of Parliament* (22nd ed., Butterworths London 1997),
     p. 341 fn 2.
146 *Register*, 19 May 1858, p. 3.
147 *Register*, 12 May 1858, p. 3; 19 May 1858, p. 3.
148 Documents in the possession of Mr K.T. Borrow (and to be given to the
     Flinders University of South Australia) show that this was so.
149 *Register*, 28 May 1858, p. 3; see also *Register*, 24 May 1858, p. 3.
150 *Register*, 12 July 1858, p. 3.
151 *Register*, 20 December 1858, p. 2.
152 *Register*, 9 February 1859, p. 3.
153 *Register*, 11 December 1858, p. 3. See also *Register*, 16 December 1858, p. 3;
     28 January 1859, p. 3.
154 *South Australian Government Gazette*, 7 April 1859, p. 323.
155 Pike, *Paradise of Dissent*, pp. 429f, 466.
156 *Register*, 23 July 1862, p. 5; *Observer*, 13 August 1887, p. 35.
157 GRG 24/6/1855/579; 24/6/1855/648. Allen, *Royal South Australian Almanac
     for 1858* (Adelaide, Register & Observer Offices, 1858), p. 33 shows that

Borrow's appointment, originally made under Act No. 18 of 1854, survived the enactment of the Act No. 27 of 1855–56.

158 South Australian Parliamentary Papers, no. 128/1865, pp. 2f. The middle name of Mr Goodiar varies slightly in different records, but it may be assumed that it is the same man.

159 See also GRG 53/271.

160 South Australian Parliamentary Papers, no. 3/1873, p. 3 (emphasis in original). See also Hammerton, *Water South Australia: A History of the Engineering and Water Supply Department* (Wakefield, Netley 1986), pp. 24, 41, 42 fn 27.

161 The procedure under the Act was in fact sometimes called a 'petition of right': *Bloch* v. *Smith* [1922] SASR 95, 96; *William Charlick* v. *Smith* [1922] SASR 364, 366; *Siebert* v. *Hunkin* [1934] SASR 347, 357; (1934) 51 CLR 538, 539; *Miesiewicz* v. *South Australian Railways Commissioner* [1961] SASR 190, 194; and see South Australian Parliamentary Debates, House of Assembly, 28 March 1972, p. 4346 (King A.-G. Q.C.).

162 See above, p. 64.

163 *Adelaide Times*, 30 October 1851, p. 3. The report in the *Register* (30 October 1851, p. 3) is similar, although it omits Mr Gwynne's express mention of the law of torts.

164 Robertson, *Law and Practice of Civil Proceedings by and against The Crown and Departments of the Government* (Stevens & Sons, London 1908), p. 350 (emphasis added).

165 This includes, for reasons which the author explains elsewhere, the *dictum* of Chief Justice Hanson in *North Australian Company* v. *Blackmore* (1871) 5 SALR 157, 176 quoted by some authors.

166 South Australian Parliamentary Debates, 27 October 1874, col. 2162.

167 See the Index to the Parliamentary Debates for 1874, House of Assembly, *s.v.* 'Railway Accident', which lists no fewer than four claims by five people.

168 4 September 1874, p. 4.

169 Finn, *Law and Government*, p. 142.

170 [1913] SALR 144.

171 [1922] SASR 95.

172 His Honour had stated as late as 1915 that the Crown was not liable in tort in South Australia: *Folland* v. *Stevens* [1915] SALR 25, 39.

173 [1922] SASR 95, 106.

174 *Hall* v. *Bonnett* [1956] SASR 10, 22. See also Canaway, 'Actions Against the Commonwealth for Torts' (1904) 1 Clth LR 241, 244.

175 Bell, *Crown Proceedings, being a Full Statement of the Law relating to Action by and against the Crown as affected by the* Crown Proceedings Act 1947 (Sweet & Maxwell, London 1948), p. 22 fn n.

176 *Downs* v. *Williams* (1971) 126 CLR 61, 78; see also *Mewett*, (1997) 191 CLR 471, 544f.

177 See above, p. 90.

5. Clubs and Societies Legislation

1. Background of the innovation

Because the law, generally speaking, does not prevent people from gathering together and talking about whatever they like, no permission from the law is required to form a not-for-profit club, society or association. It is in fact a basic human right to do so, recognised in such august instruments as the International Covenant on Civil and Political Rights.[1] But thanks to a South Australian legal innovation which has spread throughout Australia, Australian law positively assists people who wish to associate. It does so by permitting them to have their associations registered and incorporated as legally recognised entities.

Incorporation enables an association to hold land and other forms of property, and to enter into legal relationships such as contracts, in its own right and in its own name rather than using the names of some or all of its members. Under modern legislation, this has two main advantages. First, it means that when members leave associations, or die, the association need not note that fact on any contract or record of property ownership – for example, on records of the ownership of land kept under the Torrens system.

Secondly, it does away with the risk that the officers and even members of the association, although not personally at fault, might be successfully sued and made liable for any debts the association as a whole may incur or any damages it might have to pay.[2]

These advantages were first offered to associations by the *Associations*

Incorporation Act 1858 of South Australia. The legislation, it will be observed, is a South Australian innovation from the same year as the Torrens system. The Act provided a simple and cheap method of incorporating and running an association formed for community purposes. It has been copied in all other Australian jurisdictions.

The current version of the Act in South Australia[3] establishes the following list of purposes for which not-for-profit associations may be recognised and incorporated:

(a) for a religious, educational, charitable or benevolent purpose; or

(b) for the purpose of promoting or encouraging literature, science or the arts; or

(c) for the purpose of providing medical treatment or attention, or promoting the interests of persons who suffer from a particular physical, mental or intellectual disability; or

(d) for the purpose of sport, recreation or amusement; or

(e) for the purpose of establishing, carrying on, or improving a community centre, or promoting the interests of a local community or a particular section of a local community; or

(f) for conserving resources or preserving any part of the environmental, historical or cultural heritage of the State; or

(g) for the purpose of promoting the interests of students or staff of an educational institution; or

(h) for political purposes; or

(i) for the purpose of administering any scheme or fund for the payment of superannuation or retiring benefits to the members of any organisation or the employees of any body corporate, firm or person; or

(j) for the purpose of promoting the common interests of persons who are engaged in, or interested in, a particular business, trade or industry; or

(k) for any purpose approved by the Minister.

In other words, the Act embraces a great deal of the community's life and endeavours.

The South Australian innovation of 1858 was copied across Australia, although much more slowly than the Torrens system, partly because it was not quite as epoch-making as the Torrens system and partly because a less satisfactory alternative was available in the rest of Australia to clubs and societies – namely, incorporation as a company under the companies statutes. This was the method used in the eastern States until they adopted the modern version of the South Australian statute in the 1980s, as had been recommended by bodies such as the Law Reform Commission of New South Wales.[4]

Using the companies legislation for the purpose of incorporating clubs and societies was not ideal since companies legislation assumes that organisations have shareholders and are trading for profit, and that there is a need for the safeguards and paperwork that apply to companies. As the Law Reform Commission of New South Wales put it in 1982,

> In the result, although today the *Companies Act* provides a means for the incorporation and regulation of non-profit associations, the means is neither simple nor inexpensive. The complexity and expense of registration and consequent regulation under the *Companies Act* leads many non-profit associations to look for simpler and less expensive ways to achieve incorporation.[5]

Figures show that what is, for the eastern States, a new way of incorporating clubs and societies has been taken up very rapidly over there,[6] proving the continuing value of the South Australian innovation, a century and a quarter after it was conceived, to the whole of Australian society. 'With hindsight', writes Sally Sievers, 'it seems amazing that it took so long for associations incorporation Acts to be introduced in Australia's three largest States.'[7] Other States were not quite as slow to catch on. Western Australia adopted the South Australian legislation as early as 1895,[8] and Tasmania and the A.C.T. and the Northern Territory in the 1950s and 1960s.[9]

A fairly recent count indicated that about 125 000 societies existed in Australia which have been incorporated under the legislation initiated in South Australia.[10] In all likelihood most of these would have been formed anyway, but the existence of associations incorporation legislation makes them much easier and cheaper to run, and conserves their resources for their real purpose.

2. Drafting, introduction and passage of the Act

The Bill for the Act, as introduced by Captain Charles Hervey Bagot into the Legislative Council on 21 January 1858, only a few days before the *Real Property Act* finally passed through Parliament, is preserved in South Australia's Parliamentary Library. With some minor exceptions, it is very similar to the Act as finally enacted. The Bill, like the Act, establishes a scheme of incorporation by means of a grant of a certificate by the Master of the Supreme Court following the making of an application to the Court. Eligibility for incorporation was to be restricted to non-profit community organisations such as churches, schools, hospitals, benevolent and charitable institutions, mechanics' institutes and institutes for the purpose of promoting literature, science and the arts. This was a shorter version of the list just quoted which may still be found in South Australian law today. There were some other minor differences between the Bill and the Act as finally enacted, but none of great significance.

The preamble to the legislation indicated why Parliament introduced it. The preamble said that

> great inconvenience has arisen in cases where property belonging to institutions established for the promotion of religion, education, and benevolent and useful objects, has become vested in trustees, by the refusal of such trustees to act, and by the necessity for the frequent change of trustees; and great expense is often incurred by reason of such change, and the appointment of other trustees, and the transfer of property to such other trustees.

The Act did not confer on associations limited liability for debts as exists for some companies, and indeed expressly provided that the existing liability of the members of the association for its debts remained unaffected. More modern legislation has since changed this.[11] Nor did it make any 'provision for members' rights or for the termination of the association'.[12] Again, these defects were to be remedied, some in inter-State versions of the innovation,[13] and the remedy was then imported to South Australia.

'Hansard', the Parliamentary debates, shows that Captain Bagot referred, in introducing the Bill, in a general way to the assistance he had received from a member of the legal profession.[14] This in itself was nothing remarkable given that South Australia did not at the time possess a parliamentary drafter and that Bagot was not himself legally trained.[15] However, the newspaper reports of the parliamentary debates, which include more detail than 'Hansard', make the role played by Captain Bagot's legal adviser appear quite decisive. The *Adelaide Times*[16] states that Captain Bagot told Parliament that 'the Bill had been placed in his hand by a member of the legal profession, who stated it was most desirable'. When the Bill was re-introduced in September 1858, the Bill of January 1858 having lapsed in the meantime, the *Register*[17] reported Captain Bagot as saying that the Bill 'had been got up under the superintendence of a legal gentleman of considerable eminence'.

One recent writer calls the clubs and societies legislation 'the Bagot idea' and 'Bagot's legislation',[18] but Bagot's statements show that this is wrong. Bagot was the mere parliamentary agent of an unnamed external instigator whose idea the Bill was and who drafted it himself. To Captain Bagot belongs the credit for recognising a good idea, bringing it before Parliament and persisting with it, but not, if the statements reported in the newspapers are correctly reported and true, the credit for originating the idea.

But who was this 'legal gentleman of considerable eminence'? Who stood behind the Bill?

The South Australian legal profession was not large in 1858. A local directory[19] lists a total of forty-five practising lawyers. Many of these men were also members of Parliament, including almost all of the most eminent lawyers such as Messrs R.D. Hanson, E.C. Gwynne,[20] W. Bakewell, J.T. Bagot (Captain Bagot's nephew),[21] J.H. Fisher, and

R.B. Andrews. It may confidently be assumed that, if one of these members of Parliament had been responsible for the Bill to the extent suggested by Captain Bagot in his speech, that fact would at least have been mentioned in the debates and, indeed, the responsible person would probably have introduced the Bill himself. Certainly there would have been no need to omit to mention the identity of the drafter.

The instigator of this idea could have been a lawyer outside Parliament who wished to remain anonymous because, in the words of one member of the House of Assembly, the Bill would 'cut off a large amount of revenue from the profession to which he had the honor to belong'.[22] There were in fact one or two fairly high-profile practising lawyers who were not members of Parliament, such as Rupert Ingleby, W.H. Burford and H.W. Parker. But there is no particular reason to associate any of them with the drafting of the Act; it would have been something of an exaggeration to describe them as 'of considerable eminence'; and there is no really compelling reason why they would not have been named as the instigator if that had been the case: surely the wrath of their practitioner colleagues would have been short-lived and bearable, as no one would have derived his entire livelihood from acting for associations, and legal help would be required by those incorporating under the new Act anyway.[23] The Crown Solicitor, W.A. Wearing, might also have instigated the Bill, although he would surely have been named as its source if he had acted in his official capacity, and he would not even have to fear the wrath of his colleagues, as a private practitioner possibly might, for drafting a Bill which deprived them of fees. Any such secrets would, at any rate, have been hard to keep in the small legal profession in Adelaide in those days. Of course, the drafter might simply have been modest and unwilling to have his name mentioned in Parliament, but there is no reason to suspect this.

The fact that there was no rush to incorporate after the Act was enacted – the first incorporated association, as we shall see, was formed in 1860, almost two years later, and very few in the first decade thereafter[24] – suggests that the Act was not the product of a legal practitioner's desire to solve a pressing practical issue on behalf of a particular association, but the work of someone with a longer-term interest in promoting voluntary associations.

The fact that Schedule A to the Bill used the term 'Act of Council', a designation which had become out of date after the opening of the first bicameral Parliament of South Australia in 1857, also suggests that this was a project which had been in someone's top drawer for some time rather than something proposed as the result of some immediate practical need.

So we are looking for someone who is, so to speak, above the dust of the arena. I suggest that the chief clue to the source of the Act lies in the combination of eminence and anonymity which are to be found in Captain Bagot's utterances. These criteria are best fulfilled by a Judge: such a person is an eminent member of the legal profession *par excellence* and is also compelled to remain anonymous, at least officially, by the constraints surrounding the judicial role. And if we examine the Bench of South Australia at this stage in its history, we can identify a prime candidate for the honour of being the drafter of the Act: Mr Acting Justice Charles Mann.

The other Judges seem much less likely to have been the source of the Act. Chief Justice Cooper was absent on leave in England from the end of 1856 to May 1858.[25] It cannot of course be ruled out that he had presented Captain Bagot with a draft of the Bill before he left or sent one by post during his absence, although it seems unlikely even having regard to his role in the formation of the first association to incorporate under the Act two years later.[26] If Chief Justice Cooper had presented the Bill to Captain Bagot in late 1856, just before he left, why did Captain Bagot wait so long to introduce it? Furthermore, the Chief Justice appears to have adopted the more traditional method of writing to the government and making a suggestion for legislation in cases in which he felt he had something to contribute.[27] Finally, a recent biographer of Sir Charles Cooper has been unable to find any material linking him with the Act[28] and points out that his suggestions for legislation 'did not reflect the mind of an inspired law reformer. Rather, they were limited to legislative housekeeping and deference to

English models',[29] which excludes a statute like the *Associations Incorporation Act* 1858, for which there was no English precedent. And although a generous obituary-writer was able to say of Acting Chief Justice Boothby[30] that he 'exhibited proofs of originality and acuteness' and 'could be a bold innovating reformer',[31] and his Honour also was occasionally the anonymous author of pamphlets,[32] it seems most unlikely that a Judge with such a 'rooted dislike of colonial innovations'[33] would have contributed one to the South Australian statute book. These two Judges can therefore, it seems, be ruled out. But the case for Mr Acting Justice Mann does not rest merely on this process of exclusion.

Charles Mann had been one of the very first settlers in South Australia and its first Advocate-General.[34] By 1858, the year in which the Act was enacted, he had been Justice of the Peace, Special Magistrate, Commissioner of the Court of Insolvency[35] (in which capacity we met him in a previous chapter) and Acting Justice of the Supreme Court (during Chief Justice Cooper's absence).[36] Douglas Pike comments that his 'major public interest was the advancement of education, particularly by means of mechanics' institutes and libraries. ... As a public functionary he was forbidden an active part in the struggle for civil and religious liberty, but there can be little doubt that he was discreetly active behind the scenes',[37] which might of course include being the instigator of legislation. Pike's statement that Mann was interested in education, mechanics' institutes and libraries is correct: in the early days of South Australia, Mann had been on the committees of the Literary Association, the Mechanics' Institute and the subscription library.[38] Mechanics' institutes and institutes for promoting literature, it will be recalled, were some of the bodies eligible for incorporation under the Act.

The *Southern Australian*, a newspaper which Mann co-founded and edited in opposition to the pro-government *Register* in 1838 and 1839,[39] was full of exhortations to establish and support societies of various sorts to improve the standard of life in early South Australia.[40] It was probably Mann himself who, in an editorial on 7 August 1839,[41] explained that 'Among those features which distinguish our colony

Charles Mann,
photographic reproduction of a painting
SSL:MLSA:B6620

from every other with which we are acquainted, none is more striking than the determination evinced here to employ and keep in active operation every known engine for moral, mental and social improvement. This characteristic ensures future greatness.' It might well have been the debates on what became the *Real Property Act* which led Mr Acting Justice Mann to pull the draft of the Act out of his top drawer and to have it debated in Parliament as an adjunct to the real property legislation and as a means of enabling associations to hold property in a convenient manner.

Also eligible for incorporation under the Act were religious bodies. Mann had also been a trustee of the first church to be built on South Australian soil (Holy Trinity Church, North Terrace),[42] in which capacity he had been faced with the consequences of the trustees' personal liability for debts incurred on behalf of the organisation they represented.[43] Mann was also an opponent of state aid to religion (one of the major controversies in early South Australia), believing that all denominations should provide for their own sustenance and government.[44] Here he had a good deal in common with Captain Bagot. Bagot was also an opponent of state aid to religion,[45] as a result of which Bagot 'fell out with many Anglicans'.[46] It is quite consistent with their shared view on this question to wish to provide legal facilities for religious bodies to set up their own self-administering corporations – especially when we remember that the alternative is the passing of an incorporation Act for individual denominations on an *ad hoc* basis. This might be thought – as the Church of England found when it attempted to have a special incorporation Act passed for itself in the early 1860s[47] – to carry a whiff of state endorsement of those denominations favoured with such measures as against those that are not. Furthermore, personal relationships between the two may be assumed to have been at least cordial. Captain Bagot had gone on the public record in appreciation of Mann's services as an Acting Judge in 1849, something which Mann had not forgotten in 1852 when he used Bagot's opinion of his services as a Judge in support of his application for the judicial vacancy which had arisen on the early death of Mr Justice Crawford (and which, most unfortunately as it turned out, was given to one Benjamin Boothby).[48] It is therefore probable that Captain Bagot would have been willing to do Mr Acting Justice Mann's parliamentary work for him.

Pike also records that Mann, when Advocate-General, had quibbled over the enacting words of ordinances,[49] and this matches up very nicely with a statement in 'Hansard'[50] that the enacting words of the Act had to be changed to what had become the usual South Australian form during the Bill's passage through the Legislative Council.

Mann's interest in the sort of public institutions which could be incorporated under the Act had not ceased by the 1850s. He gave a well-received lecture to the Mechanics' Institute in the late 1840s;[51] he gave evidence to a select committee of the Legislative Council in 1853 which considered the question of the future of literary, scientific and similar institutions in South Australia;[52] in 1853 he developed a plan for rescuing the Mechanics' Institute involving the establishment by it of a free public library in return for government grants;[53] and he provided answers to questions proposed by the 'General Committee of the Adelaide Library and Mechanics' Institute appointed at the General Quarterly Meeting on the 15th day of January 1853' on the history of attempts to establish libraries and public institutes in South Australia.[54] These are all the types of bodies which the Act of 1858 was aimed at assisting.

All this would have been very well known to the members of Parliament considering the Bill. Thus, those who had not already been initiated might well have been able to guess that the eminent legal gentleman to whom Captain Bagot referred was none other than Charles Mann. Given Mann's well-known positive attitude towards voluntary associations and his agreement with Captain Bagot on the question of state aid to religion, the hint would have been quite easily understood by leading citizens of the late 1850s. The identity of the brains behind the Bill was therefore not really a secret at all to those who heard Captain Bagot's words. The identity of its instigator could not be publicly announced, because of his role as a Judge, but everyone who mattered knew who it was.

If the Act was Mr Acting Justice Mann's work, he did not live long to see it in operation. He died on the Queen's Birthday, 24 May 1860, 'after an illness which had for some time past compelled him to retire from the active duties of the Court [of Insolvency] over which he presided',[55] but which clearly did not affect him in early 1858 (when the Act was first proposed in Parliament) to an extent which prevented him from being re-appointed as Commissioner of Insolvency.[56]

My conclusion that Charles Mann was the real author of the Act is based on circumstantial evidence only. He left no papers to posterity. At some later time, conclusive proof might be found that someone else was the instigator. But on the state of the evidence currently available, the credit for the *Associations Incorporation Act* 1858 and for the second great South Australian legal innovation of that year should be given to Mr Acting Justice Mann.

Let us return briefly to Dr Ulrich Hübbe, whom we have already met in connexion with the *Real Property Act*. Could he be the drafter of this legislation? This thought arises because of the striking fact that Torrens,[57] in introducing the Bill for the *Real Property Act*, referred in a mysterious way, as did Captain Bagot, to assistance he had received in drafting the Bill from an unnamed legal person. However, it seems even more unlikely that Dr Hübbe was the source of the *Associations Incorporation Act* 1858 than that he produced the *Real Property Act* single-handedly. Although the method of incorporation required by the *Associations Incorporation Act* 1858 involved, as does modern German law,[58] procedures before a Court,[59] this is probably just coincidence again. This feature of German law cannot be traced back much further than the beginnings of modern German associations law in the late 1860s, over ten years after the South Australian Act was enacted.[60] Furthermore, Dr Hübbe had not written a book advocating reform of the law relating to voluntary associations, as he had in relation to real property law.

What about the reverse possibility? As far as I am aware, however, no one has ever suggested Mr Acting Justice Mann as the possible helper in the development of the *Real Property Act* whom Torrens did not wish to name.

3. The repeal and revival of the Act

The Act was repealed in 1864 by s 184 of the *Companies Act* 1864. If Charles Mann was the true author and drafter of the Act, it is not surprising that the repeal went through virtually unchallenged, as he was no longer alive to defend his creation. His Act was, however, brought back into force the next year by Act No. 12 of 1865 ('the Revival Act'). What is going on here?

Although there was a change of government between the repeal and revival of the Act, there is nothing to suggest that there were any significant political differences which led to this about-face by the legislature. Rather, the surviving sources suggest a number of reasons for the passing of the Revival Act in 1865; it was stated in the second reading speech for the Revival Act that the repeal of the Act had affected the trustees of educational establishments and religious bodies injuriously, that the repeal had been 'inadvertent'[61] and that the Port Adelaide Grammar School had found that it could not incorporate 'except it underwent all the formula[e] of the *Joint-Stock Companies Act*'.[62]

The repeal-and-revival episode is best understood, I suggest, as a reflection of the tension between the role of colonial legislatures in the nineteenth century as mere transmitters of English reforms to the colonies and their role as innovative law reformers in their own right. For the South Australian *Companies Act* 1864, which repealed the Act, was (in its substantive provisions) 'nearly a reprint of the English Act',[63] 'in all its essential provisions a copy of an English Act',[64] namely, the *Companies Act* 1862. It was quite common for the Australian colonies to copy English legislation in this era, and this is one of the numerous examples. The English legislation, however, contained no special provision for community associations as distinct from the trading companies with which it was designed to deal.

We do not know who added the *Associations Incorporation Act* 1858 to the list of Acts which were to be repealed in favour of the English import which became the South Australian *Companies Act* 1864. Whoever it was, however, probably did not do so 'inadvertent[ly]', in the sense of by accident or through inattention – although the full implications of repealing the Act may not have been apparent to all the legislators of 1864. Rather, the repeal of the Act in 1864 occurred because the person responsible for drafting the *Companies Act* 1864 came to the conclusion that the South Australian innovation could be abandoned now that English legislation had arrived and that the English legislation, being more elaborate, was better.

As was shown the next year, however, the South Australian legislation did in fact fill a need which the companies legislation catered for less well – the need for a simple and cheap method of incorporation available to non-profit entities such as the Port Adelaide Grammar School. The companies legislation was too complicated for such organisations, and was drafted on the assumption that those incorporating under it were aiming to make a profit, which the Port Adelaide Grammar School was not. There was therefore no need for things like shares and safeguards for investors. The revival of the Act was not therefore so much the correction of an 'inadvertent' error as it was a belated realisation by the South Australian Parliament that it had in fact created a legal innovation in 1858 which was worth keeping because it suited the community's needs better than the English legislation.

The Port Adelaide Grammar School, a Church-affiliated school established in 1862,[65] was indeed incorporated under the Act,[66] although its incorporation was cancelled in 1938 after the school had ceased to function.[67] By that time, however, it had played its part in South Australian legal history.

And when South Australia came to adopt the English *Companies Act* 1867, it omitted s 23 of that Act relating to the incorporation of not-for-profit entities as companies.[68] As was stated in Parliament,[69] this was because South Australia already had its own indigenous statute for this purpose – a statute which was better suited to the needs of non-profit associations than the English one. Despite the existence of later English legislation attempting to deal with the same area of law, then, the South Australian legislature stood by the decision it had made in 1865 to prefer its own statute to possible imports. It was only in the eastern States that such imports were required, at least until they got around to adopting the South Australian innovation of 1858, which remained a superior solution to the needs of community associations.

4. An upper-class plot?

Why was legislation to assist community associations first enacted in South Australia? The answer to this question sheds light on some interesting features of the early South Australian community.

To answer this question, one could of course point to the Province's general reputation for legislative innovation which also produced the other legislation discussed in this book. One commentator suggests, however, that the Act was meant to serve 'the then dominant liberal economic and political ideology of *laissez-faire* individualism' and that it was 'formulated by the upper class in colonial South Australia, and it was used for the immediate benefit of that same class'.[70] However, this rather heavy-handed Marxist conclusion is not really supported by facts. Nor is it obviously correct, as people of virtually any social class can form and join associations of one type or another. There is nothing in the Act which suggests that it could be right either.

Admittedly the very first society to incorporate under the Act was the Church of England Endowment Society,[71] the trustees of which all called themselves Honourables or Esquires in the notice which, as required by the Act, they published in the *Government Gazette* on 24 May 1860,[72] which was coincidentally the day of Charles Mann's death. Later successful applications in the 1860s and 1870s came, however, from the ranks of artisans, working men or what today would be called small business-people. A machinist and brewer sought the incorporation of the Gawler Institute[73] and two store-keepers and one telegraph station-master applied for the incorporation of the Mount Gambier Institute.[74] Further early applications were approved from such non-Establishment, even 'outsider' bodies as the German Club,[75] the Adelaide Hebrew Philanthropic Society,[76] the Jesuits,[77] the Penola Mechanics' Institute[78] and the Prince Alfred Sailors' Home, the object of which was (in part) 'to provide board and lodging for seamen frequenting or resorting to the Port of Adelaide at as low a charge as possible',[79] a facility which was perhaps unlikely to appeal to the upper class. Looking at the sorts of organisations which incorporated under the Act in the first few years after it was passed, we cannot identify a noticeable bias towards the upper class. If anything there is a bias towards outsiders of various sorts.

My survey of the first one hundred associations incorporated under the Act, which takes us to 1888, thirty years after its passing,[80] indicates that exactly half were religious. (The high number is explained by the fact that many of these were individual parishes). Of these fifty, thirty-seven were of the dissenting denominations, or forty-one if the established Church of Scotland is included, and only six from the Church of England. The six employers' and professional associations were outnumbered by the seven philanthropic societies, eight institutes and nine clubs of various types (two ethnic and one each musical, youth, bushman's, gardeners', freethinkers', yachting and lodge societies). The rest were a miscellaneous assortment including schools (three), show societies (three), hospitals and health institutes (five) and Aborigines' benefit organisations (two).

The Marxist explanation is also inconsistent with the fact that the legislation spread so slowly throughout the rest of Australia. After all, other colonies had upper classes as well which might have been expected to adopt the legislation if it really did offer such great advantages to the upper class. The comparatively rapid adoption throughout Australia of the *Real Property Act* suggests that that piece of legislation did indeed serve the interests of those who held the levers of power – who were very often landowners or well connected to landowners – although of course that statute also served the interests of the large and growing class of more humble landowners, and this broad appeal doubtless explains its popularity and rapid adoption throughout Australia. But the *Associations Incorporation Act* 1858 was not adopted anywhere nearly as rapidly throughout Australia, as we might expect it would be if it were really such a boon to those in power. In fact, it serves, at least judging it on its face, no identifiable class of people (other than people in clubs and societies, who can be of any social class).

What was it, then, about South Australia which led to its being the pioneer in this field – other than its general record for legislative innovations? Part of the answer may be found in the spirit of religious freedom and absence of state interference in religious matters that has already been mentioned. Such a climate was hostile to special Acts incorporating religious bodies – as the Church of England found when it petitioned for its own special incorporation Act in 1862[81] and the cry went up that its petition 'shewed the desire of the Church to become an Established Church'.[82] On the other hand, nineteenth-century South Australian society was not in any way irreligious and was quite content to promote religion on an equal basis for all by providing a general incorporation Act open to all comers.

A more significant reason for the Act's enactment may be found in the marked sense of difference from – even superiority to – the other Australian colonies which existed in South Australian public life until well into the twentieth century. As one historian explained in 1911, 'the Province [of South Australia] was founded by a superior class of men and women'[83] – the implicit contrast here is with the other Australian colonies, which were founded by convicts[84] – and the superior nature of the founders of South Australia, our author continued, was proved by the formation, early on, of such elevated bodies as the South Australian Literary Association. Charles Mann, as has already been mentioned, also referred to a related difference between South Australia and the other colonies he knew: 'the determination ... to employ and keep in active operation every known engine for moral, mental and social improvement. This characteristic ensures future greatness.'

Thus, official encouragement was given (by separate legislation)[85] to the formation of the South Australian Institute in Adelaide and, later, to equivalents in the country districts. It was therefore entirely in accordance with the Province's self-image as a beacon of freedom and high-mindedness in a sea of convict settlements that a statute should be passed facilitating the formation of further voluntary associations among its free and high-minded citizenry in order to ensure the continued edification and improvement of the 'superior class of men and women' who had settled in South Australia. This does not, of course, mean that voluntary associations in early South Australia always lived up to the hopes of their founders,[86] but this was all the more reason to attempt to encourage them by legal as well as other means.

All this does not however mean that the Act was intended to serve the purposes of the upper class (whatever that may be). The 'superior class of men and women' did not form a society consisting solely of the upper class (is such a thing possible?), but also included honest artisans and labourers untainted by the convict stain. As we have seen, one of the chief concerns of the time – and of Charles Mann – was the establishment of a Mechanics' Institute and equivalent institutes for country districts, which were designed to serve the educational and recreational needs of those with little formal education – even if some of them belonged to the artisan class, and thus to the aristocracy of labour.[87] Mechanics' institutes and similar bodies were specifically mentioned in s 11 of the Act as the sort of association which might be incorporated under it,[88] as were benevolent and charitable institutions, which at most might be the recipients of money from the upper class but would be unlikely to provide anything to them other than an outlet for their charitable instincts. Thus, the Act seems to be quite neutral, at least on its face, towards all classes of society, and expressly includes some things which benefit less well-off people.

Clearly the Act was designed to facilitate the holding of property, and in particular real property, by voluntary associations, and thus assumed that the associations which would be its beneficiaries would have at least some assets. However, associations such as country and mechanics' institutes, which received their funds from government grants and numerous small contributions from the strata of society below the upper class, typically owned merely a small piece of land and a modest building for their needs which, with some books, constituted virtually the whole of their assets. Anyone who drives around country South Australia, or even some suburbs of Adelaide such as Magill and Goodwood, will have seen institute buildings from those days. The same applies to institutions such as the German Club. It is precisely this sort of association, which might be have one fairly large asset (its building) but be income poor,[89] that was in need of a means of ensuring that its real property could be held in a simple and cheap manner which avoided ongoing expense caused by repeated transfers consequent on changes of trustees. The gentry would be able to look after itself in this respect much more easily than could middle- and lower-class institutions, which might often struggle to raise the money necessary for the upkeep of their buildings, let alone for legal fees. And the upper class had much more to lose from the personal liability of members of associations for the associations' debts, something which the Act (s 4) expressly preserved.[90] The Act therefore would have appeared something of a failure or an irrelevance from the point of view of an upper-class person.

Now it might possibly be said that promoting the education of the artisan and working classes (in mechanics' institutes and the like) as well as of their children (in institutions such as the Port Adelaide Grammar School) might assist the upper class in keeping a lid on the discontent of the lower classes, although this seems rather a long bow to draw in nineteenth-century South Australia, which was hardly a seething cauldron of revolutionary thought. But it is difficult to see that even this aim could be pursued by facilitating the establishment of the German Club or the Adelaide Hebrew Philanthropic Society. The Act, by doing this, did not serve the upper class, but rather enhanced the ability of all classes of people, including those multicultural groups which were present in early South Australia, to have their associations recognised by the law as legal persons.

Although the number of associations incorporated under the Act in its early years was small, the fact that there was such a mixed and in part humble set of associations incorporated under it makes the failure of the upper class in other parts of Australia to seize on the South Australian innovation as a means to promoting their own interests less than surprising. As we have seen, the South Australian legislation was originated in South Australia because of the unique origins and pretensions of that society as a free settlement, not because of any characteristics it shared with other Australian colonies such as the existence of an upper class.

Notes

1 Article 22 (1).
2 Examples and relevant cases may be found in Fletcher, *The Law Relating to Non-Profit Associations in Australia and New Zealand* (Law Book, Sydney 1986), Chh. 7, 8.
3 *Associations Incorporation Act* 1985 s 18 (1) (part).
4 *Report on Incorporation of Associations* (L.R.C. (N.S.W.) 30/1982).
5 *Ibid.*, p. 13. The report also mentions the possibility of creating a company limited by guarantee and deals with the drawbacks of that option.
6 Sievers, (2001) 13 Aust Jo Corp Law 124, 129, 142.
7 Sievers, (2001) 13 Aust Jo Corp Law 124, 129.
8 *Associations Incorporation Act* 1895; Huntly, *A Most Useful Enactment: the Legislative History, Function and Legal Philosophy of the Associations Incorporation Legislation in Western Australia* (unpublished, M.Comm. thesis, Curtin University of Technology, 1999).
9 The history is traced in Fletcher, *Law Relating to Non-Profit Associations*, Ch. 12; Sievers, 'Incorporation and Regulation of Non-Profit Associations in Australia and other Common-Law Jurisdictions' (2001) 13 Aust Jo Corp Law 124, 128–135.
10 See the statistics collected by the Centre of Philanthropy and Non-profit Studies, Queensland University of Technology, available at: http://www.cpns.qut.edu.au/Statistics%20251002.pdf. The figure given is that for 31 December 2001. See also Sievers, (2001) 13 Aust Jo Corp Law 124, 142.
11 This did, however, take some time. The liability of members of incorporated associations for the association's debts was not excluded until the enactment of the *Companies Act* 1934 s 401, on which see *Report of the Joint Select Committee of the Legislative Council and House of Assembly on the Companies Bill 1933* (Parliamentary Paper no. 70/1934), pp. 4, 8; Re *Proprietary Articles Trade Association of South Australia* [1949] SASR 88, 97.
12 Fletcher, *Law Relating to Non-Profit Associations*, pp. 209f. Provision for winding up was made by the *Associations Incorporation Act 1890 Amendment Act* 1897 s 5, or rather once the printer's error in that section was corrected by Act No. 757 (1901).
13 See, for example, *Associations Incorporation Act* 1895 (W.A.) s 8 (conferring limited liability).
14 South Australian Parliamentary Debates, Legislative Council, 7 September 1858, col. 56.
15 Biographies of Bagot may be found in Bagot, *A Holograph Memoir of Captain Charles Hervey Bagot of the 8th Regiment* (Pioneers' Association of South Australia, Adelaide 1942); Loyau, *The Representative Men of South Australia* (George Howell, Adelaide 1893), pp. 48f; *Observer*, 31 July 1880, p. 187 (obituary following Bagot's death on 29 July).
16 22 January 1858, p. 3.
17 8 September 1858, p. 2.
18 Fletcher, *Law Relating to Non-Profit Associations*, pp. 219, 209.
19 *Howell's Directory for the City and Port of Adelaide and South Australian Almanac for the Year 1858* (David Gall, Adelaide 1858), p. 95.

20 Gwynne may also be ruled out as the source because, in the reports of parliamentary debates on 21 January 1858, both the *Register* and the *Adelaide Times* (both at p. 3 in the editions of 22 January 1858) agree that Captain Bagot had said words to the effect that he would be interested to hear whether Mr Gwynne was in favour of the principle of the Bill when he returned to his seat. Unless there was some unusually elaborate coded message here, this suggests that Mr Gwynne had not seen the Bill before its introduction. It is, however, worth noting that E.C. Gwynne had been a partner (in a law firm) with Charles Mann, and the ostentatious enquiries about his views may be explained on this basis.

21 See Coxon *et al.*, *Biographical Register of the South Australian Parliament 1857–1957* (Wakefield, Netley 1985), p. 9. Although Captain Bagot and the lawyer J.T. Bagot M.P. were related, there is, as with the other members of Parliament, no reason to suppose that J.T. Bagot would not have introduced the Bill into Parliament himself had it been his production; or, at the very least, that some reference would have been made to that fact in the debates. As a further indication of J.T. Bagot's lack of interest in the subject, he was in fact absent from Parliament during a crucial week of debate on the Bill in early December 1858: Votes and Proceedings, House of Assembly, p. 175.

22 South Australian Parliamentary Debates, House of Assembly, 3 December 1858, col. 752.

23 Thus, for example, s 1 required affidavits to be sworn, something which it is difficult to do without the help of a lawyer.

24 Mr Richard Lawley of the Corporate Affairs Commission (Office of Consumer and Business Affairs) has informed the author that association no. A10, *i.e.* the tenth association incorporated under the Act, was incorporated on 21 February 1870. As late as 1887 it was said in Parliament that the Act 'had not been very largely availed of, but it had been to a certain extent, and of late years it had been availed of to a larger extent than previously': South Australian Parliamentary Debates, House of Assembly, 10 August 1887, col. 460. As we shall see below, the one-hundredth association incorporated under the Act was incorporated in 1888, thirty years after its passing.

25 *South Australian Government Gazette*, 12 February 1857, p. 142; 27 May 1858, p. 388.

26 This was the Church of England Endowment Society, although it was not formed (even as an unincorporated body) until January 1860, so that Chief Justice Cooper would have had to plan many years in advance for the prospect of the formation of such a society to be in his mind before he left for England in late 1856 and for him to propose a statute under which it could be incorporated before he left.

27 See, *e.g.*, the letter from Chief Justice Cooper to the Chief Secretary in file CSO 3045/1855, GRG 1/21/2, and the references in Bennett, *Cooper C.J.*, pp. 86–88. (All CSO files cited in this book may also be found in the South Australian archives.)

28 Personal communication with Dr J.M. Bennett (letter dated 7 October 2002).

29 Bennett, *Cooper C.J.*, p. 89.

30 See above, p. 61 fn 47.

31 *Register*, 22 June 1868, p. 2.

32 Hague, *The Judicial Career of Benjamin Boothby* (unpublished, Adelaide 1992), pp. 11f, 21, 190.

33 Hague, *Boothby J.*, p. 38.

34 See the biography in the *Australian Dictionary of Biography*, vol. 2, pp. 200f.

35 *South Australian Government Gazette*, 6 March 1856, p. 164 (all three appointments mentioned in the text, the last on an acting basis); 10 April 1856, p. 267, and 2 March 1858, p. 171 (permanent appointment as Commissioner of the Court of Insolvency).

36 *South Australian Government Gazette*, 16 April 1857, p. 326. Mann had also been an Acting Judge in 1849: *ibid.*, 1 March 1849, p. 93; 6 September 1849, p. 410; 4 October 1849, p. 445.

37 Pike, *Paradise of Dissent*, p. 110.

38 Bridge, *A Trunk Full of Books: History of the State Library of South Australia and its Forerunners* (Wakefield, Adelaide 1986), pp. 6f, 10, 14. Chief Justice Cooper, however, also supported mechanics' institutes occasionally: see *Register*, 15 August 1854, p. 3.

39 Pitt, *Press in South Australia 1836–1850* (Wakefield, Adelaide 1946), pp. 14, 30.

40 See, *e.g.*, the issues of 30 June 1838, p. 3 (welcoming the establishment of the Mechanics' Institute); 7 July 1838, p. 3 (three separate articles on voluntary associations); 14 July 1838, p. 2 (recording that the rules of the Mechanics' Institute could be inspected at the newspaper's offices); 4 August 1838, p. 2 (noticing the election of the officers of the Mechanics' Institute, including Charles Mann); 11 August 1838, Supplement, p. 1 (establishment of South Australian Club); 18 August 1838, p. 2 (Mechanics' Institute to open shortly); 1 September 1838, p. 4 (proposal to establish a hospital; notice signed by Charles Mann, among others) and Supplement, p. 1 (reports on opening of Mechanics' Institute); 22 September 1838, p. 3 (lectures given at Mechanics' Institute, including one by Charles Mann; also, clubrooms of South Australian Club almost complete); 29 September 1838, p. 2 (clubrooms now ready); 22 December 1838, p. 3 (formation of Natural History Society of South Australia); 27 March 1839, p. 3 (formation of South Australian Church Building Society); 24 April 1839, p. 3 (first anniversary meeting of South Australian School Society about to be held, urges attendance); 1 May 1839, p. 4 (reports on that meeting); 26 June 1839, p. 3 (report on difficulties of the Mechanics' Institute and personal liability of several persons involved in it for its debts); 24 July 1839, p. 3 (urging attendance at a meeting to consider the future of the Mechanics' Institute); 31 July 1839, p. 3 (similar); 7 August 1839, pp. 2f (reports on unification of Mechanics' Institute with Scientific and Literary Association; committee includes Charles Mann); 14 August 1839, p. 2 (financial contributions including that of Charles Mann); 28 August, 4 September and 18 September 1839, each at p. 3 (reports of lectures at unified society); 16 October 1839, p. 3 (rejoicing at establishment of Agricultural Society, Charles Mann being one of the committee members); 13 November 1839, p. 3 (reporting that the value of a Mechanics' Institute,

'we rejoice to perceive, is every day becoming more apparent, and more fully appreciated by the public').

41   At pp. 2f.

42   Dickey, *Holy Trinity Adelaide 1836–1988: the History of a City Church* (Adelaide, Trinity Church Trust, 1988), pp. 24f, 200; Pike, *Paradise of Dissent*, p. 265.

43   Dickey, *Holy Trinity Adelaide*, p. 47; Pike, *Paradise of Dissent*, pp. 268f.

44   Pike, *Paradise of Dissent*, p. 272.

45   Pike, *Paradise of Dissent*, p. 435.

46   *Australian Dictionary of Biography*, Vol. 1, pp. 47f.

47   South Australian Parliamentary Debates, Legislative Council, 29 July 1862, col. 550. For a similar objection connected with the Church of England, see South Australian Parliamentary Debates, House of Assembly, 18 November 1891, col. 2064.

48   Mann's application for the Judgeship may be found in the Colonial Office files, CO 13/78 (A.J.C.P. 786), as the Governor forwarded it to Downing Street attached to despatch no. 54 of 2 October 1852. Appendix 2 of Mann's job application reproduces a resolution passed by the Legislative Council in 1849 thanking Mr Acting Justice Mann for his services; Captain Bagot is shown as supporting it. For the contemporary report, see the *Register*, 15 December 1849, p. 2. The resolution, but not Captain Bagot's support of it, is recorded in the Votes and Proceedings of the Legislative Council, 12 December 1849, p. 28. The petition in favour of appointing Mr Acting Justice Mann to a permanent Judgeship is attached to the Governor's Despatch of 23 October 1849 (State Archives of South Australia, GRG 2/5/11, despatch no. 145), but unfortunately there is no indication of who signed it.

49   Pike, *Paradise of Dissent*, p. 226; see further *Register*, 6 January 1838, p. 1.

50   21 September 1858, col. 176; similar *Advertiser*, 22 September 1858, p. 3; unfortunately, there is nothing in any other sources which might make the precise nature of the amendment made here clearer. Although 'Hansard' refers to the 'preamble', it seems quite clear that the enacting words are meant given that the preamble contained no words even remotely like those referred to in 'Hansard'.

51   Pike, *Paradise of Dissent*, p. 504.

52   *Report from the Select Committee of the Legislative Council of South Australia to Report if it be Expedient that a Bill to Establish a National Institute should be Introduced* (Parliamentary Papers no. 80/1854), pp. 7–10; Bridge, *A Trunk Full of Books*, pp. 24f, 29.

53   Talbot, *A Chance to Read: A History of the Institutes Movement in South Australia* (Libraries Board, Adelaide 1992), p. 28.

54   GRG 19/320.

55   *Register*, 25 May 1860, p. 2.

56   *South Australian Government Gazette*, 2 March 1858, p. 171.

57   See above, p. 43 fn 46.

58   § 55 of the Civil Code.

59   Although actually the similarity is not as great as it appears, as the Master of the Supreme Court was acting as the Registrar of Companies in this respect:

see *Registrar of Companies (Miscellaneous Functions) Act* 1924; South
Australian Parliamentary Debates, House of Assembly, 18 November 1924,
p. 1733.

60 Laws such as the Prussian *Ordinance relating to the Prevention of the Misuse of
the Freedom of Assembly and of Association calculated to endanger Public Freedom
and Order* of 11 March 1850 (*Gesetz-Sammlung für die Königlich Preußischen
Staaten*, 30 March 1850, pp. 277ff), for example, are pre-modern in the
sense that they do not provide for any form of incorporation and are
principally concerned, as the title suggests, with public order. See, *e.g.*,
Hauser, 'Die neueste Bayerische Gesetzgebung über Vereine, Erwerbs- und
Wirthschaftsgenossenschaften sowie über Nicht-Handels-
Actiengesellschaften' ZHR 14 (1870), 341, 341–347; Kögler,
*Arbeiterbewegung und Vereinsrecht: Ein Beitrag zur Entstehungsgeschichte des
BGB* (Duncker & Humblot, Berlin 1974), pp. 11–14, 47–49; Oppenheimer,
'Die beiden Vereinsklassen des Bürgerlichen Gesetzbuches (§§ 21, 22)'
JherJb 47 (1904), 99, 99–115; Vormbaum, *Die Rechtsfähigkeit der Vereine im
19. Jahrhundert: ein Beitrag zur Entstehungsgeschichte des BGB* (Walter de
Gruyter, Berlin 1976), pp. 44–93; Weick in Staudinger *et al.* (eds.),
*Kommentar zum Bürgerlichen Gesetzbuch mit Einführungsgesetz und
Nebengesetzen* 1. Buch, §§ 21–103 (13th ed., Sellier-de Gruyter, Berlin 1995),
pp. 67–69. The author has no direct information about the associations law
of Hamburg in particular, but the sources just quoted strongly suggest that
it was not ahead of its time in this respect.

61 South Australian Parliamentary Debates, House of Assembly, 19 July 1865,
col. 840.

62 *Advertiser*, 12 July 1858, p. 3.

63 *Advertiser*, 5 November 1864, p. 3.

64 *Register*, 2 November 1864, p. 2.

65 See Ross, *Private School Education at St Paul's, Port Adelaide, 1846–1927*
(unpublished, 1992).

66 The Master's certificate to that effect, dated 30 August 1867, is filed in the
Lands Titles Office: GRO 190/1867. Further information may be found in
the Anglican Archives, Adelaide, file no. 272 (D179).

67 On 28 July 1938 according to a note in file no. 272 (D179), Anglican
Archives, Adelaide; *South Australian Government Gazette*, 28 July 1938,
p. 219.

68 The English legislation, minus s 23, was adopted in South Australia by Act
No. 22 of 1870–71. A provision similar to s 23 of the English Act was not
included in South Australian legislation until the enactment of the
Companies Act 1934 s 28. See now *Corporations Act* 2001 (Clth) ss 150, 151.
Registration under the companies legislation was long the only available
means of achieving incorporation in those States which adopted the South
Australian idea only after many decades: Sievers, (2001) 13 Aust Jo Corp
Law 124, 128.

69 South Australian Parliamentary Debates, Legislative Council,
29 November 1870, p. 1499.

70 Bottomley, 'The Corporate Form and Regulation: Associations
Incorporation Legislation in Australia' in Tomasic/Lucas (eds.), *Power,*

Regulation and Resistance: Studies in the Sociology of Law (Canberra College of Advanced Education, Canberra 1986), p. 53.

71   Association no. A1 in the records of the Corporate Affairs Commission, incorporated on 25 September 1863 (according to the records of the Commission, although the date may be too late having regard to the certificate of incorporation which may be found in the Lands Titles Office, GRO 321/1860; it is however the same as that found in the *Church of England Endowment Society Act* [1891] (S.A.) s 2). The Dean and Chapter of the Diocese of Adelaide also applied in 1863 for incorporation under the Act after their request for a special incorporation Act for the Church had been rejected in 1862. See the certificate of incorporation preserved in the Anglican Archives, Adelaide, file no. 124 (D178); records of the Corporate Affairs Commission, association no. A3. See also *South Australian Government Gazette*, 29 September 1870, p. 1309.

72   At p. 475.

73   *South Australian Government Gazette*, 13 August 1863, pp. 680f; incorporated on 15 September 1864 as association no. A4 (records of the Corporate Affairs Commission) and apparently still incorporated under the Act.

74   *South Australian Government Gazette*, 10 January 1867, p. 39; incorporated on 26 April 1867 as association no. A5 (records of the Corporate Affairs Commission).

75   *South Australian Government Gazette*, 21 February 1867, p. 189; incorporated on 9 December 1886 as association no. A91 (records of the Corporate Affairs Commission).

76   *South Australian Government Gazette*, 9 December 1869, p. 1765. This organisation is stated to be incorporated in Boothby, *The Adelaide Almanac and Directory for South Australia 1872 together with Official, Ecclesiastical, Legal, Banking and Mercantile Directory* (9th ed., J. Williams, Adelaide 1872), Part II p. 40. It is shown as incorporated in the State Archives of South Australia, GRS 885/3, no. A11. The association's file, preserved in the State Archives of South Australia, GRS 885/1, indicates that it was wound up in 1974 and the property transferred to the Jewish Welfare Society (S.A. Division) pursuant to a resolution of the association.

77   *South Australian Government Gazette*, 24 October 1872, p. 1533; association no A18, State Archives of South Australia, GRS 885/3 (which notes that the name of the association, originally the Society of Jesus Inc., was later changed to the Manresa Society Inc.).

78   *South Australian Government Gazette*, 11 December 1873, p. 2138; incorporated on 12 May 1874 as association no. A19 (records of the Corporate Affairs Commission).

79   *South Australian Government Gazette*, 30 September 1875, p. 1846; shown as incorporated in *Sands and McDougall's South Australian Directory for 1884* (21st ed., Sands & McDougall, Adelaide 1884), p. 773 and succeeding editions; association no A22, State Archives of South Australia, GRS 885/3. For the cancellation of the incorporation, see *South Australian Government Gazette*, 28 July 1938, p. 219.

80 And is based on the register of associations held in the State Archives of
    South Australia, GRS 885/3.
81 *Report of the Select Committee of the Legislative Council on the* Church of
    England Incorporation Bill (Parliamentary Paper No. 179/1862); Pike,
    Paradise, p. 486. See also Parliamentary Paper No. 49/1862. The despatch
    of 19 September 1861 referred to there may be found in GRG 2/6/9. The
    special Bill for the Church of England seems to have been an idea of the
    Colonial Office: see further GRG 2/38 P.S.O. file no. 566 (1861); GRG 2/2,
    despatch of 15 January 1861.
82 See above, fn 47.
83 Blacket, *History of South Australia: A Romantic and Successful Experiment in
    Colonisation* (2nd ed., Hussey & Gillingham, Adelaide 1911), p. 122.
84 Except Western Australia, which was founded by free settlers but took
    convicts later.
85 Act No. 16 of 1855–56. See also such later enactments as the *Suburban and
    Country Institutes Act* 1874. Note, too, the invitation to apply for grants in
    the *South Australian Government Gazette*, 18 February 1858, p. 141.
86 See, *e.g.*, Pike, *Paradise of Dissent*, pp. 504ff.
87 See generally Talbot, *A Chance to Read*, Ch. 1 and p. 13.
88 Although, once the legislative framework for suburban and country
    institutes had become somewhat more elaborate and the advantages of
    having all institutes under the one legal umbrella had become apparent (see
    South Australian Parliamentary Debates, Legislative Council, 19 July 1887,
    coll. 243f; GRG 19/12a/3/569; GRG 19/12a/5/270; GRG 19/355/4/414;
    GRG 19/355/4/418f, 421), institutes were prohibited from incorporating
    under the Act: *Suburban and Country Institutes Act* 1874 s 9; South Australian
    Parliamentary Debates, Legislative Council, 1 July 1874, p. 746. This
    prohibition survived a number of legislative 'paradigm changes' until it was
    eventually repealed by the *Libraries and Institutes Act Amendment Act* 1950
    s 4; see further *Williams* v. *Coulthard* [1948] SASR 183, 190f.
89 On the general poverty of institutes in this period, see Ryan, *The
    Development of State Libraries and their Effect on the Public Library Movement
    in Australia* (unpublished, M.A. thesis, Graduate Library School (University
    of Chicago), 1964), p. 39; Talbot, *A Chance to Read*, p. 15.
90 This was not altered until the 1930s: see above, fn 11.

6. Defendants giving evidence

1. Enforced silence under English law

In a recent article in the *Australian Law Journal*,[1] Justice Bruce Debelle writes that it 'was not until 1898 that an accused could give evidence on his own behalf'. But the right of the accused to give evidence on his own behalf in all criminal cases dates, in South Australia, not from 1898, when the British enacted legislation to that effect, but from 30 August 1882, over a decade and a half beforehand. It was on that day that the South Australian *Accused Persons Evidence Act* 1882[2] ('APEA') came into force as the first such legislation in the British Empire[3] (although some American States got in even earlier).[4]

Perhaps it is not surprising that this South Australian innovation has been forgotten. The South Australian legislature repealed the APEA in 1925[5] and replaced it with a statute which was virtually a copy of the English reform of 1898 in order to follow the English statute with its 'fuller provisions [which] protect [the accused] against questions likely to prejudice him in the eyes of the jury'.[6]

This chapter will first consider why the APEA was enacted so far in advance of the English reform which South Australia later adopted, and its immediate impact on the practice of the law in South Australia. Then the truth of the claim by the author of the APEA, Sir John Downer, that the pioneering South Australian measure was 'adopted by the Legislatures of Australia and Canada, and, to crown the triumph, adopted by the Imperial [*i.e.* the British] Parliament'[7] will be tested.

It is necessary to describe the law before 1882 before considering the South Australian innovation. Before 1882, the common law applied. By the middle third of the nineteenth century,[8] the common law disqualified from being a witness 'every person having an interest, however minute, in the result of the proceedings'.[9] This, of course, included accused persons in criminal trials as well as their spouses (subject to an exception for cases in which spouses inflicted injury on each other, which mostly benefited the victims of domestic violence). It did not however include the mistresses of accused persons. This incidentally had the amusing consequence that an alibi to the effect that the accused was at home in bed with his wife could not be proved unless someone else observed them there, as neither the accused nor the wife could give evidence, but it was easy to prove an alibi that one was in bed with one's mistress and/or someone else's spouse.[10]

In civil but not criminal trials, the rules against interested witnesses were gradually abolished in the middle of the nineteenth century. South Australia loyally copied these English reforms, including their deliberate lack of reform in criminal trials. Section 3 of Act no. 2 of 1852 of South Australia is virtually a carbon copy of s 3 of the English *Evidence Act* 1851 which, while reforming the rules in civil trials, continued to exclude accused persons from giving evidence in criminal trials.

But South Australia broke new ground in legislating about criminal trials in 1882. The APEA's key provision was s 1, which provided as follows:

Notwithstanding any law or ordinance to the contrary, from and after the passing of this Act any person accused of any felony, misdemeanor, or other indictable offence, or of any offence punishable on summary conviction, shall, if such person so desires, be competent and entitled to be sworn and give evidence as a witness on the trial of the felony, misdemeanor, or offence with which he is charged, and also in like manner may give evidence on any preliminary investigation into the said felony, misdemeanor, or offence, before Justices prior to the said trial: Provided that no presumption of guilt shall be made from the fact of such person electing not to give evidence.

The Act had only four other sections. Sections 2 and 4 were procedural. Section 3 ensured that the permission to give evidence was extended to spouses of accused persons. Section 5 said that the accused:

> shall be liable to be cross-examined as in the case of any other witness, and shall not be excused from answering any question on the ground that the answer may tend to criminate himself, and shall be liable to be prosecuted and punished for any perjury committed in such evidence in the same way as any other person now or heretofore competent to be examined as a witness: Provided always, any husband or wife of any accused person so giving evidence as aforesaid shall be excused from answering any question on the ground that the answer may tend to criminate himself or herself, as the case may be.

2. The passing of the APEA

In this case, there is no difficulty in identifying the author of the legislative innovation we're discussing. The APEA's champion was quite clearly J.W. (later Sir John) Downer Q.C. M.P., Attorney-General for South Australia in the ministry of J.C. Bray which was appointed on 24 June 1881. He was the grandfather of Alexander Downer, Minister for Foreign Affairs in the Howard government.

Even in opposition, Downer had urged the adoption of reforms permitting accused persons to give evidence. On 30 October 1878, he moved a motion in Parliament aimed at securing consensus for three reforms in the criminal law, one of which was permitting the accused to give evidence in criminal cases.[11] He made two points: that the inability of the accused to make an answer to the allegations against him meant that injustice was sometimes done because of a lack of explanation by the accused; and that, on the other hand, juries sometimes acquitted guilty people because they were not able to rule out a possible explanation which might have been tested by cross-examination if the accused could give evidence. Downer thought that innocent people would be anxious to present their stories, while guilty people should receive an opportunity to betray their guilt by giving evidence. Indeed, in his view the accused should not just be able to give evidence, but

SIR JOHN.

John Downer, by Chinner

should be compelled to do so. For the government, Attorney-General Bundey stated that he did not agree, and otherwise was not prepared to commit himself to any changes to the law. Mr Downer's motion was lost by three votes. As the *Advertiser*[12] suggested in its editorial the next day, this may well have been because of Downer's advocacy of compulsory testimony by the accused – coupled with his failure to explain that the principle of compulsion would not mean that an accused could be found guilty of an offence of failing to answer questions, merely that the Judge could make comments along the lines that it was curious that the accused failed to take an opportunity to put his side of the story and in effect invite the jury to conclude that the accused's silence indicated guilt.

This emphasis on securing the conviction of the guilty as well as the acquittal of the innocent became a principal theme of the debates in South Australia. As one leading text on the law of evidence points out,[13] the inability of the accused to give evidence did indeed have advantages for the guilty. Not only were they spared the decision about whether to subject themselves to cross-examination, but 'the jury could be left with the impression that [the accused] had a complete defence to the charge but [was] unfortunately prevented from deposing to its exact nature'. If the jury were also told that any doubts as to the accused's innocence had to be resolved in his favour, the advantages of silence to the accused are apparent. Of course, the accused could always stand up in the dock and make an unsworn statement,[14] but could not be cross-examined by the prosecution about it.

Mr Downer revived the project of making the accused a witness when he was appointed Attorney-General in June 1881. A letter supporting the proposal was published in the *Register* on 23 May 1882[15] from R. Homburg, a lawyer (and later a Judge). His view, which he said was shared by colleagues and judicial officers whose opinion he had asked, was that the law as it stood protected the guilty and injured the innocent. He gave examples of cases in which the existing law had produced injustices, and said that he had been 'met with expressions of surprise and indignation when I have told persons accused of crimes that neither they nor their wives would be able to testify to their innocence', whereas the guilty had usually been pleased to learn of this state of the law.

Homburg did not have to wait long for his hopes to be realised, for on 13 June 1882 Downer introduced into Parliament the Bill for the APEA.[16] The second reading did not occur until 6 July, but in the meantime public reaction seems to have been fairly positive. The editor of the *Register*,[17] for example, who had not reacted favourably to the proposals of 1878,[18] now stated that 'wisdom and common sense', not to mention the views of Jeremy Bentham,[19] united to support the Attorney-General's proposals. Some indication of the reason for this change of heart on the part of the editor may be gleaned from an editorial on 22 June, in which he writes that the omission of any provision for compelling the accused to give evidence was wise.

Also on 22 June,[20] the leader writer[21] raised a number of practical problems with which, he thought, the Bill should deal, even if its brevity were sacrificed as a result. He foresaw difficulties in cases in which there was more than one defendant, and pointed out that any defendant would be able to hear the evidence of all prosecution witnesses before giving his own evidence, which would enable the accused to alter his evidence to suit. Most importantly, the leader writer asked whether cross-examination of a defendant by the Crown about his character defects – in particular about any prior criminal convictions he might have – should be permitted, as they would be under the Bill as drafted. He made the very sensible suggestion that cross-examination of an accused person 'should be confined to matters bearing on the specific offence with which he is charged'. But the *Register* continued to support the Bill. A week later, it published an extract from the *Law Times* in which an attempt in England to bring about a similar reform was noted with approval.[22]

Downer, on moving the Bill's second reading on 6 July,[23] 'true to his well-known leanings in this matter, entered *con amore* into the exposition of the principle of the Bill'.[24] Again the argument was that the proposed reform would assist the innocent and assist in the conviction of the guilty. It was also pointed out that similar reforms had been proposed in England and that assorted distinguished legal figures in England had approved of the principle. In relation to the cross-examination of the accused, Mr Downer professed himself able to accept amendments such as those suggested by the *Register* on 22 June, but did not move any himself. Commenting on this speech, the *Advertiser*[25] repeated its approval of the Bill and added, rather presciently, that the proviso that no presumption of guilt should be made against a silent defendant would be mostly inoperative, for 'all the statutes in the world cannot prevent a jury from being biased, consciously or unconsciously, against a person who, when accused of a crime, listens to particular statements that if believed demonstrate his guilt, and yet has not a word to say for himself'. This point had occurred to the politicians, too.[26]

Any illusion of unanimity among the legal profession was however dispelled by the second reading debate. Two influential lawyers who were also members of Parliament and had experience in the criminal law rose to oppose the Bill: Josiah Symon Q.C. and Charles Cameron Kingston, later Premier of South Australia. Symon believed that the Bill would not confer a new privilege, but rather take two privileges away: the privilege to give an unsworn statement, and the freedom from cross-examination. Furthermore, he argued, the inability of the accused to give evidence reinforced the presumption of innocence by ensuring that every possible presumption was made in favour of the accused. And if Imperial legislation could be expected, it would be better to wait for that, as it would contain all necessary safeguards for the accused (as, indeed, turned out to be the case – sixteen years later).[27] Kingston referred to the temptation to perjury which would exist if the accused were permitted to give sworn evidence and the unfairness involved in permitting the cross-examination of the accused on all aspects of his past life.[28]

Symon's objections did not convince the *Register*,[29] however, which repeated its endorsement of the Bill on the day after his speech; nor could Messrs Symon and Kingston together convince the House of Assembly, for on 18 July, after a short further debate in which the possibilities of convicting the guilty from their own evidence were gleefully re-emphasised,[30] the Bill passed its second reading by twenty-six votes to six.[31] Such a large majority assured the Bill of passage through the

Committee stage and of a third reading. In Committee, an attempt was again made to make the giving of evidence by accused persons compulsory rather than optional, but this was rejected by Downer not on the grounds that it was a bad idea, but on the grounds that enabling an accused person to give evidence amounted 'practically'[32] to compulsion. The debate in the Legislative Council was quite short and, except for the insertion of the proviso to clause 5 protecting spouses (quoted above), devoid of interest; the Bill quickly moved through its second and third readings in the Upper House in late July and early August.[33]

Having thus passed through Parliament, the APEA received the Royal assent on 30 August 1882. It was then sent, in accordance with usual practice, to the Colonial Office in Whitehall so that the question could be considered whether The Queen's power of disallowance should be exercised.[34] Disallowance was not seriously considered;[35] by this time, over thirty years after the non-assent to the first claimants' relief legislation of 1851, the colonies were on a very long leash. One official in the Colonial Office reviewing the APEA noted, perhaps somewhat wistfully, that 'it would be interesting to observe the working of this provision',[36] as the issue was a disputed one in England as well. The real question, as the official in the Colonial Office perspicaciously saw, would be how the legislation would operate in practice.

3. The Act is applied

As the Supreme Court of South Australia was not conducting criminal trials when the APEA came into force, it was first applied in lower Courts such as the Police Court of the City of Adelaide. Since 1 January 1857, the Magistrate had been Samuel Beddome. A contemporary pen portrait of his Worship,[37] while lamenting his tendency to impose fines too high for poorer people to pay, praised his ability at 'detecting the many barefaced falsehoods uttered by the unscrupulous police'.[38] This talent was now to be directed to the evidence not just of police officers, but also of defendants.

a. The first cases

The APEA was first applied in the prosecution of one Richard Newell, a mason, for the assault of Constable Northey in the execution of the latter's duty on 1 September 1882. The case was heard before Mr Beddome on Saturday 2 September 1882. The *Advertiser*[39] reported helpfully that this 'was the first case in which the defendant was allowed under the *Accused Persons Oaths Act* to get in the witness-box and give evidence on his own behalf'. (Presumably this reflects some appropriate statement to this effect made in the Court at the time.) The constable's story was that he had intervened in a fight between two men at what was then the Exhibition Ground (that is, somewhere near the north-western corner of North Terrace and Frome Road)[40] and for his trouble was assaulted by Newell. It was none other than C.C. Kingston M.P. who thereupon put the defendant into the witness-box to give evidence under the Act which he had opposed in Parliament. (It was still common, at this stage, for legally qualified Members of Parliament to practise as lawyers as well.)

Newell's story was 'that he saw the constable wrangling with a friend of his, and to prevent a row he asked the constable to have a dance'[41] – an idiom since regrettably lost to the English language, or at least its Australian branch, but the meaning of which might be guessed at. Newell's evidence was corroborated 'by a number of witnesses, including his wife',[42] now able to give evidence under s 3 of the APEA. These witnesses said that he had been prevented from striking the constable by his wife.[43] Perhaps Newell was not pleased at having his wife introduced into the story in this way; we do not know; but at any rate he was acquitted. Thus, the first test of the APEA, from Mr Kingston's point of view at least, confirmed the theory that it enabled the innocent accused person (together with his wife!) to secure his acquittal.

The score was evened up when two German seamen, Gustave Muller and Albert Hase, were fined 5 shillings each for riotous behaviour (although acquitted of assault) at the Corporation Wharf, Port Adelaide, having given evidence themselves before R.J. Turner S.M. sitting at the local Police Court on 4 September. The *Register*[44] reported that H.C.E. Muecke acted as interpreter, and so it may be assumed that the seamen not only heard the evidence translated, but actually gave their evidence in German.

By 8 September, however, a problem with the interpretation of the APEA had already become apparent. Jane Simpson, charged with threatening Ellen Wainwright that she would 'tear out her liver and eat the pieces', 'was about to be sworn when Mr Beddome intimated that it could not be done, as the accused was not charged with a penal offence under the Act, but was only brought before the Court with the object of being bound over to keep the peace'.[45] His Worship rejected counsel's arguments to the contrary, but on the following Monday announced that he now believed that he had been wrong, 'and that in future cases of the kind he would accept the evidence of the defendant until a superior Court had decided otherwise'.[46]

The first conviction in what might be called an 'oath against oath' case came on 11 September. William Muldone swore that Elizabeth Willis had put her hand in his pocket and taken three-and-sixpence, but Willis denied this on oath. For reasons which are not given in the newspaper reports, Willis's story was not believed, and she was sentenced to a month's hard labour.[47] Another such case occurred on 18 September, when William Myers was charged with stealing a pair of boots that had been found in the possession of one Schultz, who swore that Myers had given the boots to him. Myers swore that Schultz was the culprit. He was not believed and received three months' hard labour.[48]

The newspapers from this point on contain an increasing number of reports showing that defendants had given evidence. The APEA seems to have quickly become part of the landscape in the lower Courts. The pressure to give evidence must have mounted as more accused people did so. Indeed, some defendants were so enthusiastic about their new-found right that they even gave sworn evidence at the committal hearing,[49] although the reports rarely indicate that this was a successful gambit[50] and this no doubt ensured that sworn evidence by the accused at committal became the rarity that it is today.

One further case should be noted before we leave the lower Courts. In *Police* v. *Ward*, Louisa Ward was charged with loitering, *etc.* – clearly a euphemism. She pleaded not guilty and said that she would make the constable prove that she was a prostitute. According to the newspaper report,[51] the Magistrate, Mr Beddome, asked her, 'Do you wish to be sworn to repudiate the charge?', and received the response, 'No, thank God'. Mr Beddome replied, 'Then you will pay a fine of 20 s'. Clearly, as some had hoped, and others had feared, the proviso to s 1 purporting to protect the silent accused had rather limited usefulness.

b. The first Supreme Court cases

While the cases in the lower Courts were no doubt of importance to those who appeared in them, the real test of the APEA came only with the October criminal sessions of the Supreme Court. The first such test was a joint trial: Thomas Roach and Henry Johnson were accused of assault and robbery. Both gave evidence. Counsel for Roach attempted to have the jury accept that Johnson was the sole guilty party, and also cross-examined Johnson with a view to suggesting that he had a bad character. 'This appeared to provoke resentment in Johnson, and he blurted out that he had intended to plead guilty, but had not done so at Roach's request.'[52] Not surprisingly, both accused were then found guilty by the jury and sentenced to four years' hard labour each, but the *Advertiser* reported that 'the prisoners, who seemed pleased with their light sentence, left the dock smiling'.[53] This case showed that the APEA could cause the conviction of the guilty as a result of their being cross-examined. But not all accused persons were giving evidence at this stage. There were at least two cases during the October sessions[54] in which the accused did not do so, no recorded comment on this was made by anyone and the accused was acquitted.

Editorialising on the APEA on 18 November, the *Register*[55] thought that it was too early to pass judgment on the APEA, but that it was 'highly probable that it may have to be amended'. It quickly became apparent, for example, that prejudice to the accused could arise if his past character was canvassed before the jury. When James Ryan was charged before Mr Justice Andrews in November 1882 with false pretences, there was nothing in the APEA to prevent cross-examination on his prior convictions for assault and unlawful possession, which the

Crown duly undertook,[56] or to prevent the prosecutor from stating that that the accused's 'reputation was, to say the least, mildewed'.[57]

In December 1882, during the joint trial of four prisoners for assault and robbery before Chief Justice Way, the Crown Prosecutor asked whether it would be possible for him to cross-examine the prisoners on the criminal history of the co-accused. Way, having in mind the traditional dislike of the law for arguments that the accused must have committed the offence in question because he had committed offences beforehand, said that it would be 'unfair'[58] to allow that to occur, but could point to no provision in the APEA preventing it. Thus, his Honour was unable to make the leap made by the *Advertiser*, which called the proposed cross-examination 'unfair *and illegal*'.[59] Way was no doubt relieved when the Crown Prosecutor decided not to press the point and no judicial decision on it was required. A further uncertainty with which the legislature might have dealt emerged in early December 1882, when Way expressed doubts about whether the right to make an unsworn statement had survived the APEA, although his Honour stated that he would not decide that point in the absence of his brother Judges and in the meantime would give the prisoner the benefit of the doubt.[60]

c. The murder and manslaughter trials of December 1882

While all these difficulties in the administration of the APEA were coming to light, the *Advertiser*,[61] referring chiefly to the trials in the Police Court, was happy to say that the APEA 'has worked satisfactorily', mostly owing to the assistance it gave to the guilty to ensure their own convictions. But the APEA received its most severe test in two murder trials and one manslaughter trial before Chief Justice Way in December 1882.

On 15 November 1882, a report appeared in the *Advertiser*[62] relating to a recent murder in Hamley Bridge. The victim was Christian Renderup, a Swede, who had been staying in the house of Patrick and Elizabeth Magree and 'had been in the habit for some time past of meeting once a week at the [Magrees'] house ... for the purpose of carousing'. A constable had responded to a cry of alarm from the house and found Renderup dead. A coroner's jury committed the Magrees, and their eldest daughter Margaret, for trial on the charge of murdering Renderup.

Shortly afterwards, the *Douglas*, a British ship, docked at Port Adelaide, having arrived from the Baltic with a cargo of imported wooden material and 'a small, insignificant-looking man of very unpleasing appearance'[63] named William Burns. Burns was accused of murdering the second officer, Henry Loton,[64] on the high seas on 23 September. The Supreme Court of South Australia had statutory jurisdiction to try this offence using its own procedures.[65] Finally, a young man named Henry Page was accused of the manslaughter of Alice Tree. This case was tried first.

Page had been seen assaulting Tree on the night before her death; there was blood on his shirt next morning; he had failed to deny an accusation made in his presence shortly after the discovery of the body;[66] and the accused and Tree had frequently quarrelled. That was about all the evidence linking Page to the death of Tree, although there was strong evidence that she had died a violent death at someone's hands. Page had no lawyer, and accordingly there was no one other than Chief Justice Way to give him advice about whether he should give evidence. His Honour said to the accused that it would be foolish to seek to give evidence and expose himself to cross-examination. That might only strengthen a weak Crown case. His Honour added that the 'very imperfect' APEA placed him in 'a most painful position', as it required him either to leave the prisoner exposed to the perils of cross-examination or to warn him and thus 'prevent the truth from being elicited'. Way thought that insufficient consideration had been given to 'the difficult position in which the prisoner is placed' – to which the prosecutor, Charles Mann Q.C.,[67] added, 'Not only the prisoner, but the Crown and the Judge, and every one concerned'.[68] The accused thereupon elected to make an unsworn statement denying his guilt, and was acquitted.

The *Advertiser*[69] criticised Chief Justice Way's warnings to Page in strong terms, saying that it would have been sufficient if his Honour had merely informed the prisoner of the consequences of giving evidence rather than warned him against doing so. The Chief Justice was accused of permitting an 'obstruction of justice' by preventing 'an accused person from placing himself in peril when the danger can only arise from his own guilt'. The APEA, continued the newspaper, could not be misunderstood 'by an intelligent person accustomed to dealing with statutes', and that the views of the Chief Justice were merely an expression of judicial opposition to a principle approved by Parliament. It was 'a matter of common report that at least two of our Judges are strongly opposed to' the APEA, but 'Parliament will not allow either Judge or law officer of the Crown to throw hindrances in the way of carrying out the law of the land'. Some months later, the *Register*[70] expressed the same opinion, if more moderately. These views illustrate the strength of local opinion backing Downer's aim of permitting the guilty to convict themselves by allowing them to give evidence.

After this reproof, Chief Justice Way must have been relieved to find that the next major case before him, the Magree murder trial, involved no accused persons without lawyers. The prosecutor was again the Crown Solicitor, Charles Mann Q.C.[71] Again Symon and Kingston, acting for the defence, applied the Act they had opposed in Parliament. Symon represented Patrick Magree, and Kingston defended Elizabeth, his wife; their daughter Margaret remained somewhat in the background, as the evidence against her was very weak. In the result, only Mrs Magree gave evidence. Perhaps this decision was made by the defendants in the hope that the jury would be more inclined to feel sympathy for a woman and that, if convicted, she would be less likely to be sent to the gallows than a man.

In his opening address Kingston told the jury that Mrs Magree 'demanded to be put in the witness box' even though 'under the close cross-examination she would be sure to be subjected to, the unhappy woman might be led to contradict herself'. Her motive for wishing to give evidence 'elevated her to the status of a heroine', for 'she would tell the jury that the hand which laid Christian Renderup low was the same hand that was taking up the sacred book to swear the truth upon'.[72] Her story was that she had defended herself against a sexual

Charles Kingston, on the announcement that he had been
chosen to be the first Federal Customs Minister.
Quiz 27 December 1900

attack by Renderup while her husband slept. This contradicted her story before the coroner in important respects[73] and was also cast into doubt by circumstantial evidence and the evidence of independent witnesses who, for example, heard cries coming from the Magree house which suggested that the male accused was involved in a struggle. After the trial, the *Advertiser*[74] neatly summarised the objections to Mrs Magree's evidence by stating that it 'was opposed to the [story] that she told at the inquest; it contained inherent improbabilities; it was contradicted in some material points by independent witnesses; and it was inconsistent with circumstantial evidence such as the blood-stained clothes of Patrick Magree'.

In his final address to the jury, Charles Mann, prosecuting, argued that Mrs Magree's evidence was 'absolutely false' and stated that he 'regretted' that, for 'the first time in the annals of English jurisprudence', a prosecutor 'had been put in the painful position of cross-examining a defendant on a trial for murder',[75] a state of affairs which the APEA had brought about. Josiah Symon, on the other hand, argued that Mrs Magree's evidence was true and that she had absolved her husband of responsibility.[76]

Summing up the next day, Chief Justice Way said that Mrs Magree's evidence 'is the evidence of a person who has very important interests hanging upon the impression it creates',[77] a statement which might today result in a successful appeal.[78] His Honour also raised the possibility that Mrs Magree's evidence might be 'colourable and biased for the purpose of getting [her husband] out of trouble', but urged the jury to be lenient in assessing the demeanour in the witness-box of one on trial for her life. He also noted that her story was 'substantially not shaken in any particular by the cross-examination'. Way was also careful to express greater enthusiasm for the APEA than he had in the Page trial, and one can only speculate whether this was because the *Advertiser*'s recent censure of him had either convinced him, or had convinced him that further resistance to public opinion was useless. The Chief Justice said:

Whatever our opinion may be as to the policy of the recent alteration of the law which allows persons who are placed upon their trial to give evidence, whatever may be our opinion as to the exact way in which the evidence is to be given, and the conditions under which it may be called for, we must feel that in a case like this, which is involved in so much difficulty without the evidence of the prisoner, that it is an assistance to us to have the version which the principal party concerned is able to give of what actually transpired.

The jury, however, clearly did not believe Mrs Magree, and, after deliberating for just under three hours, found both her and her husband guilty of murder, while acquitting their daughter. Sentence of death was passed on both prisoners. However, a jury of matrons – a very curious institution which has since been abolished in South Australia[79] and which involved a jury of women selected in order to determine whether a woman was pregnant – found on 21 December, after seeking the help of a medical practitioner, that Mrs Magree was pregnant and that her execution must therefore be delayed.[80]

The *Register*'s[81] verdict was that Mrs Magree's evidence was 'fully calculated' and a 'generous effort to save the life of her husband and child', but despite this doubted whether the guilty verdicts would be generally approved by the public, no doubt because of the sentence of death implied by them. The *Advertiser*[82] agreed. The next step in proceedings was the consideration of any possible commutation of the sentence by the Executive.

Meanwhile, however, the Chief Justice had another murder trial to preside over, that of William Burns, the ship's mate accused of murdering his second officer. Burns had an interesting personal history: he had taken part in the war between Peru and Chile that was raging at the time, and was serving on the Peruvian ship *Huascar* when it was captured.[83] Reports of the carnage on the *Huascar* were clearly still fresh in the communal memory, as it is mentioned in South Australian newspapers of the time[84] without further explanation. Nowadays, it is no longer well known. A contemporary report describes the scene on the *Huascar* which Burns experienced at its capture by the Chileans:

Dead and mutilated bodies were lying about in all directions, whilst the captain's cabin was blocked up by a heap of mangled corpses. Both upper and lower decks presented a shocking spectacle, being literally strewn with fragments of human remains. Out of a complement of 193 officers and men, with which the *Huascar* began the action, sixty-four, or nearly one-third, were killed or wounded.[85]

Quite possibly Burns, having experienced such horrors, had suffered some form of psychological damage equivalent to that suffered by soldiers returning from Vietnam.

The evidence in Burns' trial indicated that he had stabbed the second officer on the *Douglas* for very little reason indeed: a trivial argument about taking down some sails, during which the second officer stated that he would have no more of Burns' insolence, was followed almost immediately by Burns' stabbing him. There was little hope of acquittal, and Thomas Pater, Burns' counsel, asked the jury to convict his client of manslaughter rather than murder (thus saving him from the gallows). Mr Pater must have concluded that it was also wise or necessary, in aid of this cause, for the accused himself to give evidence. The jury must have known by now of this change in the law – in his summing up, Chief Justice Way stated that he had previously explained the elements of murder to some of them, presumably in the Magree trial[86] – and Burns or his counsel probably thought that the jury would have little time for a man putting forward a story of manslaughter if he did not give evidence.

Burns' evidence, however, was not very helpful to his cause. He could not say how he had come to stab the deceased; he had struck at the deceased's hand, not his throat. Cross-examined by Charles Mann, he denied that he had been in the Melbourne Gaol, saying that he had merely been boasting idly of being a jailbird. The *Register*[87] reported that one of the answers given by Burns in cross-examination 'invested his act more clearly with the guilt of murder than did his answers during his examination-in-chief', although it is not obvious from the reports which answer this was; presumably it was clear to those attending the trial. The Chief Justice 'summed up against'[88] Burns, and, after retiring for only half an hour, the jury brought in a verdict of murder.

Both morning newspapers[89] thought that there could be little sympathy for Burns, and the *Register*[90] added its approval of the APEA to that of the *Advertiser*, noting that it was desirable to allow murderers to convict themselves out of their own mouths and dismissing 'the purely sentimental objection against the operation of the *Accused Persons Evidence Act*, that it may entrap a prisoner into admissions which may be fatal to him'.

Executive Council met on 5 January 1883 to deal with the fate of the Magrees and Burns. The records of its meeting[91] show that the Chief Justice attended the Council and advised in favour of the commutation of the Magrees' death sentences[92] but against mercy for Burns. All members of the Council agreed with these recommendations (except the Treasurer, Mr Glyde, who rather oddly thought that there was no evidence that Burns had committed the deed with malice aforethought), and it was so ordered. As a letter-writer stated in the *Advertiser*[93] a few days later, this was not a decision that would have surprised the public in any way.

Reports of Burns' last days do not do anything to rebut the suggestion that he was suffering from some sort of post-traumatic stress and was quite willing to see his life end. On Tuesday 16 January, the *Register*[94] stated that he was 'very quiet, and appears to be thoroughly resigned to his fate'. On Thursday 18 January he was executed. He 'ascended the steps [of the scaffold] quickly, rather running than walking, and appearing to regard his approaching death most cheerfully'.[95] A reporter wrote that, in the face of death, Burns turned to religion – he was of the same denomination as Chief Justice Way, a Bible Christian[96] – and repented of his former 'wild and reckless life';[97] it may well be that he was rehabilitated by the very sentence which rendered his rehabilitation pointless. It was discovered that he had indeed been in gaol in Melbourne, for stabbing a man in a hotel.[98]

d. Later cases

By the criminal sittings of March and April 1883, it was becoming quite common for accused persons to give evidence, and the change in the law must have been well known to juries – at the latest after their first experience of a trial at which the accused did so, but, given the public discussion about the APEA, possibly even before their first case.[99] This put informal pressure on accused persons to give evidence – even if it meant revealing past felonies similar to those with which they were charged[100] – in case the jury should wonder what the accused had to hide. The pressure was increased when Mr Justice Andrews ruled in August 1883 that prosecutors and Judges had a right to comment on the fact that an accused had made an unsworn statement only and not exposed himself to cross-examination by the Crown, provided that this was not used to convict the prisoner of the offence (as prohibited by s 1 of the APEA).[101] Much later, this ruling was in effect adopted by the State's Full Court.[102]

Some concern was expressed during the settling-in period about the increasing amount of perjury that was being committed as a result of the APEA.[103] Even the *Advertiser*[104] admitted that it had provided 'fresh incitement to perjury'. The antidote, according to the *Advertiser*, was prosecuting accused persons for perjury if they committed it – a remedy which was, fortunately, never adopted generally, even though it was authorised by s 5 of the APEA.[105] There is, however, a record of one case in 1883 in which the brothers Hatswell were successfully prosecuted for perjury, having sworn falsely in the Police Court in November 1882 in order to avoid the imposition of a trivial fine on Hatswell for allowing a horse to stray on to the highway in the vicinity of Victoria Street, Goodwood. The prosecution for perjury was justified by the fact that, as the trial Judge stated, the perjury was particularly gross.[106]

The *Register*,[107] which had been equivocal in its support of the APEA, hailed it by May 1883 as an illustration of the 'readiness [with which] men in a young colony can free themselves from long centuries of inherited tradition and sentiment'.

What was the situation in the other young Australian colonies at this time? Were they following the South Australian lead?

4. The principle is adopted elsewhere

After South Australia, the next colonies to enact accused persons' evidence legislation were New Zealand, New South Wales and Victoria. Both Australian colonies did so in 1891, while New Zealand enacted its legislation in 1889.

New Zealand's legislation was the *Criminal Evidence Act* 1889.[108] There appears to have been little to no reliance in New Zealand on South Australian experience. Indeed, one newspaper said that the idea of accused persons giving evidence had 'worked satisfactorily' in some of the United States and should be 'borrow[ed]'[109] by New Zealand, but wasted no words on the seven years of experience which had by then been accumulated in South Australia. Nor was any mention made of the South Australian experience in the recorded Parliamentary debates. It is easy to understand why, in Canada,[110] the experience in the United States might have been referred to relatively frequently in the debates on the enactment of its legislation[111] and certainly more frequently than the Australian experience;[112] but the fact that New Zealand ignored South Australian experience is harder to understand.

In New South Wales, accused persons' evidence legislation was adopted by s 6 of the *Criminal Law and Evidence Amendment Act* 1891, which received the Royal assent on 14 December 1891. It stated that

> Every person charged with an indictable offence, and the husband or wife, as the case may be, of the person so charged, shall be competent, but not compellable, to give evidence in every Court on the hearing of such charge: Provided that the person so charged shall not be liable to be called as a witness on behalf of the prosecution nor to be questioned on cross-examination without the leave of the Judge as to his or her previous character or antecedents.[113]

This statute is not a copy of any other jurisdiction's legislation or proposed legislation, and, unlike the APEA, the N.S.W. statute provided some protection to the accused from being questioned about his prior convictions.[114]

Possibly the principal reason for the speedy success of the Bill in the

Parliamentary debate in New South Wales in 1891 was the fact that 'there were no legal members present' during at least part of the debate on it, and it consequently enjoyed 'a most rapid passage through committee'.[115] There was no one in Sydney to play the role of Messrs Symon and Kingston. At another stage in the debate, however, the Attorney-General for New South Wales did refer to South Australian experience, saying that he had been informed by a colleague in the Legislative Council, Sir Alfred Stephen, formerly the Chief Justice of New South Wales, that 'the Chief Justice of South Australia has stated that what I am now proposing has been the law in South Australia for some time, and that it has answered very well indeed'.[116] So there was some vague awareness of the South Australian innovation, if not of its exact terms.

Sir Alfred Stephen and Chief Justice Way were regular correspondents,[117] but I have found no letters between them on this issue. Perhaps they discussed it when Stephen visited Adelaide in 1887.[118] And perhaps it was Way who suggested the inclusion of a protection for the accused against the revelation in evidence of his past life given the trouble he had had with the APEA's failure to grant such protection.

On 23 December 1891, nine days after the New South Wales legislation was passed, the *Crimes Act* 1891 of Victoria received the Royal assent. Being based on the proposed English legislation, the Victorian legislation contained both a protection for the accused against being asked 'any question not relevant to the particular offence with which he is charged unless [he] has given evidence of good character'[119] and a provision preventing comment on an accused's failure to give evidence.

Again, the newspapers and debates on the proposed measure show little awareness of the operation of the system across the border in South Australia. The *Argus*,[120] like its New Zealand counterpart, mentioned at one stage the United States experience, but not the South Australian one. In Parliament, a trial in Chicago[121] and American experience in general[122] were mentioned at greater length than the experience in South Australia, although, immediately before the second reading of the Bill was agreed to in the Lower House, one member stated that he 'had seen in South Australia the operation of the system now proposed, and he thought its introduction into Victoria, properly guarded in the way that had been pointed out, would be of public advantage'.[123]

Attempts to enact accused persons' evidence legislation in England pre-dated the South Australian experiment: the earliest of the numerous Bills was dated 1858.[124] But the law was not finally changed until, after a long debate, the *Criminal Evidence Act* 1898 was enacted. The English discussion was a lively one, and was carried out not only in legal periodicals, but also, for example, in the columns of *The Times*.

While this debate on the desirability of allowing all accused persons to give evidence was going on, about two dozen[125] statutes were passed from the early 1870s allowing persons accused only of specific named crimes or classes of crimes to give evidence in their defence. In this way, a growing number of statutory exceptions to the common-law rule prohibiting testimony by the accused developed for specific crimes – with associated anomalies as the division between trials in which the accused could and those in which he could not give evidence became rather haphazard.[126] The most significant of these statutes, the *Criminal Law Amendment Act* 1885,[127] famously permitted Oscar Wilde to give evidence in his trial[128] although it was held over three years before the *Criminal Evidence Act* 1898 came into effect.

It was not chiefly opposition to the principle of permitting all accused persons to give evidence that caused the failure of each successive Bill until 1898. Sometimes, earlier Bills were not dealt with before the end of the Parliamentary session, while a limited sort of opposition was provided by certain Irish members, who had no objections to the enactment of accused persons' evidence legislation for England but opposed any Bill which also applied to Ireland on the grounds that the allegedly different prosecutorial style in that country would make any such Bill a means of oppression.[129] (The *Criminal Evidence Act* 1898, as finally enacted, did not apply in Ireland,[130] and accused persons could not give evidence there until just after partition in the 1920s.)[131] There was, however, opposition to the general principle of the Bill which grew as its enactment became more probable, and it is in relation to this that the English discussion on the Bill considered experience in the colonies.

As time went on, experience of accused persons giving evidence was also available in England itself, for the number of statutes under which the accused could give evidence grew with every passing year, and the advocates of generalising this principle were, of course, able to argue that the new principle had proved satisfactory.[132] On the other hand, Sir Herbert Stephen, a leading and well-connected commentator of the day, was converted by his experience of the mixed English system of the mid-1890s to the view that it was a mistake to permit any accused persons to give evidence at all.[133] His reasons were chiefly that innocent prisoners might make such a bad impression on a jury, and guilty prisoners might make such a good impression if sufficiently skilled at lying, that the reform was likely to promote the conviction of some innocent persons and the acquittal of some guilty ones. He claimed that his opposition to the Bill was shared by most 'persons having practical experience of the giving of evidence by prisoners'.[134]

In the face of such claims, supporters needed experienced testimony in favour of the proposed reform. Only colonial voices could speak with experience of a system in which all accused could give evidence. In a long piece published in *The Times* on 6 June 1896,[135] Mr Justice Windeyer of the Supreme Court of New South Wales mentioned that he had been a reluctant convert to the reform. But experience of its operation had converted him to a supporter, and:

> As far as I have been able to ascertain from conversation with them, the experience of all other Judges in the colonies of Victoria, South Australia, and Queensland, where the law has been reformed, is the same, whilst public opinion, as far as there has been any expression of it through the press, is entirely in favour of the reform.

The influence of Mr Justice Windeyer's letter on the debate appears to have been significant. Certainly his Honour was not entirely unknown in London. His letter to *The Times* was sent from the Athenaeum. And, writing to Sir Alfred Stephen in 1891, South Australian Chief Justice Way had stated that 'Windeyer is well known to all the Members of the Judicial Committee; some of them are amused and some are a little irritated with the fresh manner in which he has dealt with their judgments'.[136] Be that as it may, some indication of the importance of his letter may be gauged from a further letter to the editor of *The Times*[137] over five months later from Sir Harry Poland Q.C. of the Temple. In his letter, Sir Harry, a very prominent criminal prosecutor with a great reputation for fairness,[138]

> ask[ed] the opponents of [the Criminal Evidence] Bill – if there are any left – to read the very able letter of Sir William Windeyer (for many years the senior puisne Judge of the Supreme Court of New South Wales) which appeared in *The Times* of June 6 last. I think the lawyers and the public have pretty well made up their minds by this time on the subject.

But the colonial influence on the debates on the Criminal Evidence Bills should not be overstated. *The Times*[139] published leading articles in which the colonial experience was not mentioned at all, and the debate on the proposal, while referring to experience in other jurisdictions, concentrated mostly on the merits of the proposal as such.

Nevertheless, in the Parliamentary debate on the Bill of 1898, which finally became law, colonial experience was used as an argument for the Bill. Colonial (and United States) experience was also cited more generally by the proponents of the Bill, the Attorney-General stating that 'all the civilised countries in which prisoners can give evidence are ... satisfied with the system'.[140]

However, colonial experience was also cited against the proposal. One opponent of the Bill stated that Sir John Madden, Chief Justice of Victoria, had told him

> that the opinion of the majority of the Judges in the land where this change of the law had taken place was distinctly against it. Every year the Judges of Victoria have to report upon the cases which have been tried

before them [and] have, year after year, reported that they are against the present position of the law in Victoria, which is what this House is now asked to make law in this country. ... There is not ... a single Judge who is in favour of the law as it now stands. ... [The Judges] have called the attention of the Parliament of Victoria to the constantly increasing number of cases of perjury which have been brought about by this change of the law.[141]

Three days later, one of the Irish members went even further, declaring that 'the very Chief Justice of one of these colonies had declared that practically everybody in the Colonies' – not just that Chief Justice's colony! – 'was dissatisfied with the working of the Bill, and desired the old order of things to be reverted to'.[142]

These statements, however, exaggerated the extent of judicial dissatisfaction with the law in Victoria. The Judges' Report for the year 1894[143] shows that Sir John Madden, the Chief Justice, and his colleagues had in their sights only paragraph (3) of the proviso to s 34 of the *Crimes Act* 1891, which provided that an accused person could not be asked or required to answer 'any question not relevant to the particular offence with which he is charged unless such person has given evidence of good character'.[144] The Judges' objection to the Victorian provision was that it allowed 'a prisoner who has been several times convicted [to] swear that he did not commit it without any risk of the jury knowing what his oath is worth', and that several prosecutions for perjury had resulted from such false swearing. If 'it' refers to the accused person's previous offences, it is hard to follow this line of reasoning, for an assertion that an accused has not committed offences in the past would certainly be regarded today as 'evidence of good character'.

It may of course be that Mr Richards M.P. had become privy to more thorough-going opinions of the reform when he spoke to Sir John Madden and his colleagues. But all this could not stop the triumphal progress of the Bill through the House of Commons and on to the statute book. Clearly, not even the apparent exaggeration of judicial dissatisfaction with the proposed reform in Victoria could prevent its enactment, and this can only be because public opinion and the opinion of the House was already so much in favour of the reform that these exaggerations were ignored.

The colonial experience represented by Mr Justice Windeyer played some small part in developing that wide degree of consensus in favour of the reform in England. Once England had reformed the law, it was only a matter of time before all common-law countries followed the lead first set by South Australia in 1882.

Nevertheless, Sir John Downer's boast that his statute had been 'adopted' by the other Australian colonies, Canada and the United Kingdom was only partially justified. The South Australian experience played quite a modest role in the enactment of accused persons' evidence legislation in the colonies of New South Wales and Victoria.

On the other hand, the combined experience of those colonies and South Australia in the application of such legislation does seem to have had more than a modest influence on the debate in England.

Notes

1   'Judicial Independence and the Rule of Law' (2001) 75 ALJ 556, 556.
2   The Act (no. 245) contained no short-title section and never formally received the short title here employed, but that short title was in reasonably common use on a semi-formal level until the APEA was repealed in 1925 (see below, fn 5); see also *Azzopardi* v. *R* (2001) 205 CLR 50, 57 fn 38; 65 fn 57; 103 fn 197. In its earliest days, the Act was also referred to by a variety of other names, such as the *Prisoners Evidence Act*, the *Accused Persons' Oaths Act* and other variants. Just before its repeal, Mr Justice Angas Parsons referred to it as the 'Evidence Act of 1882': *R* v. *Phillips* [1922] SASR 276, *passim*. The APEA's long title was 'An Act to enable Persons Accused of Offences to give Evidence on Oath'.
3   The usual caveat applies: see above, p. 93 fn 3. India had a provision permitting the Court to put questions to the accused: *Code of Criminal Procedure* 1872 s 342; *Code of Criminal Procedure* 1882 s 342 (and later still *Code of Criminal Procedure* 1898 s 342), each of which supplemented the *Indian Evidence Act* 1872 s 120, which enabled spouses of accused persons to give evidence. However, each of the three Codes provided (ss 345, 342 (para. 4) and 342 (4) respectively) that no oath should be administered to the accused, which meant that accused was not a witness and gave no evidence: *Subedar* v. *State* [1957] AIR All 396, 398. No account is taken here of legislation which permitted the accused to give evidence in a few criminal cases only (such as that cited below, fn 125).
4   Allen, *The Law of Evidence in Victorian England* (Cambridge U.P., 1997), pp. 176–180; Thayer, *Select Cases on Evidence at the Common Law with Notes*

(Sever, Cambridge U.S.A. 1892), p. 1071; Wigmore, *Evidence in Trials at Common Law* (4th ed., Little, Brown & Co., Boston 1979), pp. 826f (noting, in fn 2, a statement in a later edition of Thayer's work that the first such statute was passed in 1864). However, a comparison of such texts of the early U.S. statutes as are available to the author does not suggest that the APEA was directly based on them, and there is nothing in any other sources to suggest that either the words of the U.S. statutes or, more generally, the Courts' experience there influenced the South Australian legislators in any way.

5 *Evidence Amendment Act* 1925 s 12; see now *Evidence Act* 1929 s 18. Despite its repeal in South Australia in 1925, the APEA continued in operation in the Northern Territory of Australia (see *Tuckiar* v. *R* (1934) 52 CLR 335). The South Australian legislature had ceased to exercise jurisdiction over the Territory after the enactment of the APEA but before its repeal in South Australia. The APEA was repealed for the Northern Territory by the *Evidence Ordinances* 1939 ord. 2 and Schedule. This enactment finally removed the APEA from the last Australian statute book in which it had appeared.

6 South Australian Parliamentary Debates, House of Assembly, 18 August 1925, p. 485.

7 South Australian Parliamentary Debates, Legislative Council, 3 November 1908, p. 303.

8 For brief descriptions of the evolution of the common law to this point, see Allen, *The Law of Evidence in Victorian England*, pp. 123–127; Howard *et al.* (eds.), *Phipson on Evidence* (15th ed., Sweet and Maxwell, London 2000), pp. 148f; Pitt-Lewis, 'The New Great Reform in the Criminal Law' (1898) 44 Nineteenth Century 591, 591–594; 'Prisoners' Evidence' (1884) 77 LT 99, 99; Sibley, (1896) 100 LT 568, (1896) 101 LT 20; Stephen, *History of the Criminal Law of England* Vol. I (MacMillan, London 1883), pp. 439f; Stephen, 'Suggestions as to the Reform of the Criminal Law' (1877) 2 Nineteenth Century 737, 749–751.

9 Howard *et al.* (eds.), *Phipson*, p. 148.

10 Parliamentary Debates, House of Commons, 22 March 1888, col. 68; 25 April 1898, col. 982; Allen, *The Law of Evidence in Victorian England*, p. 167. See now, on the position of mistresses as compared with wives, *R* v. *Pearce* [2002] 1 WLR 1553.

11 The debate is reported in the South Australian Parliamentary Debates, House of Assembly, 30 October 1878, coll. 1407–1417, 1421f.

12 31 October 1878, p. 4; see also *Register*, 31 October 1878, p. 4.

13 Cross, *Evidence* (5th ed., London, Butterworths 1979), p. 166.

14 Further possibilities for the accused to have his side of the story told to the Court are discussed in 'Statements by Prisoners' Counsel' (1883) 76 LT 100; (1883) 76 LT 117; (1884) 76 LT 172; 'The Privileges of the Accused' (1883) 76 LT 150; 'Statements by Prisoners' (1884) 76 LT 187; Note, (1884) 76 LT 249; 'Criminal Law and the Jurisdiction of Magistrates' (1884) 77 LT 117, 117. The right to make an unsworn statement has since been abolished: *Evidence Act* 1929 s 18A.

15 At p. 6.

16   The clauses were not all in quite the form in which they were eventually enacted, as a comparison with the Bill as reproduced in the *Advertiser*, 7 July 1882, p. 4, and of the Committee stage of the Bill in Parliament will confirm. Thus, for example, the proviso to s 5 was added during debate: South Australian Parliamentary Debates, Legislative Council, 25 July 1882, coll. 448f; 3 August 1882, col. 551.

17   16 June 1882, p. 4.

18   *Register*, 31 October 1878, p. 4.

19   For a handy summary of these, see Allen, *The Law of Evidence in Victorian England*, pp. 128–132.

20   *Register*, p. 4.

21   Perhaps spurred on by an letter to the Editor which had just appeared: *Register*, 20 June 1882, p. 6.

22   29 June 1882, p. 5.

23   South Australian Parliamentary Debates, House of Assembly, 6 July 1882, coll. 277–281.

24   *Register*, 7 July 1882, p. 5.

25   7 July 1882, p. 4.

26   South Australian Parliamentary Debates, House of Assembly, 11 July 1882, coll. 314f; 12 July 1882, col. 333; see also *Advertiser*, 8 December 1882, p. 4; *Advertiser*, 27 December 1882, p. 4. For the expression of similar views in England, see Allen, *The Law of Evidence in Victorian England*, pp. 158–160.

27   South Australian Parliamentary Debates, House of Assembly, 11 July 1882, col. 310–314.

28   South Australian Parliamentary Debates, House of Assembly, 12 July 1882, coll. 328–333.

29   12 July 1882, p. 4.

30   South Australian Parliamentary Debates, House of Assembly, 18 July 1882, col. 388.

31   South Australian Parliamentary Debates, House of Assembly, 18 July 1882, col. 393.

32   South Australian Parliamentary Debates, House of Assembly, 18 July 1882, col. 395.

33   South Australian Parliamentary Debates, Legislative Council, 25 July 1882, col. 449; 9 August 1882, col. 588.

34   CO 13/140/164–179.

35   CO 13/140/178–179.

36   CO 13/140/164.

37   A title no longer used in South Australia, but clearly in use then, as the newspaper reports show.

38   *Frearson's Weekly*, 20 January 1883, p. 792. That this opinion was shared by others is shown by Pascoe, *History of Adelaide and Vicinity with a General Sketch of the Province of South Australia and Biographies of Representative Men* (Hussey & Gillingham, Adelaide 1901), p. 298, published two years after Mr Beddome's death in April 1898. His Worship is there referred to as 'a man of much wordly wisdom who had a keen, penetrating judgment, and that wise acquaintance of human character which he combined with a knowledge of close reasoning necessary to the proper administration of the

law' (p. 298). His retirement as Police Magistrate on 31 July 1890, after thirty-three and a half years' service in that position, was accompanied by 'unfeigned expressions of general regret' (*ibid.*).

39   4 September 1882, p. 7.

40   The Exhibition Grounds were near the old Exhibition Building on North Terrace. The spot where the events took place is therefore now within the grounds of the University of Adelaide, or possibly the North Terrace campus of the University of South Australia. For a plan of this area as it was then, see Jensen/Jensen, *Colonial Architecture in South Australia: A Definitive Chronicle of Development 1836–1890* (Rigby, Adelaide 1980), p. 798.

41   *Register*, 4 September 1882, p. 6.

42   *Advertiser*, 4 September 1882, p. 7.

43   *Register*, 4 September 1882, p. 6.

44   5 September 1882, p. 6. The *Advertiser*'s report (5 September 1882, p. 6) states that the seamen were 'discharged with a caution', but I am inclined to believe the more detailed report in the *Register*.

45   *Register*, 9 September 1882, p. 5; see also Supplement, p. 1; *Advertiser*, 9 September 1882, p. 4.

46   *Register*, 12 September 1882, p. 5; similar *Advertiser*, 13 September 1882, p. 5.

47   *Register*, Supplement, 12 September 1882, p. 1.

48   *Register*, Supplement, 19 September 1882, p. 2.

49   *E.g. Advertiser*, Supplement, 21 September 1882, p. 2; 23 September 1882, p. 2 (case in Moonta on 15 September); *Register*, Supplement, 7 October 1882, p. 2; *Advertiser*, Supplement, 31 October 1882, p. 2; *Register*, Supplement, 5 December 1882, p. 2; *Advertiser*, Supplement, 14 December 1882, p. 2.

50   An exception is *R* v. *Burford* (*Advertiser*, 3 October 1882, p. 6) – here it is stated that the accused 'pleaded' his defence, which presumably means that he gave evidence; the report in the *Register*, Supplement, 3 October 1882 is also ambiguous on this point.

51   *Advertiser*, Supplement, 13 October 1882, p. 1.

52   *Register*, 5 October 1882, p. 5; see also Supplement, p. 2.

53   *Advertiser*, Supplement, 5 October 1882, p. 1.

54   *Advertiser*, Supplement, 7 October 1882, p. 2 ('prisoner declined to be sworn and simply denied the allegations' of larceny from the person); *Register*, Supplement, 12 October 1882, p. 2 (robbery case).

55   18 November 1882, p. 6.

56   *Advertiser*, Supplement, 28 November 1882, p. 2.

57   *Register*, 27 November 1882, p. 6.

58   *Advertiser*, 7 December 1882, p. 7.

59   *Advertiser*, 8 December 1882, p. 4; emphasis added.

60   *Register*, 8 December 1882, p. 5. In *R* v. *Lynch* [1919] SALR 325, 341, Chief Justice Murray stated that it was by then 'generally recognised' that, as the APEA did not expressly take away the right to make an unsworn statement, it contained no sufficient indication of any intention to do so, and that accused persons accordingly had two choices. This is clearly right and in accordance with the presumption that statutes do not impliedly take away

common-law rights, although we are not told how this general recognition had emerged. It is not known, for example, whether this point had been established by an earlier Full Court decision, as none is reported and it is not possible to conduct a search of the newspapers for several decades in the absence of an index. See also *Azzopardi* v. *R* (2001) 205 CLR 50, 99f.

61   8 December 1882, p. 4.

62   At p. 6.

63   *Advertiser*, 11 December 1882, p. 5.

64   The *Advertiser*, 27 December 1882, p. 4, has 'Luton', but 'Loton' appears to be correct, as it is the name on the indictment (GRG 36/1).

65   *Admiralty Offences (Colonial) Act* 1849 (Imp.) s 1 and also, as Burns was an Englishman (his mother lived in Devonshire: *Register*, 18 January 1883, p. 5), under the *Merchant Shipping Act* 1867 (Imp.) s 11.

66   This detail is contained in the report of the *Advertiser*, Supplement, 16 December 1882, p. 1, only, and not in the *Register*'s report. In other respects, except as noted below, the reports are similar.

67   The *Advertiser*'s report places these words in the mouth of Chief Justice Way himself. In its news columns (16 December 1882, p. 5), the *Register* compromises, stating that the Chief Justice referred to 'the prisoner and the Judges'.

68   *Register*, Supplement, 16 December 1882, p. 2.

69   18 December 1882, p. 4.

70   9 May 1883, p. 4. This editorial refers to a murder rather than a manslaughter case. However, in 1883 there were no trials for murder in South Australia until October. The statement that the trial was a murder trial is therefore clearly a slip, and the reference is equally clearly to the Page case.

71   Son of Charles Mann *senior* mentioned earlier in this book.

72   *Register*, 20 December 1882, p. 7; similar *Advertiser*, Supplement, 20 December 1882, p. 1.

73   The depositions before the coroner were admitted on the trial pursuant to s 2 of the APEA: *Advertiser*, Supplement, 20 December 1882, p. 1.

74   21 December 1882, p. 5. See further *Advertiser*, 27 December 1882, p. 4.

75   *Register*, 20 December 1882, p. 7.

76   *Register*, 20 December 1882, p. 7.

77   *Register*, Supplement, 21 December 1882, p. 1; *Advertiser*, 21 December 1882, p. 6.

78   *Robinson* v. *R* (1994) 180 CLR 531. His Honour also gave the direction about the onus of proof in murder cases which was disapproved in *Woolmington* v. *D.P.P.* [1935] AC 462; and his Honour's remarks about apparent lies by the accused might also not stand up to modern appellate scrutiny.

79   *Juries Act* 1927 s 86.

80   See *Register*, Supplement, 21 December 1882, p. 1; 22 December 1882, p. 6; *Advertiser*, 21 December 1882, pp. 5, 6; 22 December 1882, p. 6.

81   21 December 1882, p. 6.

82   21 December 1882, p. 5.

83   This is stated in the reports of the evidence at Burns's trial and other newspaper reports after his sentencing, and is confirmed by an

independent source, namely Mr Juan del Campo, who maintains
a list of British men who served on the *Huascar* at
http://members.lycos.co.uk/Juan39/THE_HUASCAR.html. Mr del
Campo has stated to the author that his sources for this information are the
official records of the Peruvian Navy, the log-book of the Captain of the
Huascar, a book published by the Office of Maritime Interests (Direccion de
Intereses Maritimos) of the Peruvian Navy entitled *A La Gloria Del Gran
Almirante Del Peru Miguel Grau (To The Glory Of The Great Admiral Of Peru
Miguel Grau)* (1978 and 1995) and the primary source 'Archivo Historico de
la Marina' (Historical Archives of the Navy).

84   *E.g. Register*, 22 December 1882, p. 6.

85   Markham, *The War between Peru and Chile, 1879–1882* (Sampson Low,
Marston, Searle and Rivington, London 1882), pp. 130f. It is interesting to
note that the copy of this book in the Barr Smith Library of the University
of Adelaide bears the bookplate of none other than Chief Justice Way
himself, although the bookplate shows him as a Baronet, an honour which
had not been conferred on him in 1882. For other contemporary accounts
of the capture of the *Huascar*, see Anon, 'The Capture of the *Huascar*'
(1880) 29 Engineering 74, 182f, 189; Madan, 'Incidents of the War between
Chili and Peru, 1879–80' (1881) 25 Journal of the Royal United Service
Institution 693.

86   *Register*, 22 December 1882, p. 6.

87   22 December 1882, p. 4.

88   *Advertiser*, 22 December 1882, p. 4; this is also my impression on reading
the summing-up as reported in the *Register*, 22 December 1882, p. 6;
Advertiser, 22 December 1882, p. 6. (These reports are also the source for
otherwise unacknowledged statements about the trial in this paragraph.)

89   *Register*, 22 December 1882, p. 4; *Advertiser*, 22 December 1882, p. 4.

90   22 December 1882, p. 4; see also *Advertiser*, 27 December 1882, p. 4;
1 January 1883, p. 7.

91   GRG 40/1/12/397f; files CSO 33/1883; CSO 88/1883.

92   Magree (also spelt McGree) was discharged from gaol in June 1887: South
Australian Archives, GRG 54/41/1A/2316; *South Australian Police Gazette*,
22 June 1887, p. 100. (It may be McGree who re-appears in the *South
Australian Police Gazette*, 14 November 1894, p. 183, as having been recently
convicted of two counts of larceny. A comparison of the two Magrees'
descriptions makes this a possible state of affairs, although the matter is not
free from doubt as the descriptions vary in some respects. If it was the same
Magree in 1894, it is at least odd that neither of the daily newspapers
(*Register*, 23 August 1894, p. 7; 24 August 1894, p. 3; *Advertiser* 23 August
1894, p. 7; 24 August 1894, p. 7) mentions this fact.) The records in the
South Australian Archives relating to Mrs Magree's time in, and discharge
from, prison are missing, and a search of the *South Australian Police Gazette*
up to 1922 yielded no result.

93   17 January 1883, p. 5.

94   At p. 5; similar *Advertiser*, 19 January 1883, p. 5.

95   *Register*, 19 January 1883, p. 5; similar *Advertiser*, 19 January 1883, p. 5.

96 The Bible Christians were an offshoot of the Methodists, whom they later rejoined.

97 *Register*, 19 January 1883, p. 5.

98 *Register*, 19 January 1883, p. 6.

99 *Cf. R* v. *Lynch* [1919] SALR 325, 346, 356.

100 There are at least two further records of an accused person being cross-examined on prior convictions: *R* v. *Sheehan Register*, 6 April 1883, p. 7; *Advertiser*, 6 April 1883, p. 7; *R* v. *Howell* (1885) 19 SALR 1. Here, the prior conviction was very similar to the offence with which the accused was charged (both 'grievous bodily harm' offences), and the accused was found guilty.

101 *Register*, 8 August 1883, p. 5. The Court reports at p. 2 of the same day's Supplement indicate that the accused in this case was acquitted anyway. His defence was a lack of intent (he did not know that the coin was counterfeit), and this makes the comment by Mr Justice Andrews less surprising.

102 *R* v. *Lynch* [1919] SALR 325, 346f (although the Court here did not refer to any precedents, either English or South Australian). See, however, *Tuckiar* v. *R* (1934) 52 CLR 335, 344f, 353f.

103 See South Australian Parliamentary Debates, House of Assembly, 17 July 1883, col. 491; *Report of the Select Committee of the Legislative Council on the Abolition of Oaths Bill 1885* (S.A. Parliamentary Papers no. 125/1885), p. 12 (Mr Justice Boucaut).

104 13 April 1883, p. 4.

105 In *R* v. *Dean* (1896) 17 NSWR 35, the Supreme Court of New South Wales decided, however, that prosecutions for perjury were permissible in those circumstances even without any words authorising them in the statute. See now, however, *R* v. *Carroll* (2002) 194 ALR 1, 26.

106 *Register*, 12 April 1883, p. 7; 13 April 1883, p. 7; *Advertiser*, 12 April 1883, p. 7; 13 April 1883, p. 7.

107 9 May 1883, p. 4.

108 New Zealand had had legislation since 1875 permitting persons accused of summary offences to give evidence: *Evidence Further Amendment Act* 1875 (N.Z.) s 5; *Badham* v. *Hill* (1878) 3 NZ Jur (N.S.) SC 84. Other jurisdictions also followed similar paths before enacting accused persons' evidence legislation applicable to all offences: *cf.*, *e.g.*, the *Evidence in Summary Convictions [sic!] Act* (N.S.W.) (no. 3 of 1882); *Criminal Evidence Act* 1896 (W.A.); 52 Vic. no. 7 (1888) (Tas.).

109 *Auckland Herald*, 12 August 1889, p. 4. See also New Zealand Parliamentary Debates, House of Representatives, 27 June 1889, p. 68.

110 For references to the United States – and French – law during the debate in the Canadian Parliament, see, *e.g.*, Canadian Parliamentary Debates, House of Commons, 3 March 1893, p. 1683. On the differences between the Canadian statute as originally enacted and the U.K. statute, see *R* v. *D'Aoust* (1902) 3 OLR 653; and, for further references, see Teed, 'The Effect of s 12 of the *Canada Evidence Act* upon an Accused' (1970) 13 Crim LQ 70.

111 *Canada Evidence Act* 1893 s 4.

112 Although one Australian statute was mentioned in the debate in Canada, one Senator quoting Queensland's *Criminal Law Amendment Act* 1892 and

referring to it as the statute of 'Australia' (Canada, *Senate Debates*, 27 March 1893, p. 444). As we have seen, each Australian statute had its own unique wording, so there was no one 'Australian' model.

113 Section 6.

114 This is due to the Attorney-General's insistence on this principle: New South Wales Parliamentary Debates, Legislative Council, 28 May 1890, p. 763; 9 July 1890, p. 1931; 23 July 1890, pp. 2287–2296.

115 *Sydney Morning Herald*, 15 October 1891, p. 5.

116 New South Wales Parliamentary Debates, Legislative Council, 9 July 1890, p. 1931.

117 For example, in the State Library of South Australia, there is preserved (PRG 30/8) a letter of recommendation for F.W. Pennefather, later first Professor Law at the University of Adelaide, from Chief Justice Way to Sir A. Stephen.

118 Bedford, *Think of Stephen: A Family Chronicle* (Angus & Robertson, Sydney 1954), p. 245.

119 Section 34, proviso (3). For early cases on this provision, see *R* v. *Gray* (1895) 1 Arg LR 20; *Wise* v. *Mahoney* (1986) 2 ALT 135. For another very interesting case involving disagreement as to whether the new state of the law was applicable when a husband and wife were tried together, see *R* v. *Stowers* (1902) 8 Arg LR 134.

120 17 December 1891, p. 5. See also *Argus*, 13 August 1891, p. 4; *Age*, 21 August 1891, p. 4.

121 Victorian Parliamentary Debates, Legislative Assembly, 16 December 1891, p. 3125.

122 Victorian Parliamentary Debates, Legislative Assembly, 29 July 1891, p. 584; 16 December 1891, p. 3130.

123 Victorian Parliamentary Debates, Legislative Assembly, 16 December 1891, p. 3128.

124 Allen, *The Law of Evidence in Victorian England*, pp. 132–144.

125 Twenty-four according to the Note in (1898) 104 LT 389; twenty-six according to the Attorney-General (House of Commons Debates, 25 April 1898, col. 978); twenty-seven according to the Note in (1898) 105 LT 549. A list may be found in Archibald, Greenhalgh & Roberts, *Metropolitan Police Guide* (2nd ed., H.M.S.O., London 1896), pp. 163f.

126 See, *e.g.*, House of Commons Debates, 25 April 1898, col. 978 (Webster A.-G.); 'Evidence in Criminal Cases Bills' (1895) 99 LT 163; Allen, *The Law of Evidence in Victorian England*, pp. 165f; Ford, 'Anomalies of the Criminal Law' (1896) 100 LT 515; Lord Justice Lopes's charge to a grand jury reported in (1897) 102 LT 248; the letter from Sir H. Poland Q.C. to *The Times*, 14 February 1898, p. 5; Stephen, 'Prisoners as Witnesses' (1886) 20 Nineteenth Century 453, 453f; the leading article in *The Times* of 12 March 1898, pp. 11f; and the references to Oscar Wilde's trial below.

127 On the origins of this statute, see 'Prisoners as Witnesses' (1897) 103 LT 297.

128 See Hyde, *The Trials of Oscar Wilde* (Dover, New York 1962), pp. 165, 243ff, and the notes in (1895) 99 LT 103; (1895) 30 LJ 285 dealing with the

complications caused by the fact that Wilde was originally charged with an offence under the *Criminal Law Amendment Act* 1885 under which the accused could give evidence and a common-law offence in relation to which the accused could not give evidence.

129 '*Evidence in Criminal Cases Bill* and Ireland' (1896) 100 LT 413. See further the views of leading Irish Q.C.s reported in (1897) 102 LT 582, the extract from the *Irish Law Times* reprinted as 'Prisoners as Witnesses' (1897) 103 LT 297 and Allen, *The Law of Evidence in Victorian England*, pp. 140f, 143, 172.

130 Section 7 (1).

131 *Criminal Evidence Act (Northern Ireland)* 1923; *Criminal Justice (Evidence) Act* 1924 (Irish Free State).

132 *E.g.* Lord Justice Lopes charging a grand jury, reported in (1897) 102 LT 248; House of Commons Debates, 22 March 1888, col. 70; Stephen, (1886) 20 Nineteenth Century 453, 454.

133 'A Bill to Promote the Conviction of Innocent Prisoners' (1896) 39 Nineteenth Century 566. Sir Herbert allowed only one exception: cases in which the burden of proof is on the defendant (at p. 572). See further the letter from N.W. Sibley, (1896) 100 LT 568.

134 *The Times*, 20 July 1897, p. 14.

135 At p. 5.

136 Chief Justice Way. to Sir A. Stephen, State Library of South Australia, Mortlock Library, PRG 30/5/3/183.

137 12 November 1896, p. 4; Sir H. Stephen's response may be found in *The Times*, 14 November 1896, p. 10.

138 *Dictionary of National Biography*, Vol. 1922–1930, pp. 683f.

139 *E.g.* 22 April 1897, p. 9.

140 House of Commons Debates, 25 April 1898, col. 979; see also col. 1006 (Sir R. Reid); col. 1063 (Mr Bucknill).

141 House of Commons Debates, 27 June 1898, col. 318.

142 House of Commons Debates, 30 June 1898, col. 681.

143 Victorian Parliamentary Papers, No. 16/1894. The same criticism was repeated in the following year (Victorian Parliamentary Papers, No. 93/1895–6). There was no other criticism of the *Crimes Act* 1891 in any other years in the 1890s (despite the statement, quoted in the text, that the Judges had expressed their dissatisfaction 'year after year').

144 At p. 4.

7. An important procedural reform – that didn't work

1. Law and equity

Every first-year law student knows, or should know, the history of the fusion of the administration of the two systems of law making up the English (and thus the colonial Australian) judicial system. The fusion of the administration of the systems of law and equity occurred in the 1870s in England, and was widely and rapidly copied in all Australian colonies except New South Wales.[1]

The story leading up to that great reform is a complex one, the result of a long historical process.[2] By the start of the nineteenth century there existed in England two sets of Courts to administer two separate sets of legal rules. One was the common law and the other equity. Equity contained such important principles as the trust, and important means of enforcing rights such as the injunction. The general idea was that the common law contained the strict rules of the law, and equity was a mild corrective to it where it was unfair, although over the years equity had also hardened into a system of rules. In cases of conflict between the rules of the common law and those of equity, the rules of equity prevailed.

The Courts administering the common law found this fact so irksome that they refused to recognise most of equity's rules, deciding cases without reference to them. Equity, for its part, often would refuse to listen to people who had not yet established their rights before the Courts administering the common law.

This caused significant procedural problems, and much waste of time and money. A case often needed to be tried twice, once in the common-law Courts and once in the equitable ones, in order to establish the law applicable to one and the same set of facts. It also meant that there were many traps for the unwary caused by the existence of two systems that were quite independent of each other. In the Borrow & Goodiar case, for example, the plaintiffs had a claim under the *Claimants Relief Act* for money not paid to them under a contract. This was a claim under the common law, not a claim in equity. The government, as defendant, wanted to bring up a point under the rules of equity in its defence. It could not however do so in the Court of common law in which the plaintiffs (or their creditors) had sued it. It needed to sue separately in the equity Court, starting completely fresh proceedings and seeking the prohibition of a claim at common law which was in conflict with the rules of equity. In those proceedings, it would have been a 'plaintiff in equity', having initiated new proceedings. But it did not get past first base. The drafter of the *Claimants Relief Act* had not thought of this twist. The Supreme Court refused the government's application to appear as a plaintiff in equity on the grounds that the *Claimants Relief Act* 'did not seem to grant power to the Government to appear as plaintiff, though it was allowed to appear as defendant'.[3]

To add insult to injury, each set of Courts had its own procedures, making it necessary to comply with different procedures if moving from one set of Courts to the other. In early South Australia, there were particular complaints about the great expense and delay associated with equitable procedure, mirroring those in England at about the same time, such as may be seen, for example, in Dickens's *Bleak House*. Moreover, procedure before the Court of equity involved the drawing up of a complex and wordy bill in equity and numerous subsequent stages which seemed designed to maximise lawyers' and officials' fees. As the *Register*[4] put it in September 1852:

> It is a matter of surprise to the newly arrived stranger to find already flourishing in this colony the whole system of Chancery practice and

special pleading which has obstructed the course of justice in England, and rendered Courts of Equity, especially, what may be emphatically styled Courts of iniquity. There are at this moment cases pending in the Supreme Court of this Province which would be considered bad, in respect to delay and expense, even in that polluted Augean stable, the Court of Chancery at home.

Sometimes the rules of the so-called system of equity were felt to be unjust in principle. R.R. Torrens said that one of the reasons he designed the Torrens system was his recognition of the defects of the Courts of equity, which applied the doctrines of equity to real property law unfairly to the disadvantage of a friend or relative of his.[5] (To what extent the Torrens system succeeded in curing those defects is another question.) In property law, the rules of equity sometimes meant that land owners were lumbered with a mortgage or a lease on their land which they did not know about when buying it.

An end was finally put to this dual system in England by the *Supreme Court of Judicature Act* 1873 (U.K.), which created one Court to deal with issues of both common law and equity. This reform, known as the 'judicature system', is doubtless the most significant legal reform to take place in the nineteenth century. It was copied in South Australia by the *Supreme Court Act* 1878; it is a startling fact that the equivalent reform was not introduced in New South Wales until its *Supreme Court Act* 1970 came into effect in 1972, so that New South Wales was, for almost a century, a museum of outdated legal procedure.

Few writers have noticed the earlier attempt at reform which was made by the South Australian legislature, twenty years before the English reforms of 1873, in the *Supreme Court Procedure Amendment Act*, Act No. 5 of 1853. This appears to be the first statutory attempt to abolish the separate administration of law and equity in the British Empire, an indigenous and original South Australian reform unsupported by developments anywhere else. It was also a complete failure, the only failure we encounter in this book.

2. The need for reform

In South Australia, as in the other Australian colonies, a Court with jurisdiction both at common law and in equity was set up from the first – namely, the Supreme Court. In all the Australian colonies, however, the colonists were so wedded to English forms that they overlooked the opportunity presented by the establishment of a single Court, and perpetuated the dual system.

It would have been easy, given that (unlike in England) one Court was responsible for both law and equity, to create a more rational system of law by abandoning the separate administration of law and equity and the separate systems of procedure. But rather than doing that, the distinction between the two systems was kept up by inventing separate 'sides' of the single Court for law and equity, despite the lack of any statutory requirement for this course. To pile absurdity on absurdity, the small number of Judges in each colony meant that it was not generally possible, at least in the early stages, to restrict any one Judge to hearing cases at law only, or cases in equity only. Rather, Judges would serve on both 'sides' of the Court but pretend to have only common-law jurisdiction on one day, and only equitable juris- diction on the next, but never both at once. Similarly, the different procedures applicable in England to actions at law and suits in equity were adopted by the Australian Courts.[6] The division between the administration of law and equity was thus maintained in Australia not by the creation of different Courts for law and equity, but by dividing the procedures of one Court and the time of its Judges.

The idea of solving this problem by uniting the administration of the common law and equity was being discussed in Britain and Australia by the early 1850s at least, and not just by legal experts. For example, the *Register*, South Australia's leading daily newspaper, printed in August 1853 large parts of an article by William Smillie, formerly the Advocate-General of South Australia, in the London *Law Review* of February 1853, in which he advocated that very step.[7]

In his article, Smillie argued that there was no real difference between law and equity other than that artificially created by the acci- dents of legal history. This was shown by the fact that, in other legal systems such as the Scottish, no need was felt for the distinction; in Scots law, with which Smillie was familiar as a Scots lawyer, there was only one set of Courts, not two.[8] This demonstrated that the separate administration of the two systems could be swept away without loss. Indeed, he thought it surprising that this had not already happened in some of the colonies. But inertia stood in the way of this.

> As showing how potent is the agency of mere formalism in fettering the judicial energies, reference may also be made to the Charters of Justice of the colonies; where, under the name and style of 'The Supreme Court', a single tribunal is invested with the jurisdiction and powers of Her Majesty's Superior Courts of Common Law at Westminster, of the High Court of Chancery, and of the Ecclesiastical Courts, there being also usually a commission of Vice-Admiralty. The Judges have legislative authority in regulating practice and procedure by general rules and orders not being inconsistent with the Law of England. It might be supposed that a fairer opportunity for simplifying cumbrous and inappropriate forms could hardly be offered. ... Time has not yet reared on the spot a structure of *vested interests* to oppose improvement; nor can there be any conflict of rival authority, where all power is in the same undivided hands, and because there is a mixed population actively engaged, more inclined to get through business readily than to go in a roundabout way from excessive deference to mere legal antiquities. In such favourable circumstances no doubt considerable relaxation has already been achieved to disarm the terrors of sharp practice. Yet it is often disconcerting to see how many difficulties arise, and how frequently parties are turned round on mere points of practice. In the absence of consolidated rules of procedure, the powers of the Court are said to be distributive, and to be construed referribly [*sic*] with the constitution of the Judicature in England represented in the particular matter. Thus, where no express provision can be pointed to, the question always recurs, 'What is the practice at home?', and litigants and lawyers are alike launched on a sea of doubts all the wider and more perilous by its involving the *moot points* of all the Courts in England. Thus also, the learned Judge takes no notice of any matter depending before himself in

another capacity. The Chancellor [judging cases in equity] cannot act Mr Justice [at common law], nor can the civilian-Admiral help out the Consistory, except according to established precedents at Westminster, Chancery Lane, or Doctors' Commons, as the case may be. Nor, peradventure, would His Honour look into the proceedings on his table, unless put in and proved as coming from the proper custody; although throughout it may be one individual, sitting in the same seat, assisted by the same officials, and with the same parties present and cognisant.[9]

Smillie accordingly called for the abolition of the distinction between equitable and legal jurisdiction in accordance with reforms that had been introduced in New York in 1848.[10]

3. The South Australian experiment

It was in this context that the *Supreme Court Procedure Amendment Act* (S.A.) was enacted in 1853. Its first 174 sections were taken directly from British legislation, mostly the *Common Law Procedure Act* 1852. The novel, uniquely South Australian provisions were at the end, in a section headed 'Claims and Defences' and introduced by a preamble:

And whereas great expenses and delay are oftentimes occasioned to suitors by reason of the inability of the Supreme Court of this Province [of South Australia] to give effect to certain claims and defences, excepting through the medium of the equitable jurisdiction of the said Court, and it is expedient to remove such inability and to provide for the due investigation and decision of such claims and defences – Be it Enacted as follows:

Plaintiff may enforce equitable claims by actions-at-law.

175. It shall be lawful for any plaintiff to sue for and enforce by action-at-law any claim to which he may be entitled on any account or in any capacity whatsoever, although the cause of action or complaint in any such action may have been heretofore cognizable and remediable only under the equitable jurisdiction of the said Court.

Equitable defences may be pleaded.

176. In every action in the Supreme Court it shall be lawful for any

defendant, by leave of the said Court or of any Judge thereof, to avail himself of any defence in equity to the claim sought to be enforced by such action, provided such defence be specially pleaded to the same.

Further sections permitted Courts administering the common law to make orders previously reserved for Courts of equity alone as well as the referral of cases of 'complicated accounts between the plaintiff and the defendant' to a 'Master of the said Court, or to a person to be approved of' by it. None of these provisions had any counterpart in British legislation or in legislation from any other colony that I have been able to find.

In order to understand the purpose and impact on the legal system of ss 175 and 176, we need to be clear about what those sections did and did not do. They were not exactly the same as the English judicature system of 1873, which abandoned the distinct administration of law and equity altogether. Nor did ss 175 and 176 compel anyone to do anything. Rather, s 175 left the existing division between common law and equity intact, but enabled everything that could have been done in Courts of equity also to be done by Courts of common law. Owing to the dissatisfaction expressed with equitable procedure in the nineteenth century, the reverse was not permitted: actions at common law could not be conducted according to the equitable procedure, only *vice versa*.

Section 176 gave effect to a principle that was in fact shortly afterwards to be embodied, in somewhat different words and rather different effect, in the *Common Law Procedure Act* 1854 (U.K.): it enabled a plaintiff to plead equitable defences in actions at law. (Yet again we see that different communities can invent similar solutions to important legal problems at about the same time.) But s 175, permitting entire cases in equity to be conducted under common-law procedures, had no counterpart at all in any British legislation, past or future.

After the introduction of this South Australian innovation, it remained entirely lawful to conduct equitable actions according to the time-honoured equitable procedure. However, a judiciary and Bar which were anxious to carry out the spirit of these sections could easily have brought about an almost total withering-away of equitable procedure. It could simply have been bypassed, and the procedure at law adopted for all cases. However, this did not happen.

4. The passing of the Act

Part of the reason for the limited use made of ss 175 and 176 was the lack of thought given to their practical operation before the Act was passed. This is illustrated by the debates on the Bill in the Legislative Council.

The Bill was introduced into the Legislative Council on 21 July 1853 by the Advocate-General, Richard Hanson, whom we have met wearing various hats at earlier stages in this book. At the second reading on 2 August, Hanson said:

> The Bill was principally founded on an English Act, though there was one part of it entirely new. It would enable a person to plead an equitable defence in a Court of law. In this respect it had gone beyond the English Act in point of reform, but he believed the alteration would be beneficial.

He then referred to objections that had been raised to South Australia's going it alone with this reform.

> It had been objected that all the consequences of such a change could not be foreseen. He did not suppose they could be, and he thought it likely that in twelve months' time further legislation on the subject would be necessary, but he was willing to learn by experience.[11]

There is an interesting anticipation here of the learning by experience that took place after the enactment of the *Real Property Act* four years later and the discovery of defects in it which required amendment.

However, it will be noted that the permission to use common-law procedure in all equitable cases had already been watered down in the speech just quoted into a permission to plead only equitable defences

Richard Davies Hanson, c. 1880
Photograph courtesy of the State Library of South Australia, SLSA: B 5988

in common-law Courts. Indeed, the tone of the Advocate-General's remarks is that of an under-prepared speaker. The other speeches on the Bill, as far as relevant, only add to the impression that the legislature was not quite sure exactly what it was doing. The first was by Edward Gwynne. A few years later, he would become the first locally appointed Judge of the Supreme Court of South Australia.

> Mr GWYNNE felt great satisfaction in being able to add his mite of testimony in approval of the Bill. ... As far as he understood the matter, from perhaps rather a hurried perusal of the Bill, it was not intended to amalgamate the two systems of equity and law. He was free to confess that nothing was more monstrous than the system of equity in vogue in the colony. ... Of all the cases in the Court of equity ... not more than ten had arrived at a legal [!] termination. He would say that however liberal the measure, it would be a dead letter unless it was taken up by the profession; but he had no difficulty in saying that all the members of the profession would lend their aid in forwarding the measure, notwithstanding that some diminution of profits might be the result. In conclusion, he rejoiced to see this first step taken in the onward march of legal reform. ...
>
> Mr FISHER ... would observe that, whilst much, as his hon. and learned friend had observed, depended on the co-operation of the profession to secure to the public all the advantages of the proposed Bill, still more depended on the cordial co-operation of the Judges, the administrators of the law ...[12]

What the attitude of the local legal profession might be was indicated by a letter appearing in the *Register* a few days later from W.C. Belt. Belt was commenting both on the Bill and on the article referred to above by William Smillie that had been reproduced in the *Register* on 12 August, ten days after the second reading debate on the Bill.

> No lawyer who is at all conversant with the distinction that exists between law and equity, as each system is administered in the English Courts of Justice, and who knows that both the subject matters which

fall under the jurisdiction of the Courts of Equity are entirely different from those which are subject to the jurisdiction of Courts of law; and likewise that the remedies administered in these separate Courts also differ in their character and form, will for a moment dream that [the novel provisions of the Bill assimilating law and equity] are really capable of placing law and equity upon a uniform footing in our Courts of Justice. I hesitate not to assert, that no Act could be framed to effect such an object. The only means by which it could be effected is by rules and orders of Court, carefully and deliberately framed, for which no provision whatever has been made in this Bill.[13]

In response to this, 'Aliquis' expressed the view that, if the Bill were passed, 'it will be absurd, and not only absurd, but positively injurious, to maintain the distinction of jurisdictions'[14] between equity and law. But that is just what the Court did.

Debate on the Bill resumed in the Legislative Council on 20 September. According to the *Register*,[15]

On clause 175 being read, which gives power to plead equitable cases in a Court of law,

Mr [J.T.[16]] BAGOT opposed its passing. He differed from the Advocate-General with diffidence, but he was supported in his own opinion by several gentlemen of the legal profession out of doors. The first part of the Bill swept away useless and cumbrous forms, but this and following clauses introduced a new principle. While the Advocate-General followed the law reformers of England he was willing to accompany him; but now he was venturing on new and doubtful alterations.

The objection from J.H. Fisher, another lawyer, to the Bill was based on more solid and practical fears. He

could not quite agree with Mr Bagot. In England it began to be felt necessary to amalgamate law and equity. His difficulty was not one of principle but one of practice. He did not see how the Bill would be able to work practically. ... He thought it would be necessary to give the Judge power to make rules. Perhaps too it would be better for the Bill to amend proceedings in equity to pass before mentioning the present clauses.

In reply, Hanson repeated the lukewarm endorsement of the Bill that he had given on other occasions, although he did at least not misrepresent its effect on this occasion. Hanson

was quite aware that the present Act would need further amendment hereafter, but if we waited to reform till we could see all the consequences of reform we should never do it. He wished to put an end to the anomaly and absurdity of the present system, whereby the same Judge decided the same case on two different principles, according as his face was turned in the legal or equitable direction. ...

It was hard for anyone to disagree with that, and so:

After a few remarks from Messrs FISHER and BAGOT, the clause was passed.

The Advocate-General's lukewarm support for clauses 175 and 176 make one doubt whether he was the source of the ideas contained in them at all.

5. Whose idea was it?

Yet again we find that there is a great deal of uncertainty about who the author of an early South Australian legal innovation was.

a. A Scots lawyer

William Smillie – the Scots lawyer who accepted service of proceedings against the Governor under protest that the Governor could not be compelled to submit to the jurisdiction of the local Courts[17] – did not, unlike Sir Richard Hanson, live long enough to leave many memorials to his presence in South Australia. The *Biographical Index of South*

Australians[18] tells us that he was born in 1811; his memorial in the cemetery at Nairne states that the date of his birth was 25 May 1810. He arrived in South Australia in 1839 and rose rapidly through the ranks. After his first government appointment as a chief clerk and secretary to a government enquiry,[19] he was appointed Emigration Agent in July 1839[20] – an important post in a Province which relied so heavily on free emigration – and then, on 28 March 1840, became the infant Province's Advocate-General, as well as its Crown Solicitor and Public Prosecutor.[21]

Although he relinquished the post of Crown Solicitor on 1 January 1850 to Charles Mann,[22] he occupied the post of Advocate-General until 1851, when his health began to fail although he was only about forty years old. The *South Australian Government Gazette* of 5 June 1851[23] records the granting of eighteen months' sick leave to him and the temporary assumption of the office of Advocate-General by Mann. Smillie left Adelaide for Europe on Saturday 5 July 1851[24] in an effort to restore himself to health. Two weeks later, on 17 July 1851, a further notice appeared in the *Gazette*, signed by the noted explorer Charles Sturt, who was then Colonial Secretary. It stated that Hanson had been appointed 'to act as Advocate-General (during the absence of Mr Smillie)'.[25] Smillie never again filled the office of Advocate-General; he died in Paris on 11 December 1852. In those days of slow communications, the news of his death reached his former friends and colleagues in Adelaide late in April of the next year.[26]

The principal memorial to Smillie the lawyer is the article published posthumously in volume 17 of the *Law Review* of February 1853 entitled 'Civil Procedure in England, America, and Scotland, Collated: A Travelling Opinion', and quoted at length earlier. The writer was named simply as 'a colonial Crown lawyer', but in a discussion of the desirability of fusing the administration of law and equity in the same issue,[27] Smillie is mentioned as the author. The commentary records Smillie's death in Paris on 11 December 1852 and adds, 'He was much esteemed by all who knew him, and we consider his early death a great loss to the cause of scientific Law Reform'.

It could be argued, however, that Smillie could not be responsible for the Act of 1853, however much he might have sympathised with its aims, for the Bill was introduced into the Legislative Council more than seven months after his death in Paris. The date of the Bill is, however, moved back at least a year by my discovery in the South Australian Archives[28] of a first draft of it. Although this handwritten draft is undated, it bears a notation, signed by N.S. Quick, who was Clerk to the Advocate-General,[29] indicating that it was printed on 2 August 1852. As the Legislative Council did not sit on this date, this can mean only that the Bill was printed for internal purposes within the department.

As well as this handwritten draft of the Bill, there are also in the Archives several printed versions of the Bill, all of which bear the date 1852 and include various alterations and emendations in handwriting.

Intriguingly, the draft Bills contain only sections corresponding to the 'Claims and Defences' portion of the Act of 1853, that is, to the uniquely South Australian sections beginning at s 175. The Bill clearly underwent development during its various printings, as what appear to be later versions of it contain more and more of the sections which eventually became part of that portion of the Act. But in all these drafts of the Bill, the sections are by themselves. They are not part of a larger Bill also, and principally, adopting English measures, as the Act eventually did. This strengthens the supposition that the idea of fusing the administration of law and equity was a South Australian invention prior to any developments in England.

We cannot know whether Smillie was ultimately responsible for the idea behind the Act of 1853. Certainly, the issue was close to his heart. It may be his handwriting in the draft of the original Bill.[30] Alternatively, Smillie may have suggested the idea to Hanson, or left behind in the Advocate-General's office, at his departure in the middle of 1851, some indication of the contents of the Bill or of his forth-coming article in the *Law Review* in February 1853. Having regard to the delays in publishing and communication in those days, the article could easily have been drafted eighteen months or so before it was finally printed. Hanson, it seems, merely seized on the idea of fusion when pressed for suggestions for the reform of the law.

b. Hanson's contribution

Although Richard Hanson introduced the Bill which became the Act of 1853, the evidence suggests that he merely seized on the idea contained in ss 175 and 176 in order to please the Governor, Sir Henry Young.

The story of Hanson's involvement in the Act of 1853 starts with a proposal to establish in the Province of South Australia what today would be called a law reform commission. This had been proposed by John Baker on 5 November 1852, as he was waiting to hear what the Colonial Office would say about the first attempt at passing legislation to permit Borrow & Goodiar and the other claimants to sue the government. Baker mentioned a large number of defects in the law which he hoped that such a commission would look at, although the division between law and equity was not one of them.[31]

The proposed law reform commission – an idea which was far ahead of its time – was never set up. Although the Legislative Council agreed to it, neither the Governor, Sir Henry Young,[32] nor Hanson was keen on the idea, the latter apparently fearing the cost involved and the lack of political recognition and reward until several years of work had been done.[33] Some indication of Hanson's attitude towards colonial reforms at this time may also be gleaned from his speech on the Proceedings in Equity Regulation Bill in September 1852, in which he said that he 'would have hesitated to do more than follow in the wake of the English legislature' and that 'he had, at first, some doubts as to the expediency of introducing the Bill to the consideration of the House, until the views of the English government were first ascertained'.[34]

However, the Governor clearly felt unable to ignore completely the call for law reform, and, on 18 December 1852, a letter was sent from the Colonial Secretary's Office on the Governor's instructions to the Law Officers of the Crown in South Australia, a designation that surprisingly included Mr Justice Cooper as well as Hanson and the Crown Solicitor. It said that, although the Governor

has not felt it expedient to accede – under existing circumstances – to the Address of the Legislative Council of this Province, moving him to appoint a Commission of Legal Inquiry, yet he would esteem it an important service rendered to the Public, and calculated, therefore, to enhance your own reputation in the eyes of Her Majesty's Government, if you would report to him any plans of reform that may have occurred to you in your local experience as desirable to introduce into the Law and Practice now governing the Court of Justice and its office[r]s ...

His Excellency would request your consideration of the expediency of abolishing the technical forms which distinguish Equity from Law, and of providing for the fusion of Law and Equity into one and the same system and mode of procedure; the Court in Equity deciding the questions before it, without the delays and costs of reference to the Master, and the Court in Common Law exercising its jurisdiction as freed from antiquated forms and technicalities ...[35]

After suggesting reforms to the law of registration of deeds, the letter closed by expressing the hope, in terms similar to those in Smillie's article in the *Law Review*, that 'it will be found possible in South Australia, during its infancy and consequently before the pre-scription of age and usage shall be pleaded against reforms', to reform the practice and procedure of the higher Courts. It is not surprising that the Governor should be aware of legal matters, for Sir Henry Young had been educated at the Inner Temple and served as a Judge in British Guiana.[36] Clearly, however, Sir Henry was not the initiator of the Bill for the Act of 1853, for it had been printed over four months before the letter from the Colonial Secretary's Office.

The response from the Law Officers to his request for suggestions was initially unenthusiastic. It was necessary for the Colonial Secretary to write to Mr Justice Cooper, Hanson and the Crown Solicitor almost five months later, on 7 May 1853, to remind them that a reply to the Governor's request was still outstanding.[37] This prompted responses both from Cooper,[38] which is of little interest for our purposes, and Hanson. Hanson's reply was dated 16 May 1853, that is, nine days after the reminder was sent. Given its length – more than five pages of closely written handwriting on A3-size pages – I suspect that, in the time available, Hanson did little more than search around for proposals already in existence in order to cover up his failure to reply earlier. One of those proposals was the merger of the administration of common law and equity in the manner already suggested by the Governor.

After referring at some length to the difficulties of reform, Hanson's letter suggests:

> This division [between common law and equity] appears to me to be indefensible in principle and cumbrous and inconvenient in practice. It is difficult indeed to imagine that a System can be either wise or just under which the same individual acting as Judge in the same Court at the same time and in reference to the same subject matter applies a different rule according as the proceedings before him are or are not entitled 'Equitable Jurisdiction'. Either the Rules of Equity or those of law should prevail, and at any rate the practical absurdity should no longer be permitted to exist of allowing one party to enforce a claim or the other to avail himself of a defence on one side of the Court of which the same Judge sitting upon the other side restrains him by injunction from reaping the fruit. I think therefore that one principal object of legislation as regards procedure should be to abolish the distinction between Courts of law and Equity, substituting for the two inconsistent and conflicting rules which at present exist one rule which shall be enforced in the same Court and by the same method of proceeding.[39]

He went on to suggest a procedure for enforcing claims under a fused system. Responding to this letter on 26 May 1853, the Colonial Secretary, acting on the Governor's instructions, requested Hanson to prepare a Bill 'to abolish [the] distinction of equity and law'.[40] As we have already seen, however, there was no need for Hanson to do this, as a Bill had already been prepared. One wonders, if he had known of this fact when writing on 16 May, why he did not mention it then. Indeed, one wonders why he did not reply sooner if he had known all along that the Bill existed. It may be that this fact became known to Hanson only after he had asked his officers to assist him to comply with the Governor's request of 26 May.

At all events, on opening the fourth session of the Legislative

Council on 21 July, the Governor said that he had not agreed to the proposal for a general law reform commission. However, he did have certain plans for law reform. One of these was to adopt an English Act reforming procedure, which had proved successful in England. His Excellency expressed the hope

> that equal success will attend those portions of the proposed measure which are not based upon an English precedent – in which it is proposed to facilitate references to arbitration, and to enable equitable claims and defences to be made available by means of the simpler and less costly forms of common law.[41]

It was this Bill that became the Act of 1853.

If Hanson did copy the provisions of the Bill for the Act of 1853 from Smillie, it may not have been the first time. On 22 September 1852, a letter to the editor of the *Adelaide Times*[42] had appeared, charging Hanson with appropriating the labours of others in the drafting of Bills. But given the inadequacy of the surviving evidence, other possible explanations cannot be ruled out. It may be merely coincidental that Hanson proposed a reform which had just been put forward by his predecessor in office.

c. A British idea?

After all, fusing the administration of law and equity was a topic that was being discussed by many lawyers at this time. On 19 November 1852, James Whiteside, Solicitor-General for Ireland, introduced into the House of Commons the Bill for the Act that eventually became the *Common Law Procedure Amendment Act (Ireland) 1853*. The long title of the Bill, unlike that of the Act, gave as one of its objectives 'to enable the Superior Courts of Common Law to give effect to certain legal rights and just defences, so far as might be, without the expense and delay of a resort to a Court of Equity'.[43] It proposed to make certain equitable rights enforceable in Courts of law. Although these proposals did not go nearly as far as the South Australian Act of 1853, and, in particular, did not even reach the statute book, it was stated in the

House of Lords during debate that the Bill adopted 'the principle of fusion'[44] in certain areas.

Some form of fusion or blending of jurisdiction was also considered by the Commissioners appointed to Inquire into the Process, Practice and System of Pleading in the (English) Court of Chancery, whose report the House of Commons ordered to be printed on 30 March 1852. Those Commissioners recommended that without:

> abolishing the distinction between Law and Equity, or blending the Courts into one Court of universal Jurisdiction, a practical and effectual remedy for many of the evils in question may be found in such a transfer or blending of jurisdiction, coupled with such other practical amendments, as will render each Court competent to administer complete justice in the cases which fall under its cognizance. We think that the jurisdiction now exercised by Courts of Equity may be conferred upon Courts of Law, and that the jurisdiction now exercised by Courts of Law may be conferred upon Courts of Equity, to such an extent as to render both Courts competent to administer entire justice, without the parties in the one Court being obliged to resort to the aid of the other. Under such a system the number of cases where persons may, at their option, resort to either a Court of Law or to a Court of Equity, will doubtless be considerably increased. But this does not appear to us to constitute any substantial objection. There is, at present, a large ground common to the jurisdiction and procedure of both Courts.[45]

This solution is similar to that adopted in South Australia by the Act of 1853. The obvious difference is that the South Australian Act permitted Courts of common law to exercise equitable jurisdiction, but not the reverse. The reason for this was simply the low regard in which equitable procedures were held in South Australia in the 1850s. Did the Commissioners' Report had some influence on the South Australian legislation?

As with the Torrens system, the introduction of which also coincided with the publication of an English report with a vaguely similar thrust, it seems very unlikely that this is anything more than coincidence. Admittedly, an article in the *Register* of 9 September 1852[46] appears to imply that the some of the colonists were already aware of at least the general tenor of the Commissioners' Report.

But as we saw above, a hand-written draft of the Bill for the South Australian Act of 1853 bears the notation that it was printed on 2 August 1852. English news from March and April 1852 was only beginning to arrive in the Province then. The *Adelaide Times* contains in its edition of 17 July 1852 English news up to 6 April, and the *Register* has English news up to 5 April on 15 July. Even if the Commissioners' Report had been sent to Adelaide as soon as it was ordered to be printed, it could have reached Adelaide only about two weeks before the handwritten draft of the Bill was printed. This, surely, would not have been enough time for the principles contained in the Report to come to the attention of a busy Advocate-General and for him to digest them and to draft and have printed a Bill based on them. This is especially so given the glacial pace at which Hanson responded to the Governor's request of December 1852 for proposals to reform the law. And any delay in sending the Report would have been fatal, for what appears to be the next ship bearing news would have come too late: it left England on 11 April, and its arrival is recorded one day after the Bill was printed, on 3 August.[47]

Finally, and conclusively, one would expect that, if ss 175 and 176 had been based on the Commissioners' Report, Hanson would have said so when they were being considered by the Legislative Council or in the correspondence which has survived. This would have been only natural in an era in which reliance on English reforms was routine and mostly sensible given the small size of the Australian colonies and their common practice of looking mainly to English reforms (which also promoted legal uniformity within the Australian colonies). I mentioned above that Hanson said that the Bill for the Act of 1853 was 'principally founded on an English Act', although one portion of it was 'entirely new'. There is no reason to assume that only half this statement was true. Objections were made in the Legislative Council to ss 175 and 176 on the grounds of a lack of English precedent for them.

They could have been easily answered if an idea suggested in an English report had been the basis of the proposal.

Just as with the Torrens system, therefore, the similarity is pure coincidence; and it should not surprise us that, in relation to one of the great questions facing law reformers in the nineteenth century, a similar idea should have occurred to two sets of people at approximately the same time.

6. The reform fails

Alex Castles remarks that 'whether [ss 175 and 176] had a strong impact on the actual practice of the Supreme Court is a moot point'.[48] Research shows that the effect of the Act on the practice of the Court was very small indeed.

The first sign of the ineffectiveness of ss 175 and 176 became evident in the new Rules of Court made under the Act of 1853, drafted after a meeting of the legal profession held at the end of December 1853 'to assist the Judges with suggestions'[49] in relation to the content of the Rules. The Rules of Court, made by the two Judges, Mr Justice Cooper and Mr Justice Boothby, under the Act of 1853 and published in the *South Australian Government Gazette* on 5 January 1854,[50] contained no reference at all to ss 175 and 176 or to any machinery by which their potential could be realised. This was despite the fact that s 186 of the Act[51] clearly would have authorised such rules.

The Rules were forwarded by the Judges to Attorney-General Hanson without any explanation of the failure to take advantage of ss 175 and 176. But Hanson did not remark on this omission, saying merely that he did not 'at present see any ground for suggesting any alterations in these Rules'.[52] Those were hardly the words of someone committed to the idea of fusing the administration of law and equity as soon as possible. Indeed, Hanson had said in the Legislative Council on 29 November 1853, hardly more than a month after the Act of 1853 had received Royal assent, that he 'despaired of seeing any very great improvement being effected in the procedures in equity at the Supreme Court. But ... the time had scarcely arrived for abolishing its jurisdiction in matters of equity.'[53]

On 16 February 1854, shortly after the Rules under Act No. 5 of 1853 had been published, the *Gazette*[54] contained Rules under Act No. 14 of 1853, passed to simplify proceedings in the equitable jurisdiction of the Court. These Rules, too, contained no reference to the possibility of transferring cases in equity to the common-law 'side' of the Court. Rather, their very detail suggested that a separate equitable jurisdiction was expected to flourish for years to come. So too does the passing of Act No. 14 of 1853, the long title of which was 'An Act to amend the practice and proceeding in the Equitable Jurisdiction of the Supreme Court of South Australia'. It contained only one very brief mention of ss 175 and 176 of Act No. 5 of 1853.

The tendency towards separating the equitable jurisdiction of the Court from its common-law jurisdiction was continued by Act No. 31 of 1855–56, which consolidated the statute law of that time relating to the Supreme Court into one statute. Like previous statutes, it contained separate conferrals on the Court of legal and equitable jurisdiction respectively – although, also like its predecessors, it contained no statutory requirement to divide the Court into 'sides'. Such a division was, however, assumed by the *Common Law Procedure Act* 1862, which referred in its preamble to the 'Common Law Side of the Supreme Court of South Australia', and in s 1 to its 'equitable jurisdiction'. The climax of this process was undoubtedly the *Equity Act* 1866, which, while generally a mere copy of various English statutes, provided for the appointment of a Primary Judge in Equity 'to sit, hear and determine, without the assistance of the other Judges, or either of them, all causes and matters at any time depending in the said Supreme Court, in its equitable jurisdiction' – the beginnings of a separate Court of equity.

For their part, the Judges ignored ss 175 and 176 not only in drafting the Rules of Court, but also in deciding cases. Research in the early years after the passing of the Act is handicapped by the absence of regular law reports. But when the *South Australian Law Reports* do start (with volume number zero!) in 1865, the same year as the official Law Reports began in England, they are divided into cases at law and cases in equity. This practice continued until shortly after South

Benjamin Boothby, c. 1865
Photograph courtesy of the State Library of South Australia, SLSA: B 46869

Australia adopted the English reforms in 1878. And some indications of the complete neglect of ss 175 and 176 can be gleaned from other early sources. Thus, for example, in *McDonald* v. *Galbraith*[55] Mr Justice Boothby is reported to have said that a defence of partnership 'can only be raised by equitable plea. It is no answer to common law.' It is recorded that the lawyers involved looked up the books, but the report suggests that no one went to s 176 of the Act of 1853. Perhaps the greatest indication of the neglect from which ss 175 and 176 suffered is that Mr Justice Boothby never had occasion to hold them invalid because they were contrary to the law of England, as he probably would have if they had come before him.[56] Those sections are not mentioned in any of the many papers calling for his removal, in part because of his excessive invalidation of local statutes, the details of which they recite in relentless detail.[57]

The Primary Judge in Equity, appointed under the *Equity Act* 1866,[58] was Mr Justice Gwynne, whom we met earlier in this chapter as a member of the Legislative Council in 1853, when it had ss 175 and 176 in front of it for debate and adoption. Then, he expressed his opinion that ss 175 and 176 would be dead letters unless taken up by the profession. As Primary Judge in Equity, Gwynne continued the absurd division not just of the Court, but of individual Judges into 'sides', holding that he could not decide a common-law or other non-equitable case if he was sitting '*as* Primary Judge in Equity'.[59] He could not, when sitting in that capacity, step out of the role of Primary Judge in order to hear a common-law case as a 'normal' Judge with full powers. Indeed, he even caused a minor controversy and a clash with the government by claiming the right to be relieved of all common-law business.[60]

As Chief Justice of South Australia from 1861, Richard Hanson also continued to talk in terms of a division between the two jurisdictions,[61] even referring at one stage to a 'Court of Equity Appeals'[62] rather than simply to the Supreme Court sitting as an appeals Court. And just as the Primary Judge in Equity would not hear common-law cases, equitable cases could not be heard by the Court (even if it included Mr Justice Gwynne) sitting in its common-law jurisdiction,[63] despite s 175. By 1874, we find Gwynne, sitting as Primary Judge, holding that he had sole jurisdiction in equity.[64]

Attempts were, however, made by the lawyers – as Mr Gwynne M.L.C. had predicted – to breathe life into ss 175 and 176. In *Dyke* v. *Elliot*,[65] Mr Strangways for the defendant argued that s 176 gave him the right to plead an equitable defence in an action at common law. While Chief Justice Hanson, with whom Justices Gwynne and Wearing agreed, thought that he should not be allowed to do so because of excessive delay, and the technical details of the case some-what complicated the matter, the Court did not exactly go out of its way to promote the use of s 176. The Court's comments during argu-ment appear to indicate that it was anxious to avoid applying that untested and unfamiliar provision if some other procedural rule could be found to avoid the issue. Mr Justice Gwynne stated that the legis-lature 'should have provided the machinery' for the operation of s 176. It was not for the Court to 're-model the Act'[66] – although it is not explained why the Judges could not make Rules of Court to provide the machinery, as the Act contemplated.

A more determined attempt to mobilise the Act of 1853 was made in 1871 in *North Australian Company* v. *Blackmore*.[67] In this case two South Australian legal innovations were mobilised at once, for it was a case under the *Claimants Relief Act* against the government; Blackmore was the nominal defendant appointed under that Act. It was an action at common law arising out of the alleged failure of the South Australian government, then responsible for the Northern Territory, to survey land in the Territory as required by legislation. According to the report, 'the defendant applied in Chambers for leave to plead an equitable plea. The effect of the proposed plea, which was very com-plicated, was that time was not of the essence of the contract.'[68]

After attempts to plead the equitable plea under other statutes had failed, the defendant government was thrown back on the Act of 1853, clearly something which it did only as a last resort. It argued that the Court should give effect to s 175 as 'a bold attempt on the part of the Legislature to fuse law and equity altogether'.[69] In the course of an 'elaborate speech'[70] made by Rupert Ingleby, counsel for the

defendant, on 29 May 1871, in which his 'principal point' was the Act
of 1853, the following exchange took place:

> MR JUSTICE GWYNNE – Has the provision ever been acted upon?
> [Mr Ingleby:] No.
>
> *Stow Q.C. (amicus curiæ)* – There has been one case. It was simply a
> balance of partnership accounts.
>
> CHIEF JUSTICE HANSON – It was with reference to that sort of
> thing it was introduced. Wherever a jury could say 'Yes' or 'No',
> although of an equitable nature, it seemed more proper that Common
> Law should be applicable to it.[71]

When argument continued on 9 June 1871, Chief Justice Hanson,
according to a newspaper report,[72] drew counsel's attention to the
need for leave under s 176 and stated that it

> was necessary to prove, firstly, that the plea was one which could con-
> veniently be tried by a jury; and, secondly, that it was a plea upon which
> the simple judgment of the Court in the verdict would be sufficient . . .

Chief Justice Hanson is clearly engaged in some revision of history
here in order not to have to apply a moribund statute. There is no evidence in his writings or speeches almost twenty years earlier that
ss 175 and 176 had been intended merely to extend jury trial to simpler
equitable matters. As we have seen, not all his statements back then
reflected a deep knowledge of the changes proposed by the Bill. But
none of them mentioned juries. In the Committee stage in the
Legislative Council, for example, he had said that he 'wished to put an
end to the anomaly and absurdity of the present system, whereby the
same Judge decided the same case on two different principles,
according as his face was turned in the legal or equitable direction'.

Despite this discouraging start, the defendant continued to try to
breathe life into the statute, arguing that there was no reason why it
should not be applied and that the failure of the Judges to make rules
for its application under s 186[73] should not prejudice the defendant.[74]

The defendant's plea, however, was disallowed. The Chief Justice stated that he had 'formed an opinion, which I think it would be impossible to shake',[75] that the plea failed on substantive grounds relating to the defendant's ability to perform the contract concerned. A final decision on whether ss 175 and 176 could be revived was accordingly not made, but the Court did everything to discourage the use of the indigenous South Australian statute. The sections were not mentioned in the unsuccessful appeal to the Privy Council.[76] As Charles Mann, Attorney-General and son of the first Advocate-General, said in Parliament on 4 August 1871, 'Whether the colony had an equitable defence was one thing, and whether they had a legal defence was altogether another thing'.[77]

In 1876 in *McCulloch* v. *Whitting*,[78] the last recorded attempt to mobilise s 175 was also repelled by the Court on the substantive grounds that no equitable rights existed to apply at common law, and that therefore there was no need to consider the procedural reforms which that section sought to make. Until the end of the old system in 1878, the Court continued to enforce the distinction between law Courts and Courts of equity.[79]

Mr Justice Gwynne, at least, was not opposed to the adoption of the English reform of 1873, having said in Court as early as 30 May 1876 that 'I hope we shall soon have the new Judicature Bill';[80] he did not, however, consider whether the Bill was necessary at all, having regard to what had been added to the local statute book when he had been a member of the Legislative Council in 1853, and the ability of the Judges to make Rules of Court. But Mr Justice Gwynne was not alone in his amnesia. The debates in the South Australian Parliament on the introduction of the judicature system proceeded without any mention of ss 175 and 176.[81] Parliament did not even take the trouble to remove them from the statute book in favour of the new system.[82]

Chief Justice Hanson, unfortunately, did not live to see the judicature system in operation in South Australia. He died suddenly in February 1876, a few days before he was to give his inaugural address as first Chancellor of the University of Adelaide.

7. Reasons for the failure of the experiment

This is the only one of the South Australian legal innovations dealt with in this book that failed utterly to achieve any of its aims. As we saw, it was applied in one solitary case, and then disappeared from view for ever.

Why was it so unsuccessful?

It cannot be that the reform was simply not needed, for, as we have seen, a similar reform, made about twenty years later and imported from England, is still the basis of the modern law of procedure and Court structure. Other reasons will have to be sought.

The first reason may already be obvious from the discussion above: the South Australian legislature did not unambiguously decide, in this area of the law, whether it was a faithful follower of English reforms or a creative reformer in its own right. Thus, the home-grown South Australian reforms embodied in ss 175 and 176 of Act No. 5 of 1853 competed with English reforms adopted in South Australia, such as those contained in the earlier sections of Act No. 5 of 1853, in Act No. 14 of 1853 and in the *Equity Act* 1866 – and, eventually, with the major English reform of 1873 itself. The English statutes won.

One reason for the preference shown for the adopted English statutes was the incremental nature of the reforms embodied in them compared with the sudden change that would have been introduced by a thoroughgoing application of ss 175 and 176. It is much easier to introduce incremental reforms over twenty-five years from 1853 to 1878 than to change the system in one fell swoop.

The ambiguous attitude of those immediately responsible for the enactment of ss 175 and 176 also played an important role in the failure of the experiment. As we have just seen, Richard Hanson was very reluctant to apply those provisions as a Judge which he had introduced as a legislator. And even as a legislator, his despair of any improvement in the equitable jurisdiction of the Court does not sit well with his sponsorship of ss 175 and 176 in 1853.

The other Judges too failed to make use of the innovation, and the Court never made rules to allow those provisions to operate. Mr Justice Boothby's ferocious insistence that the law of South Australia must not be contrary to the law of England would certainly have deterred lawyers from relying on ss 175 and 176 before him. For the others, the familiar system triumphed over the unfamiliar. Sections 175 and 176 were trotted out by the Bar only in desperation – as a last resort when the adopted English reforms, for one reason or another, were not applicable.

From a technical point of view, the principal flaw in ss 175 and 176 was that they gave an option to litigators. Rather than effecting a compulsory fusion of the administration of law and equity by entirely abolishing the equitable jurisdiction and transferring all its cases to the legal 'side' of the Court, or directing each Judge not to apply only law or equity at any one time, ss 175 and 176 merely permitted equitable claims to be made the subject of actions at law. Inertia and familiarity with the old system meant that advantage was not taken of the opportunity offered.

It would be interesting to speculate what the result might have been if this South Australian reform adopted in 1853 had borne fruit. South Australia might have ended up, at least for a few years and possibly even up to the present day, with a procedural system based on an indigenous innovation rather than on the British model that prevailed elsewhere in the British Empire. Instead, the South Australian reforms of 1853 were destined to be of historical interest only almost from the day of their enactment. Rather than being the road to thorough procedural reform, they were a detour on which hardly anyone travelled.

Notes

1   A full list of all the statutes in each State and descriptions of the circumstances surrounding their enactment may be found in numerous sources such as Bennett, 'Historical Trends in Australian Law Reform' (1969) 9 UWALR 211, 227–232; Castles, *An Australian Legal History*, pp. 358–361.

2   More details of the system as described in this and the following paragraphs may be found in texts such as Mr Justice Meagher/Mr Justice Heydon/Leeming, *Equity: Doctrines and Remedies* (4th ed., Butterworths, Sydney 2002), Ch. 1.

3   *Register*, 23 April 1856, p. 2; *Adelaide Times*, 23 April 1856, p. 3.

4   9 September 1852, p. 2.

5   Cooper, (2003) 3 Ox U Clth Law Jo 201, 207f; Fox, (1950) 23 ALJ 489, 489f.

6 Castles, *Australian Legal History*, pp. 347f.
7 (1853) 17 Law Review 217.
8 (1853) 17 Law Review 217, 220–224.
9 (1853) 17 Law Review 217, 224f (emphases in original).
10 (1853) 17 Law Review 217, 225–230. The system in New York had already been noticed in England: see the *Supplement to the Appendix to the First Report of Her Majesty's Commissioners Appointed to Inquire into the Process, Practice and System of Pleading in the Court of Chancery &c.* (H.M.S.O., London 1852), reprinted in *British Parliamentary Papers: Legal Administration General* Vol. 8 (Irish University Press, Shannon 1970), pp. 369–388.
11 *Register*, 3 August 1853, p. 3.
12 *Register*, 3 August 1853, p. 3.
13 *Register*, 15 August 1853, p. 3.
14 *Register*, 23 August 1853, p. 3.
15 21 September 1853, pp. 2f.
16 See Pike, *Paradise of Dissent*, p. 467; above, p. 121 fn 21.
17 See above, p. 70.
18 Statton (ed.), vol. 4 p. 1500.
19 *Register*, 1 June 1839, p. 1.
20 *South Australian Government Gazette*, 11 July 1839, p. 3. The previous Emigration Agent had been removed for indulging himself in disputes with the Governor: *Register*, 13 July 1839, p. 3.
21 *South Australian Government Gazette*, 2 April 1840, p. 1.
22 *South Australian Government Gazette*, 3 January 1850, p. 1.
23 At p. 385.
24 *Register*, 7 July 1851, p. 2.
25 *South Australian Government Gazette*, 17 July 1851, p. 495.
26 Death notices appeared in the *Register* of 27 April 1853, p. 3, and 3 May 1853, p. 3. The latter consisted of an extract of a death notice published in a journal known as the *Edinburgh Witness*.
27 At pp. 439f.
28 GRG 1/15.
29 *South Australian Government Gazette*, 28 October 1847, p. 342. South Australian Parliamentary Papers, no. 10A of 1867, p. 22, recorded that Quick, Secretary to the Attorney-General, had resigned on 8 February 1866.
30 The author has compared the handwriting with that of manuscripts known to be by Smillie and other early officials' handwriting. At least to his untrained eyes, there appear to be insufficient points of distinction in Smillie's handwriting to enable a firm conclusion to be drawn on this point. Smillie's handwriting may be contrasted in this respect with, for example, that of Professor F.W. Pennefather, whose handwriting is instantly recognisable and which the author came to know intimately while writing 'Dr Pennefather's Criminal Code for South Australia' (2002) 31 CLWR 62.
31 Votes and Proceedings of the Legislative Council, 5 November 1852, paras. 4f; *Register*, 6 November 1852, p. 3.
32 Hague, *History of the Law*, p. 967.

33 Brown, *Sir Richard Davies Hanson: A Biography* (unpublished, University of Adelaide Special Collections, Adelaide 1940), p. 85.
34 *Register*, 17 September 1852, p. 3.
35 GRG 24/6/1852/1033.
36 *Australian Dictionary of Biography*, Vol. 6 p. 452.
37 GRG 24/6/1853/326.
38 GRG 24/4/1853/440; CSO 1401/1853.
39 GRG 1/6/1853/303 = CSO 1237/1853; see also GRG 1/1/7/1853/42.
40 GRG 1/1/1853/43 = GRG 24/4/1853/375.
41 South Australian Parliamentary Papers, no. 1 of 1853, p. 3.
42 At p. 3.
43 Quoted in Hansard's Parliamentary Debates, 19 November 1852, col. 257; see also *ibid.*, 29 November 1852, col. 753. The Bill is reproduced in House of Commons Papers, 1852–1853 vol. II, pp. 1ff; later versions of the Bill during its passage through Parliament are in the same volume.
44 Hansard's Parliamentary Debates, 26 July 1853, col. 804.
45 *First Report of Her Majesty's Commissioners Appointed to Inquire into the Process, Practice and System of Pleading in the Court of Chancery &c.* (H.M.S.O., London 1852), p. 3, reprinted in *British Parliamentary Papers: Legal Administration General* Vol. 8 (Irish University Press, Shannon 1970), p. 47.
46 At p. 2.
47 *Register*, 3 August 1852, p. 3.
48 Castles, *An Australian Legal History*, p. 353 fn 52.
49 *Register*, 2 January 1854, p. 3.
50 At pp. 7ff.
51 'It shall be lawful for the Judges of the said Court, from time to time, to make any such general rules and orders for the effectual execution of this Act, and of the intention and object thereof, ... and for the regulation of the forms of proceedings as in their judgment shall be necessary and proper ...'.
52 CSO 71/1854.
53 *Register*, 30 November 1853, p. 3.
54 At pp. 125ff.
55 See South Australian Parliamentary Papers, no. 22 of 1867, p. CXXXVII; for the result of the case, see *ibid.*, p. CCXXIV. The case is reported on another point in (1866) 0 SALR 71.
56 *Cf. Dawes* v. *Quarrel* (1865) 0 SALR 1, 23 (Chief Justice Hanson, dissenting). Interestingly, however, Mr Justice Boothby did apply s 182 of the Act of 1853, which authorised Judges to direct juries to find special verdicts: Hague, *Boothby J.*, p. 23.
57 *E.g.*, South Australian Parliamentary Papers, no. 22 of 1867.
58 See also Act No. 23 of 1870–71.
59 Re Real Property Act *1861*; ex parte *McEllister* (1867) 1 SALR 41, 42 (emphasis in original). *Cf.* also Re *Padman and the* Insolvent Act *1860* (1867) 1 SALR 39, 40; Ex parte *the District Council of Glanville*; Re *an order to sell section no. 89 in the Hundred of Yatala in the said district* (1872) 6 SALR 96.
60 South Australian Parliamentary Debates, 15 November 1870, col. 1336f.
61 *West Kanmantoo Mining* v. *English, Scottish and Australian Chartered Bank* (1868) 2 SALR 237, 251.

62 *West Kanmantoo Mining* v. *English, Scottish and Australian Chartered Bank* (1868) 2 SALR 279, 282.
63 Re *Winnall and the* Real Property Act *1861* (1871) 5 SALR 73.
64 Re District Councils Act *1858 and the District Council of Glanville*; ex parte *Hindmarsh* (1874) 8 SALR 255, 270f.
65 (1870) 4 SALR 128.
66 (1870) 4 SALR 128, 130.
67 (1871) 5 SALR 149.
68 (1871) 5 SALR 149, 150.
69 (1871) 5 SALR 149, 151.
70 *Advertiser*, 30 May 1871, p. 3.
71 (1871) 5 SALR 149, 152. This report was clearly taken from the *Register*'s more detailed account of proceedings: 30 May 1871, p. 3. However, the *Register*'s account adds little of relevance to this issue considered here, beyond recording that Mr Ingleby also attempted to argue the intermediate position that s 175 was applicable only 'in certain more simple cases'.
72 *Advertiser*, 10 June 1871, p. 3; a slightly less detailed report appeared in the same day's *Register*, p. 6.
73 See above, fn 51.
74 (1871) 5 SALR 149, 153f.
75 (1871) 5 SALR 149, 156.
76 *Blackmore* v. *North Australian Co.* (1873) LR 5 PC 24. As this report states (at p. 39), leave to appeal against the decision of 9 June 1871 refusing leave to plead the equitable defence under the Act of 1853 was initially refused by the Supreme Court. However, the newspaper report (*Register*, 25 September 1871, p. 3) does not make it clear whether the Court, in so doing, relied on the substantive grounds relating to the defendant's ability to perform the contract or on the pleading point based on the Act of 1853.
77 South Australian Parliamentary Debates, 4 August 1871, col. 105.
78 (1876) 10 SALR 98, 115f (decision affirmed (1877) 10 SALR 248).
79 See, *e.g.*, *van Damme* v. *Bloxam* (1875) 9 SALR 27, 32; *Ferrett* v. *Clark* (1876) 10 SALR 202, 209.
80 *Kelly* v. *Cameron* (1876) 10 SALR 65, 66.
81 The inability of an Act to operate because the Judges would not make the necessary rules was raised during the debate on the *Supreme Court Bill* 1878 in Parliament on 15 October 1878 (South Australian Parliamentary Debates, col. 1170). It was not stated, however, which Act had been thus frustrated.
82 The sections in fact remained on the South Australian statute book until repealed as part of the general tidying-up of the statute book undertaken at about the time of the State's Centenary: *Supreme Court Act* 1935 s 3 and Schedule. They remained on the statute book of the Northern Territory until 1965: *Supreme Court Ordinance Repeal Ordinance* 1965 Ord. 2 (2) & Second Schedule. It would seem, however, that ss 175 and 176 were repealed impliedly by the *Supreme Court Act* 1878, for s 4 provided that the procedure and practice of the Court should be exercised 'in the manner provided by this Act or by Rules of Court, and not otherwise'. See also *Supreme Court Procedure Further Amendment Act* 1858 s 1; *Palmer* v. *Andrews* (1874) 8 SALR 281, 282f.

8. Concluding remarks

All the reforms, other than the procedural reform of 1853, that have been dealt with in this book were outstanding successes, and most spread more or less rapidly to the rest of Australia and, in some cases, to other parts of the world. Not only the outstanding example of the Torrens system, successful probably beyond the wildest dreams of anyone when it was proposed, but also the *Associations Incorporation Act* 1858 and the *Claimants Relief Act*, demonstrate that there were situations in which the tiny South Australian legislature could come up with innovations which were decidedly superior to the inherited English common law and contemporary English statutes.[1] This was so despite the vastly greater resources of experience, knowledge and wealth that were available in the centre of the Empire at the time.

There was, it can now be seen, an outpouring of legal creativity in South Australia at around the time the colonists gained the power to govern themselves in the early 1850s. And it was that rare phenomenon, successful and useful legal creativity – change that was also progress.

This fact should not be forgotten in the debates about the origin of the Torrens system: it was not the only legal innovation South Australia ever contributed to the world, but part of a series of home-grown innovatory statutes in the 1850s.

Retrospectively, the Torrens system can be identified as the greatest of the 1850s reforms – although if the procedural reform of 1853 had been made a success by the Judges and legal profession and then spread elsewhere, the Torrens system might have faced serious competition – but it does not need to be explained on the hypothesis that it was an isolated event that can only have been inspired by an outside source. It was part of the innovatory and creative movement of the 1850s which also gave us reforms such as the associations incorporation and claims-against-the-government legislation. And all these other reforms were home-grown inventions, developed and brought into existence without any help from outside as a creative reaction to defects that had been exposed in the pre-existing law.

That the creative cast of mind extended even beyond the ranks of lawyers and the legislature is shown by the fact that a grand jury of ordinary citizens called, in May 1851, for the recognition of Aboriginal customary law, and succeeded in having it recognised as a basis in itself for pardoning prisoners – not just reducing their sentence, for example – in at least two cases in which acts had been done which were consistent with Aboriginal custom but not with the British law. The popular and press agitation which eventually resulted in the enactment of the *Claimants Relief Act* was another example of the ease with which law reform could be promoted in a small community once injustice to a few of its members had come to the notice of the whole.

In fact, if it is right to identify John Baker as the author of the *Claimants Relief Act* and Torrens of the *Real Property Act*, the first three legal reforms considered here were conceived, introduced and written by non-lawyers. That is exactly one half of the six (and a majority of the successful ones) – a remarkable record for non-lawyers, but perhaps not a particularly surprising one when the degree of ingenuity, creativity and effort needed to build a city from scratch is recalled and we suppose that such ingenuity, creativity and effort can carry over into other areas of life.

Of course, the newness, or the smallness, of the early South Australian community does not itself suffice to explain the reforming zeal of early South Australians. Otherwise, Tasmania or perhaps Norfolk Island would be responsible for most early Australian legal innovations.

There was something 'in the air' in early South Australia, something which was connected with the origins of the colony as a 'Paradise of Dissent': for dissent, although for the founders of South Australia meaning primarily religious dissent, can also include, and foster an attitude of, dissent from the existing state of the law where it is in need of reform. This is something which the South Australian colonists were always ready to do if they perceived injustice or a way in which the opportunities available to the citizen to participate in public life could be enhanced.

South Australia will recall the 150th anniversary of the opening of the first Parliament of South Australia in April 2007, and shortly afterwards, in January 2008, there will occur the 150th anniversary of the enactment of the Torrens system in its home. I hope that this book will contribute in some small way to the celebrations of those two great events in the early history of the Province of South Australia.

Note

1   This may be seen by comparing those three innovations with, respectively, the English statutes on land registration (*Land Registry Act* 1862), companies (*Companies Act* 1862) and petitions of right (*Petitions of Right Act* 1860) which were enacted at about the same time, and referred to in the relevant chapter above.

Acknowledgements

With the exception of the first, second and last chapters of this book, this book draws on material published by the author in various scholarly journals.

The author warmly thanks the publishers of the journals listed for readily granting permission to reproduce extracts from the articles published earlier:

Chapter 3. 'The Grand Jury of South Australia' (2001) 45 *American Journal of Legal History* 468

Chapter 4. 'John Baker's Act: the South Australian Origins of Australian Claims-Against-the-Government Legislation' (2004) 27 *University of New South Wales Law Journal* 736

Chapter 5. 'The Origins of Associations Incorporation Legislation – the *Associations Incorporation Act* 1858 of South Australia' (2003) 22 *University of Queensland Law Journal* 224

Chapter 6. 'The *Accused Persons Evidence Act* 1882 of South Australia: a Model for British Law?' (2002) 31 *Common Law World Review* 332

Chapter 7. 'South Australia's Judicature Act Reforms of 1853 – the First Attempt to Fuse Law and Equity in the British Empire' (2001) 22 *Journal of Legal History* 55

Index

This index is arranged alphabetically, word for word. Italic page numbers indicate illustrations.